CHRIST†
IN YOUR
CLASSROOM

Robert A. Hodgdon, M.ED.

WESTBOW
PRESS®
A DIVISION OF THOMAS NELSON
& ZONDERVAN

WestBow Press books may be ordered through booksellers or by contacting:

WestBow Press
A Division of Thomas Nelson & Zondervan
1663 Liberty Drive
Bloomington, IN 47403
www.westbowpress.com
1 (866) 928-1240

ISBN: 978-1-9736-4416-3 (sc)
ISBN: 978-1-9736-4417-0 (e)

Library of Congress Control Number: 2018913091

Print information available on the last page.

WestBow Press rev. date: 11/19/2018

CONTENTS

INTRODUCTION

The first thing anyone who reads this book needs to know is that I am a hypocrite. I desperately wish it were not so, but I am a member of a fallen race. Created in the image of God, I am never-the-less tainted by original sin. Anyone who professes to be a Christian and understands the nature of the flesh will nod his or her head in understanding. We are all hypocrites to one extent or another. We don't always practice what we preach. It's not that many of us don't have the absolute best intentions. We do. But in my case my impulsive, selfish, hypocritical, sinful nature often leads me to act contrary to what I know is right. The Apostle Paul wrote of this same frustration in his letter to the Romans:

> For I know that good itself does not dwell in me, that is, in my sinful nature. For I have the desire to do what is good, but I cannot carry it out. For I do not do the good I want to do, but the evil I do not want to do—this I keep on doing.
>
> Romans 7:18-19 New International Version

I did not write this book, therefore, because I have mastered all the things that are in it. On the contrary, I wrote it as a guide for myself precisely because I had mastered *none* of what is in it though I desperately want to. I think it is fair to say that much of my adult life I have primarily lived life on my own terms, not giving a whole lot of thought to honoring God with my life. In Psalm 127:1, we read, "Unless the Lord builds the house, its builder labors in vain" (NIV). I believe that the Lord built me to be a more Godly man. He has had a hand in building me, the "structure." I, on the other hand, have had a hand in weakening that structure though years of neglect. Through the process of writing, I have certainly grown and matured in my faith. I have begun to put into practice many of the things I have written about. But by no stretch of the imagination am I even close to mastering any of them. Superficially, one might observe a new coat of paint on the outside, some new cabinets on the inside. Unfortunately there is still a lot of work that needs to be accomplished. Even at the structural level, if one were to peek underneath at the supporting beams, one would discover a considerable amount of rot.

I am not a biblical scholar. I have no formal training for teaching the Bible. Faith is not something that comes naturally to me. On the contrary, I would say it is more accurate for me to say that in my life the concept of faith in general has been something I never grasped with both hands. In 1 Corinthians, Paul writes about the unique gifts assigned to each person by God. One of these gifts is the gift of faith. The study notes in the NIV for this passage suggest that a person who has the gift of faith has an extraordinary ability to believe and trust in the power of the Holy Spirit. I am not that person. Nor do I believe are most Christians, so in that sense at least I do not feel alone in my struggle. I have learned a great deal about our faith through the process of writing this book, but even now I fight every single day to hold on to that faith. Part of this struggle is a result of my past. Some is a result of my worldly knowledge. I am a life sciences teacher, but also have a formal background in history and social science. Sometimes I feel like I have demons constantly grasping at my feet, fighting to drag me back down into the pit from which I came. I had hoped that through the process of writing this book I would put some of those demons to rest, that I would finally feel that light shine on my face as I neared the surface. I have felt that light and warmth, but I have also felt those strong hands and thorny nails dig deeper into my calves, strengthen their grasp. I am still in the pit, nearer to the top some days more than others. As Paul has said, many of the things I need to do to climb out of this pit I cannot carry out. Like so many Christians who, like me, did not inherit the gift of faith, the Lord has given me a *measure* of faith, and while my faith has grown in some areas I am still by no means a good example of a *mature* Christian. Yes, I wrote a book, but I did not write it under my own power or through my own knowledge of our faith. It is very possible, probable in fact, that this book will help others who read it far more than it will help me. Why wouldn't it if I did not write this book under my own power or as a result of my own personal victories? It would seem like an awful lot of work (10,000 words) if this book had a hand in leading only me to make some changes in my own life. I believe the Lord inspired me to write this book and it is good where His wisdom and knowledge shines through. Where it is weak or perhaps even inaccurate is testimony to those times when I wrestled control of the process from Him out of my own ignorance or perhaps for some self-serving purpose. At the very least, the grammatical and formatting errors are my own as this science teacher elected to self-edit!

I remain hopeful. I have seen people pulled from a pit far deeper than my own become champions for the Lord and I pray that one day that is something that will be said of me. I hope God will give me the strength to be a champion one day. I pray that He will increase my measure of faith. God has His timeline. For the time being, count me as one who is in the thick of the struggle. In this book you will read about the battles I am fighting rather than about the wars I have won. If your experience has been anything like mine, then you know that at times when you feel like victory is at hand, the enemy army is somehow fortified, and the battle becomes even harder. Three steps forward, two steps back. Is this not often true at times in life as well as in our faith? At this stage of development, I am at best able to focus my energy on one skirmish at a time. I will go to this book time and again as a resource for me as though I had not been the one through whose hand it had been written.

I am not saying that my faith over the past several years has not grown. It certainly has. But as it has grown, so too has the intensity of the slings and arrows that are hurled at my faith. When you are fighting skirmishes behind the front, you are not aware of the intensity of the battle at the front. When I stepped out into my faith, I stepped out on the battlefield and saw for the first time the formidable army I face. Instead of one arrow at a time zipping by me, I experienced a barrage. It is formidable to me because I am new to my faith. To a seasoned veteran, a mature Christian, one who knows and feels the strength of God in his life, this enemy does not seem nearly as formidable because they feel God's infinite power and strength so much more. But I am a private in a world at war. The Bible tells us to put on the armor of God. I have done so. But I am a knight in shining armor. A veteran in the fight for the faith is a knight in dented armor. The veteran soldier runs toward the fight. Those of us who are new to the battle linger to the rear of the division, and at times still turn and run from the fight. I want to fight for my faith, for our Lord. But I am not yet ready for the front. He is not ready for me to fight at the front. I will repeat it several times in this book: I remain a work in progress.

As my faith slowly develops, I have begun to understand the expectations God has of me and the desires He has for me. To my despair, the more knowledge I gained about my faith the more I realized how far from the mark I have been and still am. I was a good father but not the father God desired me to be. I was a good husband but not the husband God wanted me to be. I was a good teacher, but it never really occurred to me that I was not the teacher God wanted me to be. After all, I work in an institution where we are one sentence away (*One nation, under God)* from eliminating any reference to God at all. The separation of church and state forbids me from referencing Jesus except in a historical frame of reference in which I must give Allah, Muhammad, Buddha, and a thousand Hindu gods equal billing.

When I learned that scripture calls us to honor God in our work, I simply gave it no thought. It was a part of the Bible like other parts that, at the time, I felt somehow did not apply to me. I guess I assumed that if I couldn't talk about Jesus there was little else I could do to honor Him in my life of work. I had an excuse. I wasn't allowed to talk about my religion with students. My excuse for not sharing the Gospel with colleagues is two-fold. First, I didn't want to be seen as a religious zealot. Secondly, I did not have the type of reputation that would make me a credible witness. I was in no way prepared to be "a light in the darkness." In my mind, I was part of the darkness.

We have the great commission to bring the Gospel to the world, but leading people to seek and hopefully find Christ requires so much more than sharing the Gospel. Our testimony is made complete in the lives we lead. We are called to live a life that stands apart from the world in a way that people will see a reflection of goodness, contentment, strength, calmness, joy, and peace that is both uncommon and compelling. Our lives should inspire others to seek the source of our harmony, and in doing so we open the door for an introduction to Jesus even though we may have never mentioned His name. Instead of hypocrisy, our aim should be its opposite: integrity. Integrity means that we make it our goal to honor God in every aspect of our lives, even when nobody else is around to observe us. Integrity strengthens our ability to lead others to Christ either directly or indirectly. Hypocrisy weakens this ability, and perhaps worse, discredits our Lord and Savior.

Like many "new" Christians, my initial thoughts were on how I could honor God by serving at my church. I chose to serve as one of the members of the church's photography corps. Over a period of three years, I took thousands of pictures at a variety of events. During that time, however, I really wasn't putting a whole lot of thought into how to honor my God as the head of my family nor in how I might honor Him through my work. I don't recall the moment when my eyes were opened, when I began to realize how superficial my faith was, but it corresponded roughly with the time of my second child's birth. It is not the purpose of this particular book to discuss how I worked to become a better father and husband except to say that I came to realize that my whole life needed work, so as I slowly began to turn things over to God I slowly began to transform in all areas of my life. That included my work as a teacher.

The Bible clearly identifies work as good. We are designed to work. Not only this, but we are expected to honor God through our work. God does not distinguish between a waitress and neurologist. If our work is honorable to begin with (which some certainly is not), then God expects us to serve Him and serve others through our work. Nowhere in the Bible do I recall any promise that our work would be easy nor that we would always find our work enjoyable. In fact, it would be more accurate to say that the Bible points out very clearly life will be full of trials and this is perhaps no more true than in issues related to our work. As teachers, we have a tremendously stressful job that is only getting more stressful with each passing year. It does not help that only another teacher could possibly understand how much is involved in being an effective and engaging teacher in today's modern classrooms. In the eyes of many, we are the people who only work 190 days per year. Talk radio hosts week after week slam the American Education System for the problems of our society as though we alone are the ones responsible for shaping our youth. I have seen estimates that in some areas of the U.S. nearly one-third to one-half of all new teachers leave the profession within the first five years. There is nothing easy about teaching, and most assuredly not everything involved in teaching is enjoyable. I can think of few professions where the presence of God is needed more than in educating and shaping the minds and the character of our children. And yet, it is by law a profession where we cannot mention Him or His Word. With colleagues, certainly we can share our faith, initially through our actions and then, if the Spirit moves them to want more, through the Gospel. With students we cannot ever share our faith. We cannot ever share the Gospel (at school). However, we can show them a glimpse of Christ through our actions. If this is the way we introduce them to the nature of Christ, I believe God will find another way to introduce Himself personally to that child. We may never learn what effect we have on our students. Only a small number of them will remain in the town of their youth. The rest we may never hear from or hear of again once they graduate from high school. If we are fortunate, we may see the seeds we plant begin to germinate as our students progress through high school and become young adults. Most likely, though, we must simply have faith that if we were truly allowing God to work through us in our job, somewhere down the line that seed will begin to germinate.

For the first thirteen years of my professional career as a teacher I worked with troubled youth. How I wish now that I was more attentive to how God was working through me then to help these students. I was not saved, and I did not realize that it was God's power and grace that enabled me to help these children. Therefore, I did not steer them toward our Lord. I taught them about personal inner strength because I was of the mind that it was my own personal inner strength that allowed me to navigate life's obstacles. Since being saved, I understand that I have accomplished nothing under my own strength. Even when I thought I was running the show, God was working through. I don't believe He would have done so forever. He knew where I was at the time, why I was there, but more importantly he knew who I would desire to become one day. More importantly, He knew what He desired for me to become. Everything I have ever done and experienced in my life prepared me for the man I would desire to become when I accepted Christ as my personal Lord and Savior. It is tough not to be able to share the Gospel with students whom I am convinced nothing and no one else will help. There have been times when I risked sharing a bit of the Gospel with students who were not members of my church, but I will be the first to admit that doing so may *not* be honoring God. The Bible says that we are to honor the laws of our government and our leaders unless they are calling us to do something sinful. I take my lead from the majority of the leaders of our nation's Christian churches. They honor that law and therefore so should I. My impulse to break the law and risk being reprimanded or worse was not based on the strength of my faith but rather was a reflection of its weakness. I did not trust that God would help me to find a more indirect way to expose these children to Him. Ultimately, we serve no one if we lose our job for violating federal law.

My original intent in writing this book or manual for myself was to develop a plan for honoring God through my teaching. Approximately fifty-five hours of my life every week are dedicated to teaching. I believe being a teacher is my calling because God blessed me with the tools to be an effective teacher. Up until a few years ago, my focus in the classroom was almost entirely on teaching the state's Life Science curriculum well. I believe God loves it when I teach about the enormous complexity and diversity of His creation. However, those of you who understand what a "calling" is know what I have only recently come to understand: though God expects me to do well at teaching science, my calling is not just to teach science *per se*. My classroom provides a setting. The subject I teach provides a context. But my calling at its core is the same as any other Christians: to lead people to a live-changing relationship with Christ. All effective teachers know that you plan with the end in mind. I wanted to develop something that would help me to live a more Godly life and to serve as a living example of Christ that could directly or indirectly lead more people to Him.

Each year about one hundred to one hundred twenty students come to me to learn science. Many are from Christian families. Usually this includes a number of students who are members of the same church as my family. The churches in my area have strong youth programs, so I trust that most of the students who participate regularly in these programs will be able to recognize Christian behavior when they see it. That means they can recognize in a heartbeat behavior that does *not* reflect our faith. Students who are not members of our faith usually come to know that I am a Christian either because they hear from students who are members of my church, see me at one of our church sponsored public events, or because they hear me mention something about church. The court rulings related to the separation of church and state prevent us from teaching about our faith, but we are certainly under no obligation to hide the fact that we are Christians. I sometimes wear ties with Christian symbols on them or mention events like the time members of the World Children's Choir performed at my church (in that instance, I was able to relate it to a social studies lesson on child soldiers of Africa). The church is a part of our community and as such comes up in conversation from time to time. We are under no obligation to pretend that we are members of a secret society. We are Christians, not Masons.

As teachers, we are in a position to have enormous influence over the minds of these children. Most teachers are aware of this influence. The course material is not the only thing that we have the opportunity to share with our students. The teaching of values has always been a part of public education, but of course that has opened the door for a whole lot of different values. In most schools, you will find the same core values: sharing, respecting others, honesty, hard work-all of which can be found in Biblical teachings. I have taught at a number of schools in my career and I have yet to come across one where humility was taught or practiced. Certainly, it was not in my classroom or in my relationship with my colleagues. There was a great deal of arrogance behind my desire to be one of the best at what I do and to be one of the most popular teachers among the students. In many ways I was a "success" if scores and popularity are the sole measures of success. I know teachers who get great scores from the kids, but the kids come to hate them in the process. I know others whom the kids absolutely adore but whose teaching skills are exceedingly poor. I experienced the best of both worlds, and though I tried to play humble and nonchalant about it, inside I was digging myself far too much. I was proud of what *I* had accomplished mostly (as I saw it) on my own. I gave token credit to God in my prayers, never in public. I did eventually graduate from near complete ignorance to the next step up, spiritual infancy, and only then did I begin to see the damage I had caused to my own reputation and the years I had wasted trying to change the world on my terms when I could have and should have been trying to change the world on God's terms. Psalm 119:21 tells us that God rebukes the arrogant, but all of us have experienced students who resist discipline and some that even laugh at our attempts to discipline them. Some of us don't even recognize that we are being rebuked and thus fail to learn or change. I tell my students all the time that a reputation is easy to earn but incredibly difficult to lose. I know this to true in my case. I may never be able to fully launder the stench of my pride from the nostrils of those who "knew me then." The damage is not so much to my ego (which thankfully has become far less of a motivating factor), than to my ability to share the Gospel with others. Never-the-less, I have come to believe and accept that I am exactly where God wants me to be at this point in my life.

I have not always been as certain of this. There have been times when I have felt I was meant for something different. During my years working with children with emotional and behavior problems I cared deeply for the children, or if I were to be absolutely honest *most* of the children, but it does not take long to start to feel burned out working almost exclusively with this particular population of student. The paperwork, regulations, and the attitudes of other teachers toward my students and me for bringing them to their classrooms (attitudes I often understood) at times contributed to that burnout. During those years, I yearned to get back to teaching either social studies or science at the secondary level. Apparently, God needed me where I was. In 2004, God changed his mission for me. I found a job teaching both science and social studies. I did not recognize it at the time, but now I see that God had work for me to do in this capacity. I do not know how long this will last before He moves me into something else, but now that I understand that I am serving God through my work my goal is to do so as well as possible until God opens the next door. I am wonderfully blessed. I said before I believe this is where God wants me to be because He has prepared me so wonderfully for this job. When I am feeling overwhelmed by the workload, I try to remember that God has blessed me with gifts that others may greatly desire but whom the Lord may not have blessed in the same way. I have seen many teachers over the years who struggle greatly in their work, and I now I wonder whether the underlying issue was that God had other plans for them. I have seen some teachers who have a deep faith in God yet seem unable to find their way at the head of the classroom. Wanting something deeply and praying for it night after night still does not guarantee God will answer our prayers the way we want Him to. I imagine Tim Tebow, a man who inspires many people because of his faith, knows this as well as anyone. For these struggling teachers, I wonder how frightening it must be to have prepared for years for a profession they felt they were meant for only to find out that may not be the case. In this economy today where college graduates are moving back home at alarming rates it must be terrifying to consider that one might have to start over. I know there are teachers who continue to teach even though they are miserable and even though they are not particularly good at it. I have been there myself. If you are there, regardless of whether you are sold on this "Christianity thing" or not, I believe God will show the path He has laid out for you. It may be teaching, but then again it may not be. If teaching is your calling, then I challenge you to take that next step toward full faith in God's power and promise by doing what the Bible tells us to do and what I have tried to do over the past few years of my career: Honor God through your work. Invite Christ to work through you in your teaching, in your relationships with your students, and in the example you set for them and your colleagues. I wish I could tell you it would be easy, but as they say in the South, "That dog won't hunt." For one thing, I learned that I cannot strategically target which areas of my life I want God to improve. I cannot honor God as a teacher unless I undergo a transformation where I am honoring God with *all* of my life. Secondly, as a teacher I think and learn in a very specific way. I like things broken down for me in a format that I can relate to. I like having a guide or a manual, or perhaps some sort of Bible Unit Plan for teachers. I figured there had to be something like that out there for me to use. I figured wrong.

There are hundreds of Christian "guidebooks" available to help us honor God through our marriage or in our parenting. There are many on the history of Christianity. There are books arguing the validity of Christ. There are analyses for every book of the Bible. There are Christian books and sermons related to just about anything one can think of. There are even books discussing how our modern educational system is damaging Christianity. What I was not able to find was a manual or guide book on how to be a Christian teacher in today's secular classroom. It makes sense, I guess. Most Christian books and scholarly articles are written by Christian theologians or by people who have a career in a Christian-based enterprise such as Christian counselors, Christian relief or charity workers, etc. Hence the problem: theologians, Christian counselors, and Christian relief workers don't work in public schools. When it comes to understanding how I can best serve Christ through my teaching, I had bits and pieces of information floating around in my mind, but in order for me to use this information effectively I needed to have it organized into a unified, coherent, outline or even manual. I searched for such a book or manual written by someone more qualified than I am, but I could not find anything that came close to what I needed. There is no "manual" for us. There is no unit plan. I came to the realization that if I wanted a manual on how to serve Christ in my classroom, I'd have to write it myself.

As a teacher, part of my job is to build and teach units. Unit plans contain the educational standards, resources, methods, vocabulary, critical foundational understandings, the essential questions that guide my instruction, assessments, activities, and many other elements. I can learn about something through reading, listening, or watching a documentary. Most teachers would attest that if one wants to truly master the material, there is no better way than to develop a unit plan and then teach it. Unit plans have the added benefit of being dynamic rather than static. Each time I teach a unit, I discover ways to make it even better. My unit plan is my guide. I keep it on my desk and refer to it frequently as I teach the unit. When my eyes were opened to what a commitment to Christ really involves, I knew for me that I needed to have everything arranged in a way that worked for me. I needed something like a unit plan. I tried to recall some of the most important messages from my study of the Bible, sermons, and other Christian resources and begin building my unit around that.

1. Understand that a commitment to God literally means that you are *giving your life to Him to do with it what He wants*. We are to offer our life as a living sacrifice. Recognize that if you really mean to hand your life over to Christ, you *must allow Him to be in control*. If you rely upon your own self-control, strength, or willpower to get things done, you will falter. Christ told His followers, "Anyone who intends to come with me has to let *me* lead. You're not in the driver's seat; I am" (Mark 8:34 The Message). Luke reminds us, "If you grasp and cling to life on your terms, you'll lose it, but if you let that life go, you'll get life on God's terms" (Luke 17:33 MSG). Long before Christ appeared on earth, the prophet Jeremiah understood that "people's lives are not their own; it is not for them to direct their steps" (Jeremiah 10:23 NIV).

2. Clothe yourself in humility. Work for the glory of God rather than our own glory. Christ, God in man's flesh, was born under the most humble conditions and lived the most humble of lives. If THE God of the universe can demonstrate such humility, then certainly we should be expected and inspired to do the same. Admit your shortcomings and ask for forgiveness. Repent daily. Put the needs of others ahead of your own. Be sincere about it. God knows what's really in your mind. The Bible warns us, "don't imagine yourself to be quite presentable when you haven't had a bath in weeks" (Proverbs 30: 12 MSG). In humility, do not consider yourself above anyone else.

3. God expects us to maintain the right frame of mind. This can only be accomplished when you have faith in God's power and promises. God wants us to trust Him *in every way* and *in every circumstance*. He does not want us to live a life of worry or anxiety for worry is sinful and unproductive most of the time. It will cripple you and make you unable to do God's work well. Accept that struggles are a necessary part of God's plan for you and embrace them. Remember that throughout your struggles, when you are afraid or anxious, God is there to provide you with whatever you need to help you through it. Do not be a complainer. Show gratitude for the blessings you have and don't complain about what you do not have. Be joyful.

4. People should be able to glimpse the character of God through your words, your actions, and your service. Treat others with love and compassion, in a loving way, even when our sinful nature interferes with our ability to *feel* love for them. Make every effort to get along with others. Lead a life of service to others. As the apostle Paul said, "Though I am free and belong to no one, I have made myself a slave to everyone, to win as many as possible" (1 Corinthians 9:19 NIV).

5. Understand that while deeds do not save, they are the manifestation of your commitment, a reflection of your humility and your gratitude. They are your "fruits" by which your heart will be known. "No good tree bears bad fruit, nor does a bad tree bear good fruit. Each tree is recognized by its own fruit. People do not pick figs from thorn bushes, or grapes from briers" (Luke 6:43-44 NIV).

6. God expects us to grow in our faith so that we may gain strength as a witness. In Peter's second letter, he writes:

Supplement your faith with a generous provision of moral excellence, and moral excellence with knowledge, and knowledge with self-control, and self-control with patient endurance, and patient endurance with godliness, and godliness with brotherly affection, and brotherly affection with love for everyone. The more you grow like this, the more productive and useful you will be in your knowledge of our Lord Jesus Christ. But those who fail to develop in this way are shortsighted or blind, forgetting that they have been cleansed from their old sin.

2 Peter 1:5-9 New Living Translation

7. If we are to pray for God to work through us in any one area of our life, we must work on developing our Christ-like character in *all* areas of our life. We all have many roles to fulfill: parent, spouse, friend, counselor, member of a church, or teacher. When we move from role to role throughout our lives, God expects us to be the same person of character, integrity, and conviction in every area. If we compare these different areas to different rooms in a house, God does not want us to flick on the humility switch when we enter one room only to shut it off when we leave and enter another. God's power is diminished through our hypocrisy. The Devil's, on the other hand, is greatly magnified by hypocrisy.

This is not an exhaustive list of the most important tenets of our faith by any means. I looked through this list with the goal of determining where to start in terms of organization. What I began to discover as God opened my eyes is that there are common threads running through the tapestry of the Bible. The genetic code for all living things on earth is made up of only four distinct types of molecules called bases: adenine, thymine, guanine, and cytosine. These bases assemble in complex arrangements to form DNA. DNA assembles to form genes which control specific traits of our physical appearance and bodily function. Being the science teacher, I found that I could narrow the code for living a life that truly honors God into one base: love. God is love, so it makes sense that all things that come from God have their root in love. The specific "traits" that are formed from love are things like commitment, faith, humility, and integrity. The particular arrangement of the bases that form genetic traits is not random. Any deviation from this arrangement can result in dysfunction, disfigurement, even death. The Bible uses the analogy of the fruit tree to demonstrate how well we reflect Godly love in our lives. We are told that we will all be judged by our fruit, both by God and by others. Our fruit does not save us, but it does reflect the depth and sincerity of our relationship with God. A tree that produces much fruit is watered by God, given sunlight from God, grows in proper soil provided by and enriched by God, and is pruned by God. We are all created *in God's image*. We produce fruit best when our character reflects His character. What I have come to understand through the process of writing this book is that while I was trying to figure out how to honor God and have Him flow through me in my role *as a teacher*, God is concerned with my whole character, the character I display in each "room" of my life. It is impossible for God's love and character to flow through me in my classroom if I do not allow it to flow through me in my role as a father, a husband, a friend, a mentor, a colleague, or a member of a church. I will spend a great deal of time talking about the specifics of what I feel a Christian teacher should look like, but the first three chapters focus on building the kind of character and integrity that God desires from us in *all* areas of our life.

I quote Biblical passages from several different translations of the Bible. Wherever italics or bold type are used when quoting scripture, the emphasis is mine. I would also like to apologize in advance to English or writing teachers. A professional edit was not in the budget and I am a science teacher with a minimal background in English/Language Arts. I hope the grammatical errors you experience will not disturb the flow of your reading. I would advise you to keep your red ink pen at the ready.

Imagine...

In all companies, on other days, on whatever occasions persons met together, Christ was to be heard of, and seen in the midst of them. Our young people, when they met, were wont to spend the time in talking of the excellency and dying love of Jesus Christ, the glory of the way of salvation, the wonderful, free, and sovereign grace of God, His glorious work in the conversion of a soul, the truth and certainty of the great things of God's word, the sweetness of the views of His perfections, etc....Many who before had labored under difficulties about their own state, had now their doubts removed by more satisfying experience, and more clear discoveries of God's love. When this work first appeared and was so extraordinarily carried on amongst us in the winter, others round about us seemed not to know what to make of it. Many scoffed at and ridiculed it; and some compared what we called conversion, to certain distempers. But it was very observable of many, who occasionally came amongst us from abroad with disregardful hearts, that what they saw here cured them of such a temper of mind. Strangers were generally surprised to find things so much beyond what they had heard, and were wont to tell others that the state of the town could not be conceived of by those who had not seen it.

Excerpts from *A Faithful Narrative of the Surprising Work of God* by Jonathan Edwards

CHAPTER ONE

What Does it Really Mean to Commit to Christ?

So here's what I want you to do, God helping you: Take your everyday, ordinary life—your sleeping, eating, going-to-work, and walking-around life—and place it before God as an offering. Embracing what God does for you is the best thing you can do for him. Don't become so well-adjusted to your culture that you fit into it without even thinking. Instead, fix your attention on God. You'll be changed from the inside out. Readily recognize what he wants from you, and quickly respond to it. Unlike the culture around you, always dragging you down to its level of immaturity, God brings the best out of you, develops well-formed maturity in you.

Romans 12:1 2 MSG

Any man who can drive safely while kissing a pretty girl is simply not giving the kiss the attention it deserves.

Albert Einstein

Remember that the Christian life is one of action, not of speech and daydreams. Let there be few words and many deeds and let them be done well.

St. Vincent Pallotti

Committing a great truth to memory is admirable; committing it to life is wisdom.

William Arthur Ward

If the highest aim of a captain were to preserve his ship, he would keep it in port forever.

Thomas Aquinas

Foundational Concepts

✝ A commitment to God means that we will honor and love Him with all your heart, all your soul, all your mind, and all your strength.

✝   When you commit to God, God will work to make you perfect.
✝   God will help you to honor your commitment.

Central Questions

1.   What does making a commitment to give your life to God involve?
2.   What will a life changing commitment to God look like?
3.   How will we, a fallen race, be able to honor a lifelong commitment to God?

A young, male athlete approaches a championship caliber coach and says, "Coach, I want to be an elite athlete. I want to play at a professional level and lead my team to a World Championship. I want to be in the Hall of Fame one day. I will do whatever you ask me to do, just help me realize my goal." The wise, old coach looks across his desk at the eager youth, leans forward in his seat and asks, "Son, do you really understand what you're getting yourself into?" You see, the old coach knows that if he agrees to take this athlete on and help him work toward realizing these goals, this young man will experience and be expected to endure an intense level of pain or discomfort. He will have to give up or sacrifice many other parts of his life, work harder than he ever thought possible, trust and obey his coach even when he disagrees, learn from his mistakes as well as his victories, and keep his eye always focused on his goals despite the many setbacks or distractions he will encounter. What he eats, how much he sleeps, how he trains, all dictated by the program developed by his coach. The commitment he would be asked to make would be life altering. But in the end the rewards would be fabulous.

I'm sure I'm not alone in admitting that when I committed my life to Christ I was not fully aware of what I was getting myself into. I thought I understood the part about believing Jesus is the Christ, the Son of the living God, and my Lord and Savior. I understood that I would need to be more conscientious about behaving "like a Christian." I understood that living a Christian lifestyle would require sacrifice, study, and self-control. I felt quite confident that I could demonstrate my faith as well as most of the people I knew to be Christians, maybe even better than those I saw as particularly hypocritical. I understood what making a commitment to Christ meant as well as any nine-year-old could. The problem was, I was forty years old at the time.

We make a lot of commitments in our lives. Sometimes we know what we are getting ourselves into, sometimes we learn the hard way. Even when we verbalize commitments like "'til death do us part" in front of a room full of witnesses, the statistics bear evidence that half of us who made that particular commitment didn't really mean it. Or, as some will say later, perhaps they meant it "at the time" but hadn't really realized what they had gotten themselves into. Commitments can be easy to make but hard to keep. Some commitments do have expiration dates. Making a commitment to give your life to God is not one of them. We are not doing God a "favor" when we commit our lives to Him. Often we hear people say they "gave themselves to God." Those who say that will hopefully come to understand that what they are truly doing is recognizing God's sovereignty over their lives. You cannot give something to someone to whom the thing already belongs. The prophet Jeremiah acknowledges what all of us should understand from the start: our lives already belong to God. "LORD, I know that people's lives are not their own; it is not for them to direct their steps" (Jeremiah 10:23 NIV). There is really no mistaking what God expects from us in terms of a commitment. It is unquestionably a call to a life of *action*. Teacher and theologian William Arthur Ward challenged us to, "Do more than belong: participate. Do more than care: help. Do more than believe: practice. Do more than be fair: be kind. Do more than forgive: forget. Do more than dream: work." Where the Bible tells us to love, it refers to action. Where it tells us to demonstrate humility it refers to action. James 1:22 (NIV) says "Do not merely *listen* to the word, and so deceive yourselves. *Do* what it says." In chapter 3, James writes, "Who is wise and understanding among you? Let them *show it* by their good life, *by deeds done in* the *humility* that comes from wisdom" (James 3:13 NIV). Christ tells us, "These words I speak to you are not incidental additions to your life, homeowner improvements to your standard of living. They are foundational words, *words to build a life on.* If you work these words into your life, you are like a smart carpenter who built his house on solid rock. Rain poured down, the river flooded, a tornado hit—but nothing moved that house. It was fixed to the rock" (Matthew 7:24-25 MSG). The apostle Paul wrote to the church in Rome, "Merely hearing God's law is a waste of your time if you don't do what he commands. *Doing*, not hearing, is what makes the difference with God" (Romans 2:13 MSG).

It doesn't matter how many times we read the Bible, how many sermons we hear, or how many books we read if none of that motivates us to obedience. Jesus said very simply, "If you love me, *keep my commands"* (John 14:15 New Living Translation). This is not the statement of a God who wants to be obeyed and revered simply for the sake of being obeyed and revered. Jesus tells us that obedience and action will benefit *us* through the bond it forms with our Father. In verses 23-24 He continues, "Anyone who loves me will obey my teaching. My Father will love them, and we will come to them and make our home with them. Anyone who does not love me will not obey my teaching. These words you hear are not my own; they belong to the Father who sent me" (John 14: 23-24 NIV). 1 John 2:3-6 (NIV) says, "We know that we have come to know him *if we keep his commands.* Whoever says, 'I know him,' but *does not do* what he commands is a liar, and the truth is not in that person. But if anyone obeys his word, love for God is truly made complete in them. This is how we know we are in him: Whoever claims to live in him *must live as Jesus did."*

Christ also warned us in the strongest language that our commitment must be sincere. An insincere commitment, a commitment that involves our mouth but not our heart, will not lead us to eternal life.

> Knowing the correct password—saying "Master, Master," for instance— isn't going to get you anywhere with me. What is required is serious obedience—**doing** what my Father wills. I can see it now—at the Final Judgment thousands strutting up to me and saying, "Master, we preached the Message, we bashed the demons, our God-sponsored projects had everyone talking." And do you know what I am going to say? "You missed the boat. All you did was use me to make yourselves important. You don't impress me one bit. You're out of here."
> Matthew 7:21-23 MSG

Not giving God your best effort at obeying Him, giving Him "inferior" offerings because you are complacent or luke-warm is offensive to Him and your "gifts" may be rejected. Consider what is written in Revelations 3:15-16 (NLT): "I know all the things you do, that you are neither hot nor cold. I wish that you were one or the other! But since you are like lukewarm water, neither hot nor cold, I will spit you out of my mouth."

Making a commitment to God literally means that you are giving Him your life to do with it what He desires. Not parts of your life, but *all* of it. In Paul's letter to the Romans, he reminds them that when they offered themselves to Christ they became a *slave to obedience*, but also that the alternative was to remain a slave to sin which would lead to death (Romans 6:16). Christ said, "Whoever wants to be my disciple must *deny themselves* and take up their cross daily and follow me. For whoever wants to save their life will lose it, but *whoever loses their life for me* will save it" (Luke 9:23-24; Matthew 10:39 NLT). Paul also wrote, "Therefore, I urge you, brothers and sisters, in view of God's mercy, to offer your bodies as a *living sacrifice*, holy and pleasing to God—this is your true and proper worship" (Romans 12:1 NIV). The Message translation of verses 1-2 reads like this:

> So here's what I want you to do, God helping you: Take your everyday, ordinary life—your sleeping, eating, going-to-work, and walking-around life—and place it before God as an offering. Embracing what God does for you is the best thing you can do for him. Don't become so well-adjusted to your culture that you fit into it without even thinking. Instead, fix your attention on God. You'll be changed from the inside out. Readily recognize what he wants from you, and quickly respond to it. Unlike the culture around you, always dragging you down to its level of immaturity, God brings the best out of you, develops well-formed maturity in you.

When asked by the religious leaders of His time what the most important commandment is, Christ answered in general terms what a sincere commitment entails: "Love the Lord your God with all your heart and with all your soul and with all your mind and with all your strength. The second is this: 'Love your neighbor as yourself.' There is no commandment greater than these" (Mark 12:30-31 NIV). When you read "through" the Bible these seem like relatively simple commandments. A commitment to Christ, however, will lead to a much deeper understanding of the Word. When you *study* the Bible, contemplate the verses, and consider how to apply them to your life (in other words, when you start to develop mature wisdom), you realize there is more to these commands than what appears. For example, you find that "love" in the Biblical sense has a number of manifestations, some of which bear little if any resemblance to the kind of love we are familiar with in our world. Similarly, you will learn who your "neighbor" is and will again be surprised at just who falls into this category. *How* you read the Bible will also determine whether simple words like *"all"* in Mark 12:30 pop out at you loud and clear or whether you unconsciously gloss over them and miss a crucial element of what Christ expects from us.

In all fairness, many people who come to Christ don't have the background knowledge to understand what a commitment to Him will be like. In Romans 2:12 (MSG), Paul tells us, "If you sin without knowing what you're doing, God takes that into account. But if you sin knowing full well what you're doing, that's a different story entirely." My own ignorance was not due to never having been exposed to the teachings of Christianity, but that I put almost no thought into developing a deeper understanding of them. It took me nearly forty years to come to a place in my life where I began to long for that deeper understanding and seek a new relationship with Christ. People come to the Lord in a number of ways. Some get a taste of The Word and go "all in" right then. These people are frequently ones are who either looking up from rock bottom or hanging on from the end of their rope. Others employ more of a Socratic method, delving into research and identifying people who are seen as mature in the faith and engaging them in a dialogue intended to weed out contradictions or inconsistencies. The outcome of this approach is not certain, but if we consider the works of C.S. Lewis and Lee Strobel it can lead some dedicated skeptics to become champions for our Lord.

Some approach making a commitment in a manner similar to how they make a major purchase. They learn everything they can about our faith then make a decision about whether they will "buy" into it or not. The outcome of this approach is also uncertain and is the approach I think has the potential to be the least effective. Any approach that does not include discourse with mature Christians has the potential to result in serious misinterpretations and misunderstandings. Through discourse, we can feel a sense of the passion of the mature believer. We get a sense of where the emphasis is, what the point is, and how it has affected him or her. If God leads us to the right set of people, we can see in the flesh what commitment looks like. We are created by God to be social beings. There is something about person-to-person contact that stirs our soul. For example, we can read about the millions of children around the world who are living lives of absolute destitution and feel the strumming of sympathy in our hearts. When we see a documentary on the life of a handful of these kids our heart gets squeezed a little tighter. *Meet* just one of these children though, and your whole being resonates with an entire symphony of grief. Whichever path leads you to Christ, if your soul is not tingling as you learn more about Him, you're approaching Him in entirely the wrong manner.

Some of us make commitments but then through the course of our busy lives don't really give a whole lot of thought on a day to day basis to whether or not we are honoring that commitment. Some people may believe they are honoring a commitment though every bit of evidence suggests otherwise. Consider this exchange between the participants in a parent-teacher meeting about a struggling student.

> Teacher: Martin is currently not passing my class. I wanted to meet with you to discuss how we can help him to be more successful.
>
> Parent: Martin knows that this is completely unacceptable to us. We value education very much in our family and he knows that. Neither of us had the opportunity to go to college, and we want to make sure that our kids have opportunities we did not have.
>
> Teacher: When did you first become aware that Martin was struggling in my class?
>
> Parent: When you called me.
>
> *Aside: Martin has been struggling for several weeks.*

Teacher: Martin, have you talked with your parents about your grades or shown them any of your test scores?

Parent : He hasn't brought home a thing!

Teacher: Well, that's not uncommon. Kids often don't want to bring home unwelcome news. Martin, why haven't you mentioned anything to your parents about your grades?

Martin: [shrugs his shoulder] I don't know. Forgot.

Teacher: Mrs. Wilson, are you familiar with the PowerSchool Parent Portal? It allows you to go online and see all of Martin's current grades in every subject.

Parent: Yes. I have been meaning to call about the password for that. I need to get that before I leave today.

Teacher: I'd be happy to help you with that after we are done meeting.

Aside- All the information on how to access PowerSchool was included in the Open House folder at the beginning of the year, including how to go online and set up the account and get a password. Teachers are able to see how often parents access their child's grades. Mrs. Wilson did, in fact, sign up for PowerSchool. The teacher's records show she logged in a few times at the beginning of the year but not since. While she did not say that she never received the information, perhaps she was trying to imply it to save face for not regularly checking up on her son's grades. Perhaps she simply forgot.

Teacher: Well, when I look at his grades I see some areas we can target for improvement. First, Martin often does not do his homework. When he does have it completed, he often isn't able to explain to me how he got his answers. Last week, another teacher caught Martin copying another student's homework which leads me to believe that he may have done this before. After doing poorly on a couple tests, Martin admitted to me that he didn't study for them. I'm sure that he is missing some of the information during class. I have him late in the afternoon, and sometimes I have to speak with him about not paying attention or even sleeping. He and I have talked about this at length, but I haven't had much luck helping him. I have tried to offer him some help first thing in the morning, but he often arrives right before the bell. He also says he is unable to stay after because he is on a travel baseball team and has practice.

Parent: I know why he's not sleeping. He stays up too late watching t.v., texting his friends, or playing video games. Why aren't you doing your homework? Whenever I ask you if you have homework you tell me 'no."

Martin: I don't know. I forget.

Parent: Ok, that's it! When I get home I'm taking your Xbox and that new smartphone we just bought for you.

Aside – A threat that is probably not going to be followed through with, that won't really matter to Martin, or that will be rescinded once he shows he has done his homework one night.

Parent: And if that doesn't work, no more baseball, mister.

Aside- A threat that has been used in the past but has also never been followed through with. You see, this is not Martin's first time at the rodeo. His parents have been in for similar meetings during past school years. Plus, being part of a travel team is often restricted to better players whose parents have a lot of time and money invested in their child. It can also serve as a kind of "status symbol."

Teacher: Martin, how often do you check the class website for help?

Martin: I don't know. Not that often. I don't usually get home from practice until late. Then I eat. I usually don't have time to check.

Parent: What website is this?

Teacher: Earlier in the year, I sent home a newsletter with information about how to access my website and what can be found there. Homework assignments, a calendar of events, helpful websites, practice tests, study guides, announcements, etc. Do you remember receiving that newsletter?

Parent: I got so many things at the beginning of the year. I don't remember. I probably got it.

Martin (who suddenly pipes up): I gave that to you mom! You signed it and I brought it back.

Parent: Well, either way, it's your responsibility to check the website, not mine. You're twelve years old.

Teacher: Here is a copy of the newsletter in case it somehow got misplaced.

Parent: I guess I need to do a better job of checking up on you. I trusted you to do this on your own, but I guess you can't be trusted. Things are going to change around our house. You can bet on that.

This exchange was not entirely fictional. In fact, it's not even an isolated incident. I have similar conversations like this almost every year. I have even sat in these meetings a couple of times when the parent across from me was also an educator. I'm not trying to bash this parent or any other by this example. I am just as guilty at times of drifting away from my own commitments to my family and in other areas of my life. I try to give the parent the benefit of the doubt: she was probably not a "bad" parent. She was probably an "overwhelmed" parent who was balancing raising kids, taking care of a home, working, being a wife, and whatever hat she wore throughout the day. I used this example to illustrate the difference between *saying* we are committed to something versus *showing* we are committed to it. Think about it. If you were the parent in the example above, would you really *expect* anybody to believe that you were as committed to your child's education as you said you were? This example is not unlike the way many of us treat our "commitment" to Christ. In my own life, there is far too often great disparity between me saying I am committed to Christ and showing I am committed to Christ.

If we call ourselves "Christians," implying a commitment to Him, yet do not appear to others to live by the very standards we speak of then not only do we lose our credibility, Christ does as well. If I have truly committed to Christ, can I expect anyone to believe it based on what they see in me? If I am truly committed to Christ, should I not do a better job of making Christ seem appealing to people? Actions speak louder than words. If we say we are committed to God but our deeds do not reflect this commitment, the commitment itself comes into question. More importantly, in the eyes of others, our faith and our God come into question. In their book *Unchristian: what a new generation really thinks about Christianity-- and why it matters*, David Kinnaman and David Lyons refer to a 1996 poll in which 85% of "non-religious" people felt Christians were hypocrites; 87% felt we were judgmental, and 70% felt we were insensitive to others (Kinnaman & Lyons, 2007). If these numbers were this high nearly twenty years ago, imagine how much of a target Christians are today now that our society has become increasingly more "liberal-minded" as a whole.

A commitment, then, is a powerful call to right action. If you make such a commitment and you are sincere about it, it becomes obvious to everyone who knows you because the proof of your conviction is tangible or observable. Certainly God knows the difference. I thought I was honoring my commitment...for the most part. God knew better. I imagine He was watching and waiting patiently for me to experience my ah-hah moment. It is indeed a humbling experience to discover what you thought you were doing satisfactorily was in fact a pitiful attempt at what is expected. Seventeenth century Puritan theologian John Owen wrote once, "All things I thought I knew; but now confess, the more I know I know, I know the less." The part of my commitment I did immediately begin to honor was learning more about my faith. In addition to studying the Bible and attending church I hit the books. I read one book after another. I read over fifty Christian books. The more I read and listened, the more I began to understand what my commitment really entailed. It is all of the things I mentioned above and more but to a degree far, far greater than what I imagined. I guess it makes sense. With the goal being a life of eternal bliss, how could the entrance to eternity cost a mere token. I began to feel the heaviness of my sin as I learned just how far from the mark I was. Like many people who are early in their walk, I pondered on what mark would be "good enough." I understood the concept of original sin and felt that would go a long way to covering my transgressions. After all, I can't expect to be perfect if I am an imperfect creation, right? That theory was dismantled one morning while reading *Mere Christianity* by C.S. Lewis (1952, 202). I came across a passage that seemed to emphasize what I have "gotten myself into."

> He will cure you all right; but He will not stop there. That may be all you asked, but if once you call Him in, He will give you the full treatment. This is why He warned people to 'count the cost' before becoming Christians. 'Make no mistake,' He says, 'if you let me in, I will make you perfect. The moment you put yourself in My hands, that is what you are in for. Nothing less, or other, than that. You have free will, and if you choose, you can push Me away. But if you do not push Me away, understand that I am going to see this job through. Whatever suffering it may cost you in your earthly life, whatever inconceivable purification it may cost you after death, whatever it costs Me, I will never rest, nor let you rest, until you are literally perfect...This I can do and will do. But I will not do anything less.

As far from the mark as I am, God is going to make *me* perfect. If I let Him. If I make a sincere commitment to Him. Not by swinging some magical wand so that I wake up one morning a new man. God is going to take a piece of raw iron ore and make me Excalibur. If I let Him. He will place me in the forge, shape my blade with hammer and anvil, fold the metal and repeat the heating and shaping again and again and again until the form of a sword starts to materialize. If you're a country boy like me perhaps a different analogy will serve better: God is going to scrub me clean like a long-haired dog that ran home yelping through the burdocks and the swamp muck after tangling with a skunk and a porcupine. Through this process, God doesn't warn us there *might* be some discomfort along the way. He *promises* there will be discomfort. But He also promises in the end I will be clean enough to present to His Father. *If I let Him.*

It is the "if I let Him" part that I admit still challenges me at times. In the fourth century AD, Augustine of Hippo wrote, "He who created us without our help will not save us without our consent." Only Christ can save us. Only we can keep Him from doing so. What a dilemma. I have a lot of areas that *need* fixing, but if I am to be totally honest there are some areas I don't *want* fixed even though I know they are sinful. How do you say, "No thanks in that particular area" to God? It isn't an option. When you ask God to fix you, His goal is to fix *all* (there's that word again) of what is broken rather than just the parts you want fixed. I want Him. I *need* Him. I'm terrified of being separated from Him for eternity. But there is simply no such thing as committing to Him a *little*. If you are content with living apart from God a little right now, then you should prepare to be content with the idea of living apart from Him for eternity.

God is reasonable, of course. He may let you get by with turning yourself over a little bit at a time at first, but at some point He is going to expect you to make a decision. In Matthew 12:30 Jesus tells His followers that anyone who isn't working with Him is working against Him. He will not be satisfied with being the relative who comes to stay with you every now and then. God has far too much work to do on you and through you, work that can only be done if you ask Him to move into your home and live with you. He has so much work to do in you and through you that He will require unconditional surrender. Unconditional surrender means accepting that *everything* we have is God's to do with what *He* wants. It means accepting that God has every right to use us and our possessions to carry out His mission for His children. It means submitting to God's plan for our life even if it is completely out of sync with what our plans are.

We are in many ways a great nation, but only the most naïve person would fail to recognize that being a member of the most prosperous nation in the world has come at a great cost to our faith: we measure our own worth and success by the standard of the world rather than by God's standard. Our success and the way we determine the success of other countries is measured in economic terms such as one's standard of living. A family of four is considered *poor* in our country if their annual income is below $40,000. In more than 80% of the countries of the world, an annual income of $40,000 would be considered fabulously rich. A person making $50,000 per year is in the top 1% of the wealthiest people on earth. Nearly half the world's population survives on $2.00 per day or less. Poverty is, of course, a relative term. Even the poorest in our country usually have access to daily food, shelter, and clothing. If a child from Malawi, one of the poorest nations on earth, were to visit a home considered "poor" or low-income by our standards, she would most likely see a sturdy structure, lots of furniture, people with many sets of clothes, televisions and video players, food in the cabinet, electricity, running water, indoor plumbing, and other amenities that would simply blow her mind.

The reason a family of four can be considered "poor" in our country is a function of supply and demand. We demand a lot. The costs of things escalate when they are in great demand and when a significant percentage of the population has the means to purchase them. In Brazil, I once bought a twenty-five-pound bag of tangerines for less than a dollar. In the United States at that time I was able to get only three tangerines for that price. If we look into our hearts, it is easy to discern why we have such an issue making a commitment to God. I love my country, but I know its culture. I know *me*. With all our privileges, opportunities, and wealth, I can think of few other cultures on earth whose people would be more reluctant to commit to turning everything we have over to anyone, even God. We love our "stuff." We love our wealth because of what it allows us to have and do, because of how it defines our success in the eyes of the world. We strive for it and feel entitled to it. On paper we are one of the most charitable nations on earth (per capita), but the amount we give to charity is still only a tiny portion of our net wealth. We forget that God blesses some people or nations with wealth, but not because they deserve it more than any other. We are blessed with wealth so that we can help those who are not. But oh how we live such lives of selfish ambition and greed even in the light of that knowledge. Whether we verbalize it or not, one of the commitments we hold tightest to in our hearts is the commitment to accumulate more wealth. It is this challenge that I believe keeps most American Christians from surrendering to God unconditionally and realizing the full potential God has for us to minister to and change the world.

We so easily lose sight of our other commitments in the glare of all that glitters. We forget that while "Humans are satisfied with what *looks* good. God probes for what *is* good" (Proverbs 16:2 NIV). With all that we have, what do we *really* do with it? The Prophet Haggai warned the people of Israel to "Give careful thought to your ways. You have planted much, but harvested little. You eat, but never have enough. You drink, but never have your fill. You put on clothes, but are not warm. You earn wages, only to put them in a purse with holes in it" (Haggai 1:5-6 NIV).

How do the affluent of this world differ from the Israelites? It shouldn't seem ironic to us that in this world the people who are most likely to surrender unconditionally to God are the people who have lost everything or who have next to nothing to begin with. The Old and New Testament contain hundreds of verses about the poor. Though some references refer to the "spiritually" poor, many refer to those who are afflicted, hungry, or needy. Christ understands the dilemma of wealth. He told His disciples, "It is easier for a camel to go through the eye of a needle than for someone who is rich to enter the kingdom of God" (Matthew 19:24 NIV). Make no mistake about it: we are rich by international standards. Making a commitment to God scares us because, while He may not ask us to sacrifice *everything* we have, He just might. In similar fashion, God may not allow us to lose "everything," but then again He may if he thinks our loss will serve a higher purpose. American pastor A.W. Tozier wrote, "The true follower of Christ will not ask, 'If I embrace this truth, what will it cost me?' Rather he will say, 'This is truth. God help me to walk in it, let come what may!'" Is not the idea of "*let come what may*" more frightening to a person who has much to lose than to a person who has little or nothing to lose?

What does any of this have to do with letting Christ loose in my classroom? Everything! When we make a commitment to Christ, it isn't limited to just one area of our lives. In Psalms 18:20 (MSG) David writes, "God made my life complete when I placed *all* the pieces before Him. When I got my act together, He gave me a fresh start." There's that word again- *all*. If we do not give our whole life to Christ, we cannot rightly expect that He will be with us completely in the areas of our life we choose. All of us wear different hats throughout the week. I am a father, a husband, a son, a friend, a member of a church, and a teacher among other things. God expects me to demonstrate my commitment to Him regardless of which hat I have on. I cannot imagine God blessing me in my role as a teacher if I make little effort to honor my commitment to Him in other areas of my life. *Honoring Christ through my teaching is impossible if I have not changed my life so that I am honoring Him through every other aspect of my life.* I cannot flip a "God switch" when I walk through the door of my classroom and expect the Light to come on. I am a member of a small community and a large church where I am constantly running into students and their parents. My former students ring up my groceries, serve me in local restaurants, take care of my children in day care, babysit for me. It is a rare thing for me to venture out into the community without running into current or past students or their parents. They see me and will always know me as their teacher regardless of where we happen to bump into each other or how much time has passed. A great deal of what I will write about has nothing to do directly with what goes on *in* your classroom. It has to do with the person you become and the life you lead outside the confines of your classroom.

So there it was laid out in plain sight before me. God is the wise old coach, heaven the Hall of Fame. In terms of my own commitment, not only did I initially not understand what I had "gotten myself into," I had mistakenly believed that there was a "good enough" standard I could maintain. After all, I reasoned, we are all sinners by nature. In addition, I have already admitted that though I want to change, I don't want to change everything *just yet*. I continue to struggle, sticking to many of my old ways even though I know full well it is not what God wants for me and is a violation of the commitment I made. I am like Augustine who in the fourth century asked God to "Give me chastity and continence, *but not yet.*"

Turning back is not an option for me. I have made a commitment and it doesn't matter that

I didn't really know what I had gotten myself into. The fact remains that I want to live a life that honors Christ, one that expresses my gratitude for His grace. I want to live a life where I lead people to Him. But my dilemma upon really learning what my commitment entailed was that I couldn't imagine how someone like me could possibly honor it! If we consider the analogy I opened this chapter with, when I first made my commitment to Christ I wasn't a "good athlete" who wanted to become great. I was analogous to an obese, chain smoking, lazy, excuse-laden, alcoholic, couch potato with a passion for fast food. I am at times (and I am careful to say *am* rather than *was* because when I turn off the God switch each of these traits can rear its ugly head) impulsive, quick-tempered, lustful, impatient, pessimistic, sarcastic, insensitive, selfish, outspoken, flirtatious, moody, and if impression truly is reality as some people say, arrogant. I can be self-righteous and display an attitude of entitlement when my feathers are ruffled. I made a commitment to God and because of it God is going to make *that* perfect? Now many years into being saved, I still can't break the twenty-minute mile. I certainly can no longer play the ignorance card. I now know more than enough to be held accountable. The Bible warns, "Don't excuse yourself by saying, 'Look, we didn't know.' For God understands all hearts, and he sees you. He who guards your soul knows you knew. He will repay all people as their actions deserve" (Proverbs 24:12 NLT). I have been so stubborn about letting go of some of my old ways, so lax at times about honoring my commitment, I find myself wondering whether God knew what He'd gotten *Himself* into.

In the end, God will honor our free will. He loves us too much and He desires a genuine love from us so much that He will never force Himself on us. Committing to God must be a choice that we make. At the end of a long and very arduous life, Joshua came before an assembly of the tribal leaders, judges, elders, and officials of Israel and reminded them how much God had blessed them. He had led them to the land God had promised to them and vanquished all the enemies in their way. This land, the major trading hub of its time between Africa, the Mediterranean, and Asia was as abundant as God had promised. Clearly the people of Israel could see without a doubt that they were indeed God's chosen people. Surely they would see this and worship the God who bestowed such blessings upon them. Joshua knew better. He knew the human heart and had seen first-hand how his people continued, despite their blessings, to turn from God time and time again. And Joshua knew God would never force Himself upon the people of Israel. Joshua knew that God would honor their free will. He would allow them to choose. Joshua acknowledged this right, then made it clear where his allegiance lay:

> But if serving the LORD seems undesirable to you, then choose for yourselves this day whom you will serve, whether the gods your ancestors served beyond the Euphrates, or the gods of the Amorites, in whose land you are living. But as for me and my household, we will serve the LORD.
>
> Joshua 24:15 NIV

If we want God to flow through us in our job as a teacher, we must make a commitment to turn over *all* aspects of our life to God. His character cannot flow in one part of our lives but not another. We must understand what is involved in this choice. Honoring such a commitment in this world and in our fallen condition will involve far more than most people can imagine. We must also recognize that it will be absolutely impossible to honor this commitment without God's help because we, as sinners, are not hard-wired to do such things. The Lord tells us to "count the cost," but He also promises us eternal life as reward for a life of honoring and obeying Him.

CHAPTER TWO

Clothe Yourself in Humility

Humility is the foundation of all the other virtues hence, in the soul in which this virtue does not exist there cannot be any other virtue except in mere appearance.

Saint Augustine of Hippo

Humble we must be, if to heaven we go; High is the roof there, but the gate is low.

Robert Herrick, 17th century English poet

The greatest test of whether the holiness we profess to seek or to attain is truth and life will be whether it produces an increasing humility in us. In man, humility is the one thing needed to allow God's holiness to dwell in him and shine through him. The chief mark of counterfeit holiness is lack of humility. The holiest will be the humblest.

Theologian Andrew Murray

Jesus told his disciples, "Learn from me, for I am gentle and humble in heart, and you will find rest for your souls." Humility is like the root of a tree, and gentleness is its fruit. We please God by humility and our neighbor by gentleness.

Anthony Mark Claret

A proud man is always looking down on things and people: and, of course as long as you are looking down, you cannot see something that is above you.

C.S. Lewis

It concerns us greatly to look at this humiliation, as one of the most essential things pertaining to true Christianity. This is the principal part of the great Christian duty of self-denial. That duty consists in two things, viz., first, in a man's denying his worldly inclinations, and in forsaking and renouncing all worldly objects and enjoyments; and, secondly, in denying his natural self-exaltation, and renouncing his own dignity and glory and in being emptied of himself; so that he does freely and from his very heart, as it were renounce himself, and annihilate himself. Thus the Christian doth in evangelical humiliation. And this latter is the greatest and most difficult part of self-denial: although they always go together, and one never truly is, where the other is not; yet natural men can come much nearer to the former than the latter.

Excerpt from Religious Affectations by Jonathan Edwards

Foundational Concepts

✝ **Our Lord and Savior Jesus lived a life characterized by humility. If we commit our lives to Him, we are called to live such a life as well.**

Central Questions

- What is the definition of humility as it applies to believers of Christ?
- What does humility look like in the life of a Christian?
- Why is humility so important?
- What is meant by "pride" in the Bible and how does God feel about it?
- How can I demonstrate humility in my role as a teacher?

Understanding Humility

In the Book of 2 Kings we are introduced to Naaman, commander of the armies of the King of Aram. Naaman was a valiant commander who had the complete favor of his king, which no doubt meant Naaman was a wealthy and powerful man. He was also afflicted with leprosy. When Naaman learned from his servants of the power of an Israelite prophet, Elisha, he was granted permission by his king to seek out this prophet for a cure. With him, Naaman took an entourage of soldiers, horses and chariots, 750 pounds of silver, and 150 pounds of gold. This they brought to the Israelite king in order to purchase the power of his God to cure Naaman. The King of Israel was dismayed. He had no power to do such a thing. His concern was that if he was unable to grant this request the King of Aram would take it as a slight and attack them. When Elisha learned of his king's plight, he told him to have Naaman seek him out. He would show Naaman the power of his God. When Naaman went to Elisha's home, Elisha did not even come out to greet him. Instead, he sent his servant to direct Naaman to do one simple task: wash himself in the Jordan River seven times and he would be cleansed. Naaman was incensed. He was a great general and yet a mere prophet had snubbed him by sending out his servant with instructions. Naaman wanted a quick and powerful cure, not something that would involve him having to do something. Naaman stormed away angry, refusing to do as Elisha had requested. Fortunately, Naaman's own servants appealed for him to give Elisha's request a chance. After all, had Naaman not been asked to do much more challenging things in his life as a soldier? Naaman relented. He swallowed his pride and washed himself in the Jordan. And he was cured. Naaman returned to Elisha a far humbler man. He offered to pay Elisha, but Elisha would take nothing. It was not Elisha who had cured but God. God demonstrating His power to a foreign leader. God taught Naaman a lesson about humility.

In 1 Peter 5:5 we are told, "All of you, clothe yourselves with humility toward one another, because, 'God opposes the proud but shows favor to the humble and oppressed" (NIV). I wonder how many of us if we left the house each day clothed in our own humility would be arrested for indecent exposure. Dictionaries define the word *humility* in a number of ways. It is a modest opinion or estimate of one's own importance or self-worth, freedom from pride or arrogance, and absence of self-assertion. Humility plays a prominent role in the Bible, as does its antithesis, pride, which in a biblical sense means "arrogance." Humility is the foundation of our relationship with Christ and it must also be the foundation of our relationship with others as well. Humility is not so much something you *have* as it is something you *do*. Being humble means making choices to behave in a certain way when that way is quite often in total opposition to what you want to do or what our culture expects us to do. In the first chapter, we read about what it means when we make a commitment to God, but in truth humility must precede that commitment if we are to have any hope of honoring the commitment. Humility from the start is essential because it demonstrates first and foremost an understanding that we can never honor our commitment to God on our own. We are not nearly strong enough or good enough. Through each stage of our walk with Christ, we will need to count on His power to help us honor our commitment. To love and worship God, we must practice humility. This humility extends vertically from us to Him and laterally from us to the people around us. Even if we were to travel as missionaries to a region where the language barrier prevents us from describing or defining humility, the act of humility is inherently easy to recognize. Anglican bishop J.C. Ryle explained it this way:

> Humility and love are precisely the graces which the men of the world can understand, if they do not comprehend doctrines. They are the graces about which there is no mystery, and they are within reach of all classes. The poorest Christian can every day find occasion for practicing love and humility.

Humility Doesn't Mean Being "Weak" in the Way We Think of Weakness

If we are to fully understand what humility is, we must also consider what it is not. In the Bible, the words "weak" and "meek" are often related to humility but in a very different way than how we view and treat weakness in our society. The term "weakness" has a very negative connotation in most cultures. The weak are often seen as unworthy of our time, non-assertive, ineffective, timid, even detestable in some cases. They are assigned very little value, are frequently marginalized or treated like doormats. People who see themselves as weak in this sense often demonstrate a degree of self-loathing that can lead to self-destruction or perhaps worse: a rage-driven outward retaliation against others in an attempt to prove they are not weak. One might argue this feeling is at the root of some of the mass shootings that have plagued our nation. This is certainly not what the Bible means when it refers to a person being "weak," "meek," or humble.

Being humble does not mean that we lack the ability to take assertive action when it is necessary. Christ was humble, but He certainly was not timid and at times He was quite assertive. Christ did not grovel at the feet of anyone though He chose the life of a servant to everyone. He taught with power and authority, but because He was so sure of His own identity He did not need to demonstrate His power or authority by lauding it over others. Paul wrote that he was made strong through his weakness because it made God's power all the more visible in him. God asks us to examine our character and acknowledge our weaknesses, but this does *not* mean He expects us to loathe ourselves in light of this self-reflection. God made us in His own image. He loves us. He desires for us to love ourselves. The old adage "hate the sin but love the sinner" applies to our own sins and loving ourselves as much as it does others.

Living a life of humility goes against so much of what we are taught by our culture. Though we talk of how we admire a humble man, in truth humility is not by any stretch of the imagination "on parade" in our culture. A tremendous amount of our energy is spent trying to "get ahead," and that is often knowingly or unknowingly at the expense of others. In our culture, and perhaps that of most advanced nations, most people are concerned with "upward mobility." Humility, by contrast, involves downward mobility. It is not my intent to shoot arrows at this country I love so much. We are only one great civilization in an extensive line over the past several millennia and I know of none that became so through abject humility including God's own chosen people. Indeed, the Israelites incurred God's wrath time and time again in large part to their lack of humility. We must accept that part of the challenge we have to become humble is that to become so is quite often contrary to what we have come to know as the American Dream. The context of the American Dream is one of the self-made man, seldom giving credit to God's role in a person or society's success. It is one of sacrifice but not necessarily the kind of Godly sacrifice we learn from the Bible. The measure of a man, likewise, is judged more often than not on what he has. God is not necessarily opposed to wealth. He blesses people with wealth, but for a very specific purpose. What God opposes is the pride that too often accompanies wealth. The belief a man holds that he has attained his wealth on his own. The tendency to value that wealth above God and above others. The unwillingness to use a greater portion of that wealth to bless or serve others. God has blessed us tremendously as a nation. We say that we are "one nation, under God." The first two sentences of the Declaration of Independence mention God. The song *America, the Beautiful*, confirms the traditional American belief that "God shed His grace on thee." But lurking in the shadows of our prosperity is the same dark spirit who has been sowing the seeds of pride throughout the soil of mankind since man first appeared on earth. Satan is real. His army is real. His power on earth is real.

Humility does not come easy or naturally to us because we are a fallen people. We must desire to become humble. We must engage in a program of prayer, study, and self-discipline designed to make humility a driving part of our character. The reason living a life of humility is so difficult is that *pride*, the opposite of humility, has supernatural origins. Pride is a tool of Satan. It is what led to Satan being cast from heaven and it is the very first tool he used to manipulate man in the Garden of Eden. It was pride, a lack of humility that led to man's fall, and because of that pride remains a deeply entrenched part of our sinful nature. Even though Satan will most likely never work on the majority of us directly (he is not omnipresent, and therefore cannot be in more than one place at any given time), the ripples that have resulted from the fall of Adam have continued throughout time. Satan revels in this. Because he can do nothing to God directly and because he knows how much God loves us, Satan and his league of demons try to get at God through His children. Pride remains a favorite "go to" tool for wreaking havoc on earth.

I'm not knowledgeable enough in my faith to understand which types of things God allows Satan to do and which are simply a result of a fallen world (remembering the entire creation groans). At my level of understanding, it seems to me that Satan and his followers wreak this havoc through us either directly or through the original sin virus. It is in no way glorifying Satan to recognize that he has real power on this earth because God has allowed him this power. We must not trivialize this power. Satan and his fallen angels were created as *supernatural* beings. They have supernatural powers which God has allowed them to unleash on earth. He, they, and the virus are supernaturally persuasive, supernaturally divisive, supernaturally destructive, and intentionally covert. Satan, the architect of evil, has the absolute best qualities of the absolute most corrupt defense attorney in the universe. Satan's goal is to, in his mind, defeat God by ultimately having more influence in the hearts and minds of God's children than God has. Remember, God will not force Himself upon us. Satan and his army are not hampered by such restraint. He has instructed his soldiers to try to force themselves into every aspect of our lives, particularly where they see the influence of God at work. They will try to interrupt your prayers, add fuel to the discord that lives in our hearts. Satan wants us to believe that they are "on our side," steering us toward his belief that our God is unreasonable, a regular killjoy. Is Satan or a demonic presence at the root of all our sinful behavior? No-not directly at least. But the ripples of the fall, the virus, man giving into temptation, affects all of us. Satan spreads a virus that can never be eliminated by *man*. Even the symptoms of this virus are supernatural in origin.

Viruses are amazing creations. They are not considered living because they do not meet the criteria for living organism. For example, they do not eat or pass waste, use energy, grow and develop, respond to their environment, or reproduce on their own. To me the most fascinating aspect of viruses is how new viruses are created. This process is an excellent analogy for how the agents of sin work on our hearts and minds. Viruses land on a target cell. The cell does not perceive the virus as a threat. For us, this could be a thought planted in our mind by an agent of evil. It sounds good, reasonable, preferable, pleasurable. The cell is deceived from the onset of the process, so much in fact that the cell opens up a passageway into the cell allowing the genetic material from the virus into the cell. So too are we deceived by the agent's message. Because we are deceived, we welcome it into our heart and mind. The viral genetic material is given VIP treatment. It is actually escorted to the host cell's nucleus, the command center for the entire cell. Once the viral genetic material is escorted into the nucleus, something fascinating takes place: the viral DNA or RNA contains a set of instructions that reprogram the host cell's DNA. Now instead of managing the functions of the cell, the host cell begins disassembling its own cellular structures and using the amino acid building blocks to manufacture more of the virus. In similar fashion, our mind becomes reprogrammed. What we once knew to be wrong now seems right. The strength of the deception multiplies. The host cell material becomes more and more depleted, making the cell vulnerable to other attacks. Our faith starts to deteriorate. In our weakened state, we become susceptible to even more sin. Once the host cell has been depleted, the millions of new viruses spill from the host cell and are carried to other cells that become infected. Once our faith is depleted, our sinful thoughts may spread to another person and another. WE became an agent of sin. Once a virus is in the body, the only thing that can defeat the virus is our body, our immune system. With sinful thoughts, the immune system is the Holy Spirit that lives within each of us. Some viruses can never be defeated. Those that do not kill us may afflict us for the remainder of our lives. With the help of the Holy Spirit, we may battle certain temptations for the remainder of our lives. Sometimes we will lose and become sick. Then perhaps we will rally. Though these types of viruses are incurable, they can be managed by maintaining our overall health and through external assistance from outside experts (physicians) and medicines. For sins that we will battle our entire lives, we can also manage them by maintaining our faith so that we can be led by the Holy Spirit, through assistance from external experts (mature Christians), and from medicine (Holy Scripture). I would also point out that vaccines exist for many infectious pathogens. A vaccine prevents the pathogen from being able to infect us. Vaccines exist against agents of sin as well. Godly parents, a strong church, knowledge of scripture, hanging out with people who come from a strong faith background. Vaccines can sometimes fail, but the likelihood of us becoming as sick for as long is greatly diminished even in this instance.

So why do sinful agents like Satan and his army have such success? It's quite simple: *WE are not supernatural beings.* We are natural beings. We may be able to fend off Satan and his army of demons or the virus for a brief period of time, but WE cannot defeat them on our own. We cannot defeat our own sinful nature, the symptoms of the virus, on our own. It takes a supernatural being to defeat a supernatural being. Even after years of developing Christian wisdom and knowledge, we are susceptible to Satan's influence. In fact, Satan and his army may work even harder to lead mature Christians astray. It is a greater victory to take down a champion than it is a rookie. Fortunately for us, we have the most powerful supernatural being behind us and inside us. To defeat the armies of evil, we must call on the power of the Holy Spirit inside us. If you call on the Holy Spirit to save you because you are prideful and feel you deserve to be saved, out of some selfish, self-deceiving desire, you will be left to battle the evil army on your own. And you will lose. If, on the other hand, you summon the Holy Spirit through humility, you will be snatched out of the devil's reach-until the next time you feel tempted. No doubt this is what Puritan minister Jonathan Edwards meant when he wrote, "Nothing sets a person so much out of the reach of the devil as humility." We should not, however, assume that all the temptation we face is from the devil or one of his fallen angels. We have the darkness of temptation in us all, constantly attacking us and we are ill-equipped to battle this on our own as well. God does expect us to use our free will, our "will power" to battle these temptations. However, our strength alone will never be enough. God ultimately wants us to turn to Him so that His power can assist us when our own meager strength fails. In chapter one, I spoke about the importance of reading each passage carefully so that you may understand the full meaning. Glossing too quickly over a word as simple as "all" can cause you to miss an essential point of the passage. In 2 Chronicles 7 (NIV) the Lord appears to Solomon and tells him, "When I shut up the heavens so that there is no rain, or command locusts to devour the land or send a plague among my people, if my people, who are called by my name, will humble themselves and pray and seek my face and turn from their wicked ways, then I will hear from heaven, and I will forgive their sin and will heal their land." There are two little words in this passage that, if overlooked, will lead to a lot of unanswered prayers. The words are "if" and "then." *If* the people humble themselves before God, *then* He will hear their prayer and help them. This passage implies that God will not even *listen to* our requests unless we humble ourselves first. For technology-minded people, God has a pop-up blocker or a firewall. Prideful requests or messages get sent to God's spam file. Humility is the password that allows us access to God. Humility is the foundation of our relationship with God. As Augustine once wrote, "Should you ask me what is the first thing in religion, I should reply that the first, second, and third thing therein is humility."

The first critical element we need to understand about humility, then, is this:

1.   The basis of a relationship with Christ is humility.

Though the Bible does not define humility for us, it certainly offers wise counsel about how to demonstrate humility and provides examples of humility in action. In his epistle to the Romans, the apostle Paul advised them, "Do not think of yourself more highly than you ought, but rather think of yourself with sober judgment" (Romans 12:3 NIV). Thomas À Kempis echoed that sentiment when he wrote, "Our own opinion of ourselves should be lower than that formed by others, for we have a better chance at our imperfections." In his letter to the Philippians, Paul wrote, "Don't be selfish; don't try to impress others. Be humble, thinking of others as better than yourselves. Don't look out only for your own interests, but take an interest in others, too" (Philippians 2:3-4 NLT). In Galatians 6:4, he advised them to, "Pay careful attention to *your own work*, for then you will get the satisfaction of a job well done, and *you won't need to compare yourself to anyone else.* For we are each responsible for our own conduct." Paul repeatedly warned followers of Christ not to be impressed with themselves or compare themselves with others to determine who is a better person or who is more worthy. "Live in harmony with one another. *Do not be proud*, but be willing to associate with people of low position. *Don't be conceited*" (Romans 12:16 NIV). I Corinthians 13:4-5 (NIV) identifies humility as a key element of Christian love: "Love is patient, love is kind. It does not envy, *it does not boast, it is not proud. It does not dishonor others*, it is *not self-seeking*, it is not easily angered, it keeps no record of wrongs."

From just these few passages, then, we further learn that humility includes:

2.   an awareness and acceptance that we must put the needs and interests of others above your own.
3.   an awareness and acceptance that we should not think ourselves better than others.
4.   an awareness and acceptance that we should not be trying to impress people with our actions (in an attempt to garner the attention and glory that more rightfully belong to God since it is He that has given us everything).

Christ, God in man's flesh, was born under the most humble conditions and lived the most humble of lives. If THE God of the universe can demonstrate such humility, then certainly we should look to Christ's examples and teachings as a model for our own humility. Putting the needs and interests of others above your own means much more than letting someone else eat the last piece of pizza or choose where you will go on vacation. From the mouth of Christ and from the actions of Christ, humility means that we are to become a servant to others. In the fourth century, though he was an influential Bishop of Caesarea, Basil the Great continued to work in a soup kitchen, volunteered in a hospital, and provided care for thieves and prostitutes. Contrast this to the passages in the Gospels of Mark and Luke where the disciples James and John are arguing about which of them is greatest. They want Jesus to tell them which of them would have a seat of honor next to Him in heaven. The text doesn't give any indication that Christ was visibly irritated by the question, but I can't see how He would not have been. He had just told them that He was going to be killed! It was as if they were saying to Jesus, "Yeah, that's a tough break. So which of us is going to sit in the position of honor in heaven with you?"

And this wasn't the first time Christ had had to deal with the thick-headedness of His disciples. Sometime before this, Christ had been asked to decide an argument between the disciples about which of them was the greatest. In that instance, Christ told them, "Anyone who wants to be first must be the very last, and the servant of all" (Mark 9:35 NIV). In Matthew 18: 3-4 (NIV) Christ described it in this way: "Truly I tell you, unless you change and become like little children, you will never enter the kingdom of heaven. Therefore, whoever takes the lowly position of this child is the greatest in the kingdom of heaven." Christ wasn't telling them to become immature. Apparently they already had that trait in spades. He was calling them to be humble. So when James and John were still in effect wanting to know who among them was the greatest, Christ reminded them again that they had missed the point: "Whoever wants to become great among you must be your servant, and whoever wants to be first must be your slave— just as the Son of Man did not come to be served, but to serve, and to give his life as a ransom for many" (Matthew 20:26-28 NIV; see also Mark 10:42-45; Luke 22:24-27).

In the last few days before His death, Christ hammered away at the need for humility. Christ Himself had lived a life of humility, but His disciples still did not seem to understand humility or the absolute necessity of humility as the basis of their relationship with Christ and others. During their last meal together, Christ did something to drive the concept of humility home. Christ took off His outer garment, wrapped a towel around his waist, then lowered Himself to the floor and did something that was typically reserved for slaves or at least the lowest ranking person in the room: He washed the callused, dirty, rank (I would imagine) feet of his disciples (see John 13:1-17). He had lived a life of humility, but He wanted to make this decisive point to His disciples. The act of washing was only part of the symbol. He could have chosen some other way to demonstrate humility, but He chose one where He literally had to lower Himself. When Peter's turn came, he protested to Jesus. He did not understand why Jesus would be washing his feet. Jesus responded by saying, "Unless I wash you, you have no part of me" (v. 8). Jesus was telling His disciples that unless they "got it," unless they understood the necessity for humility, they could never serve Him.

> When he had finished washing their feet, he put on his clothes and returned to his place. "Do you understand what I have done for you?" he asked them. "You call me 'Teacher' and 'Lord,' and rightly so, for that is what I am. Now that I, your Lord and Teacher, have washed your feet, you also should wash one another's feet. I have set you an example that you should do as I have done for you. Very truly I tell you, no servant is greater than his master, nor is a messenger greater than the one who sent him. Now that you know these things, you will be blessed if you do them.
>
> John 13: 12-17

So now we see that humility includes another element: service.

5. Humility includes an awareness and acceptance that we are to become a servant to others.

The disciples "got it," but still only to a point. Christ knew this. He had told them as He washed their feet, "You do not realize now what I am doing, but later you will understand." Christ knew that His ultimate act of humility would come a few hours later when He took the sins of the world upon His shoulders and suffered the punishment that went with them so that we could be saved. He who was without sin lowered Himself to below the gravest of sinners for our salvation. What Christ needed His disciples to understand, but what they would not fully understand until after His crucifixion and after being filled with the Holy Spirit, is that humility is the foundation for a personal, life-changing relationship with Him. None of what Christ desires for us and from us can be accomplished without humility. Humility is not just important in the life of a Christian, it is an absolute necessity. Further examples of humility exist throughout the Old and New Testaments. Abraham humbled himself before God by doing what God asked. Abraham was old and living a life of relative wealth and comfort when God called him to pack up his belongings and family and trek around a brutal desert to a place that was unknown to Abraham. When it came to divide up the land God had given Abraham, Abraham allowed Lot to have first choice of the land. Numbers 12:3 refers to Moses as "meek (humble) above all men on the face of the earth." God reminded Moses that it wasn't his own abilities that would allow him to lead but God working through him. Moses repeatedly cautioned his people to remain humble before God, and to remember that everything they have is a gift from God. Years later through the prophet Jeremiah, the Lord warned His people:

> Don't let the wise boast in their wisdom, or the powerful boast in their power, or the rich boast in their riches. But those who wish to boast should boast in this alone: That they truly know me and understand that I am the LORD who demonstrates unfailing love and who brings justice and righteousness to the earth, and that I delight in these things.
>
> Jeremiah 9:23-24 NLT

In the New Testament Gospel of Matthew, a centurion approaches Christ and asks Him to heal his servant. When Jesus told the centurion He would go with him to his home to heal his servant, the centurion responded by saying, "Lord, I do not deserve to have you come under my roof. But just say the word, and my servant will be healed" (Matthew 8:8 NIV). This powerful man humbled himself before Christ. In his epistle to the Philippians, Paul speaks of Timothy's humility: "I hope in the Lord Jesus to send Timothy to you soon, that I also may be cheered when I receive news about you. I have no one else like him, who will show genuine concern for your welfare. For everyone looks out for their own interests, not those of Jesus Christ. But you know that Timothy has proved himself, because as a son with his father he has served with me in the work of the gospel" (Philippians 2:19-22 (NIV). Paul refers to himself as "less than the least of all God's people" (Ephesians 3:8 NIV) and is in awe of Christ's choice to have him bring the message to the gentiles because he sees himself as having been so unbelievably unworthy of such an honor. The Bible has examples of the aspect of humility which discourages us from trying to impress others and draw attention to ourselves. In Galatians 1:10 (NIV), Paul asks people to consider, "Am I now trying to win the approval of human beings, or of God? Or am I trying to please people? If I were still trying to please people, I could not be a servant of Christ." In Matthew 6, Christ advises us to:

> Be especially careful when you are trying to be good so that you don't make a performance out of it. It might be good theater, but the God who made you won't be applauding. When you do something for someone else, don't call attention to yourself. You've seen them in action, I'm sure—'playactors' I call them— treating prayer meeting and street corner alike as a stage, acting compassionate as long as someone is watching, playing to the crowds. They get applause, true, but that's all they get. When you help someone out, don't think about how it looks. Just do it—quietly and unobtrusively. That is the way your God, who conceived you in love, working behind the scenes, helps you out.
>
> Matthew 6:1-4 Message

The Bible does not say that it is wrong for us to be praised, especially if it is for the right reason. Humility, though, should prevent us from self-praise. Proverbs 27:2 (NIV) says, "Let someone else praise you, and not your own mouth; an outsider, and not your own lips." Pray that you are being praised for the right reason.

Hence we learn more core characteristics of humility:

6. Humility includes an awareness and acceptance that we are unworthy, that we do not deserve the grace Christ has given us.
7. Humility includes an awareness and acceptance that everything we have comes from God.
8. Humility includes the awareness and acceptance that apart from God we are nothing.
9. Humility should prevent attention-seeking behavior that attempts to feed our own need for recognition or praise.

These humble truths breed such contempt in the hearts of so many people. It actually makes people hate the idea of such a God. As stumbling blocks go, it doesn't get much higher than this. We are raised to think we are special among men, that we have earned all that we have, that we are deserving of rewards. As I watched the 2012 Summer Olympic Games, the commentators spoke of the athlete's grit, determination, hard work, dedication, pride. For sure every one of them pushed themselves to their limit and beyond what many ever thought possible. But my favorite part of the Olympics was when a couple of remarkable young ladies with a handful of gold medals between them, undoubtedly aware of the criticism Tim Tebow has received for his public expressions of faith, never-the-less unapologetically and unwavering gave thanks to God in front of millions of viewers around the world. While the Internet was still abuzz about the reported criticism of gymnast Gabby Douglas's hair, the young lady essentially blew off the ridiculous nature of the criticism and turned her attention to God:

It is everything I thought it would be; being the Olympic champion, it definitely is an amazing feeling. And I give all the glory to God. It's kind of a win-win situation. The glory goes up to Him and the blessings fall down on me.

Later, she reportedly tweeted, "Let all that I am praise the LORD; may I never forget the good things He does for me."

In an interview with another Olympics phenom, sixteen-year-old swimming sensation Missy Franklin also gave credit to God, saying

God is always there for me. I talk with Him before, during and after practice and competitions. I pray to Him for guidance. I thank Him for this talent He has given me and promise to be a positive role model for young athletes in all sports.

If I understand her situation correctly, church and faith did not play a big role in her life as a young child. Her walk with Christ began when she entered Regis Jesuit High School. In her interview she spoke openly of how her faith and relationship with God has grown. Millions of children around the world saw these young ladies win those medals, saw their radiant and infectious personalities, and heard them give credit to God. We witnessed their humility. Missy Franklin and Gabby Douglas are the role models we needed so desperately for this generation of children. May God give them continued strength now that they are under the watchful eyes of those who are eagerly awaiting a stumble so they can tear them down and their God in the process. When we humble ourselves and openly praise God, we all become marked men or women. Some who try to take us down are from outside the faith. Too often we do it to each other.

Pride Goes Before Destruction

God is especially pleased by humility, but He is particularly angered by its antithesis-pride. Pride is an elevated sense of self, a belief that one is superior to others. Proud people feel like they alone are responsible for their own accomplishments or success. In his sermon, *Religious Affections,* Jonathan Edwards addressed the characteristics of pride, which in his explanation was the absence of evangelical humility:

It is true, that many hypocrites make great pretenses to humility, as well as other graces; and very often there is nothing whatsoever which they make a higher profession of. They endeavor to make a great show of humility in speech and behavior; but they commonly make bungling work of it, though glorious work in their own eyes. They cannot find out what a humble speech and behavior is, or how to speak and act so that there may indeed be a savor of Christian humility in what they say and do: that sweet humble air and mien is beyond their art, being not led by the Spirit, or naturally guided to a behavior becoming holy humility, by the vigor of a lowly spirit within them.

Christ was particularly disturbed by the pride and hypocrisy of the religious leaders of His time. "They tie up heavy, cumbersome loads and put them on other people's shoulders, but they themselves are not willing to lift a finger to move them. Everything they do is done for people to see: They make their phylacteries wide and the tassels on their garments long; they love the place of honor at banquets and the most important seats in the synagogues; they love to be greeted with respect in the marketplaces and to be called 'Rabbi' by others" (Matthew 23:4-7 NIV). Proverbs 15:8 (MSG) says, "God can't stand pious poses. But He delights in genuine prayers." These leaders had an exaggerated sense of self. They felt themselves above others. Jesus used the parable of the Pharisee (a religious leader) and the tax collector to contrast humility and pride. Pharisees were arguably the most important religious leaders of the Jewish people. Though John the Baptist and Christ would chastise the Pharisees and Sadducees (the other sect of powerful religious leaders) for their hypocrisy, they would have most likely been revered (albeit perhaps reluctantly) by the Jewish people. Tax collectors, on the other hand, were hated by the Jewish people. They were seen as agents of Rome who collected tribute money for the Roman Empire. It is also believed that many of these tax collectors were corrupt. When Christ discusses these two players in a parable, it is reasonable to believe that many Jews would have thought it would be the Pharisee who would serve as the protagonist. That turned out not to be the case:

> To some who were confident of their own righteousness and looked down on everyone else, Jesus told this parable: 'Two men went up to the temple to pray, one a Pharisee and the other a tax collector. The Pharisee stood by himself and prayed: 'God, I thank you that I am not like other people—robbers, evildoers, adulterers—or even like this tax collector. I fast twice a week and give a tenth of all I get.'
>
> But the tax collector stood at a distance. He would not even look up to heaven, but beat his breast and said, 'God, have mercy on me, a sinner.'
>
> I tell you that this man, rather than the other, went home justified before God. For all those who exalt themselves will be humbled, and those who humble themselves will be exalted.
>
> Luke 18:9-14 NIV

The Pharisee lacked humility. In his arrogance, he thought God would agree that he was better or more worthy than others (especially the tax collector). The Pharisee's focus was on himself. The tax collector, however, humbled himself before God. His guilt weighed heavily on his heart. He admitted to God that he was a sinner and begged for God's mercy. In this parable, Christ illustrates that we are *all* sinners, but a sinner with humility will be exalted by God while the proud will be humbled by Him. There is also another very important message that all of us must take from this parable: the only way you will ever succeed in enabling people to see the Godly person you want to be is to actually be that person day in and day out. Notice I did not say we should "act" like the person we want to be-we must *be* that person. A good actor like a skilled Pharisee can put on a good show, but Christ knew their hearts and He knows ours as well. Furthermore, if we are merely "acting," sooner or later the façade will start to fade. "Acting" is unsustainable. There are some cases where the philosophy of "fake it 'til you make it" may be necessary, but as a lifestyle it is a house built on sand.

In chapter fourteen of Luke, Christ tells the parable of the invited guest to illustrate how His followers should act when it comes to their own "importance:"

> When he noticed how the guests picked the places of honor at the table, he told them this parable: "When someone invites you to a wedding feast, do not take the place of honor, for a person more distinguished than you may have been invited. If so, the host who invited both of you will come and say to you, 'Give this person your seat.' Then, humiliated, you will have to take the least important place. But when you are invited, take the lowest place, so that when your host comes, he will say to you, 'Friend, move up to a better place.' Then you will be honored in the presence of all the other guests. For all those who exalt themselves will be humbled, and those who humble themselves will be exalted.
>
> Luke 14:7-11 NIV

Very simply, God detests pride and arrogance. Recall that it was because of pride and arrogance that He cast Satan from heaven and to some degree Adam and Eve from the Garden of Eden. Pride over and over again subjected the Israelites to God's heavy hand. Even people who have never read the Bible have no doubt heard the phrase found in Proverbs 16:18- "Pride comes before the fall." Quite simply, if humility is an absolute necessity for carrying out God's plan on earth then pride, the opposite of humility, makes that job much more difficult or even impossible. And again, God has too much for us to do to let pride slow us down. Throughout the Old and New Testament are verses condemning pride and warning of the consequences. These are but a few (all NIV unless otherwise specified):

- Proverbs 3:34 - He mocks proud mockers but shows favor to the humble and oppressed.
- Proverbs 11:2- When pride comes, then comes disgrace, but with humility comes wisdom.
- Proverbs 15:25- The LORD tears down the house of the proud, but he sets the widow's boundary stones in place.
- Proverbs 16:5- The LORD detests all the proud of heart. Be sure of this: They will not go unpunished.
- Proverbs 16:18- Pride goes before destruction, a haughty spirit before a fall.
- Proverbs 18:2- Fools find no pleasure in understanding but delight in airing their own opinions.
- Proverbs 18:12- Before a downfall the heart is haughty, but humility comes before honor.
- Proverbs 21:4- Haughty eyes, a proud heart, and evil actions are all sin.
- Proverbs 26:12- Do you see a person wise in their own eyes? There is more hope for a fool than for them.
- Proverbs 29:23 (English Standard Version)- One's pride will bring him low, but he who is lowly [humble] in spirit will obtain honor.

- Psalms 138:6- Though the LORD is exalted, he looks kindly on the lowly, but he takes notice of the proud from afar.
- Galatians 6:3- If any of you think you are something when you are nothing, you deceive yourselves.
- Psalm 75: 4-5 (NLT)- "I warned the proud, 'Stop your boasting!' I told the wicked, 'Don't raise your fists! Don't raise your fists in defiance at the heavens or speak with such arrogance.'"
- Psalm 138:6 (NLT)- Though the LORD is great, he cares for the humble, but he keeps his distance from the proud.
- 1 Samuel 2:3 (NLT)- "Stop acting so proud and haughty! Don't speak with such arrogance! For the LORD is a God who knows what you have done; he will judge your actions.

The Bible contains more verses similar to these, all of which point to the inarguable fact that God walks with the humble but opposes the proud. God will deal with pride one way or another. For people who are not believers, He may allow them to live their lives on their own terms. C.S. Lewis once wrote, "There are two kinds of people: those who say to God, 'Thy will be done,' and those to whom God says, 'All right, then, have it your way.'" This of course comes with a cost. Those whom God allows to "have it their own way" in this life will not share eternity with Him in the next life. If, however, you have made a commitment to God, I feel quite confident that if you fail to do the things you need to do to have humility become a defining part of your character, God will use something in this world *to make you* humble. Recall Christ's parable of the Pharisee and the tax collector. Christ said, "For all those who exalt themselves *will be humbled.*" He has no choice if you are truly sincere about your commitment to Him. Remember, He has to make you perfect. The Founder of the *Back to the Bible* radio broadcast, Theodore Epp wrote, "The lesson for each believer is to humble himself, not to wait for the Lord to humble him." The degree to which God will need to humble you will be related to the level of your pride and to the commitment you claimed to have made to Him. The higher you soar, the further you have to fall. Remember, though, that God is not necessarily humbling you to punish you. He is doing it because He loves you. He has a job for you on earth. He wants you to join Him in eternity, but that eternity has no rooms for the proud. God is not breaking you for *His* own good, He is breaking you for *your* own good. As many times as it takes and for as long as it takes. Theologian Smith Wigglesworth wrote, "Before God could bring me to this place [of humility] He has broken me a thousand times." In the Book of Deuteronomy, God explains (through Moses) why He put the Israelites through the trials of forty years in the desert:

> Remember how the LORD your God led you through the wilderness for these forty years, humbling you and testing you to prove your character, and to find out whether or not you would obey his commands. Yes, he humbled you by letting you go hungry and then feeding you with manna, a food previously unknown to you and your ancestors. He did it to teach you that people do not live by bread alone; rather, we live by every word that comes from the mouth of the LORD. For all these forty years your clothes didn't wear out, and your feet

didn't blister or swell. Think about it: Just as a parent disciplines a child, the LORD your God disciplines you for your own good.

Deuteronomy 8:2-6 NLT

God humbles us in a variety of ways. The Apostle Paul was humbled by what he referred to as a "thorn in his side." The Bible does not tell what this "thorn" was, but Paul himself explains that the Lord would not remove this thorn from Paul's life because it kept him from becoming arrogant or prideful. There are a number of theories about what Paul's "thorn" may have been, and we will consider some of them in Chapter Seven, but for now it is important to understand that Paul became *grateful* for his thorn because Christ had told him that His power was made perfect in Paul's weakness (humility). Thomas À Kempis expressed similar gratitude for being humbled by God for his own welfare. He wrote, "It is good for me, Lord, that Thou hast humbled me, that I may learn Thy righteous judgments, and may cast away all haughtiness of heart and all presumption."

God warns us that He will not tolerate our pride for long, and several stories prove that He does not issue hollow threats. In the Book of Daniel, God taught Babylonian King Nebuchadnezzar a hard lesson about humility:

> As he looked out across the city, he (Nebuchadnezzar) said, "Look at this great city of Babylon! By my own mighty power, I have built this beautiful city as my royal residence to display my majestic splendor.

While these words were still in his mouth, a voice called down from heaven, "O King Nebuchadnezzar, this message is for you! You are no longer ruler of this kingdom. You will be driven from human society. You will live in the fields with the wild animals, and you will eat grass like a cow. Seven periods of time will pass while you live this way, until you learn that the Most High rules over the kingdoms of the world and gives them to anyone he chooses."

That same hour the judgment was fulfilled, and Nebuchadnezzar was driven from human society. He ate grass like a cow and he was drenched with the dew of heaven. He lived this way until his hair was as long as eagles' feathers and his nails were like birds' claws.

> After this time had passed, I, Nebuchadnezzar, looked up to heaven. My sanity returned, and I praised and worshiped the Most High and honored the one who lives forever

Daniel 4:30-34 NLT

Uzziah, Judah's eleventh king, was a brilliant military tactician, politician, and statesmen who was known throughout the lands. He served as Judah's king for fifty-two years. For most of this time, Uzziah was inspired to seek out and follow God's will. As long as he did this, God continued to reward Uzziah with success. Unfortunately, as is all too often the case, Uzziah's success, prosperity, and power began to corrupt him. He became arrogant, taking credit for his own success rather than giving credit to God. When he violated God's rules for the temple, King Uzziah was stricken by God with leprosy. This mighty king lived his final days powerless and effectively alone. When he died, his disease prevented him from being buried in the royal tomb. The Lord may humble us individually as He did with Paul by allowing a humbling element to remain in our lives for our entire life if necessary or as He did with Nebuchadnezzer by humbling him with a temporary affliction. In the case of King Uzziah, God humbled him with a terminal illness. The Old Testament does not say whether Uzziah ever repented, but even if he had it appears God did not restore Uzziah to his former glory. So much does the Lord detest pride that He may also choose to humble an entire civilization. How many times did He allow the Israelites to be conquered, scattered, or enslaved by powerful outside kingdoms? Egypt. Babylon. Assyria. Rome. And it's not as though these people were not warned. The various prophets were constantly calling for the people of Judah and Israel to get their houses in order. For example, through Jeremiah (13:9), God warned that He would "rot away the pride of Judah and Jerusalem." God even sent warnings to the *enemies* of His people about the price of their pride. Consider God's warning to the Edomites in the Book of Obadiah:

> The LORD says to Edom, "I will cut you down to size among the nations; you will be greatly despised. You have been deceived by your own pride because you live in a rock fortress and make your home high in the mountains. 'Who can ever reach us way up here?' you ask boastfully. But even if you soar as high as eagles and build your nest among the stars, I will bring you crashing down," says the LORD.
>
> Obadiah 1:2-4 NLT

Some of God's harshest reaction toward pride is found in Isaiah 3:16-26. While His condemnation seems directed toward the women of Jerusalem, certainly the message was meant for all Judeans. As men were expected to be the spiritual leaders of their households, the women of their household in most cases represented the values of the male head of the household. Most women were unlikely to have been in a position to purchase the fancy clothes and jewelry they were parading around in. They were trophy wives and daughters who became living displays for the male head of household's status. As the Bible is a living document, the inspired Word of God, it is also meant to apply to people throughout the ages.

> God says, "Zion women are stuck-up, prancing around in their high heels, Making eyes at all the men in the street, swinging their hips, Tossing their hair, gaudy and garish in cheap jewelry." The Master will fix it so those Zion women will all turn bald, Scabby, bald-headed women. The Master will do it.
>
> The time is coming when the Master will strip them of their fancy baubles—the dangling earrings, anklets and bracelets, combs and mirrors and silk scarves, diamond brooches and pearl necklaces, the rings on their fingers and the rings on their toes, the latest fashions in hats, exotic perfumes and aphrodisiacs, gowns and capes, all the world's finest in fabrics and design.
>
> Instead of wearing seductive scents, these women are going to smell like rotting cabbages; Instead of modeling flowing gowns, they'll be sporting rags; Instead of their stylish hairdos, scruffy heads; Instead of beauty marks, scabs and scars.

Your finest fighting men will be killed, your soldiers left dead on the battlefield.

The entrance gate to Zion will be clotted with people mourning their dead—

A city stooped under the weight of her loss, brought to her knees by her sorrows.

My only response to this is, "Ouch!" God's disgust at the pride of these people is evident and alarmly familiar to me. The New American Standard Bible interpretation of verse 16 calls them "proud" rather than stuck up. I chose the interpretation from The Message because while not everyone may understand what the Bible means when it says someone is "proud," even a child knows that someone who is "stuck up" thinks themselves better than others. The references to flirting, wearing gaudy make-up and jewelry, dousing themselves in perfume, and wearing ankle and wrist bracelets (which "tinkle" when a person walks and draw the attention of others) are all clearly identifying the need of these people to draw attention to themselves. Flaunting one's attractiveness, being sexually suggestive, needing attention or recognition, and demonstrating our self-importance and success with a wealth of material items-the more expensive the better-sound familiar at all?

The key here is to note how people or entire societies dealt with their own sin. If they did not have enough humility to repent on their own, did they become humble and *repent* when God taught them a lesson about humility? Even the most humble person is never able to live a life free of sin. We are simply unable to avoid sinning, and because this is the case we must humble ourselves before God and repent of these sins. Only the most naïve "Christian" would believe that because Christ died for our sins we can just look at them and say, "Oh well. I sinned. No big deal. Christ took that bullet for me. I'm good to go." Such a person would believe he or she could go on sinning with impunity. That would be a grave misunderstanding of God's grace. It fails to recognize the need for humility, the need to repent for our sins. It degrades or even nullifies that person's commitment to God. The next element of humility, then, is this:

10. Humility includes the ability to sincerely acknowledge your sins and repent daily.

God Will Reward Humility

Through Christ's life, God knows how enormously challenging living a life of humility will be for us. Jesus is God, but He was also a man, and as such He must have had to deal with the same types of feelings we do. Christ lived among a *chosen* people. That alone must have bred the potential for dizzying heights of arrogance among that population. Had God the Father not seen an abundance of pride in His chosen people, He would have had no need to address it through Moses and his prophets. Likewise, had Christ not seen pride on parade everywhere in His world, He would have had no need to address it either. The abundant references to humility and pride throughout both books of the Bible testify to the need for God's attention. Being part of that culture, being God but also being human, Christ had to have been tempted by pride. The very act of allowing Himself to become human at all is an act of immense humility. If you think it is hard for you to remain humble, imagine how hard it must have been for *the* God of the universe in human form to remain humble despite all He was subjected to in His human form. But Christ remained humble. How? He was not all powerful while He was on earth. The human side of it made it impossible for Him to simply brush away the temptation of pride and make it a non-issue. Though Jesus certainly had His "own" power on earth, He frequently made it clear that much of His power came through Him from His Father in Heaven. Had Christ been "all powerful" in his human form, what need would He have had to call on God, the Father? Jesus demonstrated the need for us to humble ourselves so that we could call on God the Father's power. As His life was a model for ours, the establishment of precedence was essential.

Because He allowed himself to be subjected to this world, we can have no doubt that Christ fully understands what He is asking us to do. He is able to have *empathy*, something which is only possible for humans if we have walked in another person's shoes. Could God have felt this empathy without Christ's life? Of course. God is all powerful. He knows our mind and can feel our pain. But I imagine He knows that our human nature drives us to demand credibility, particularly when we are being asked to do something or sacrifice something. We are more trusting of people whom we feel have been through the same thing we have been through. Christ's life should remove any doubt we have that God can truly understand just how hard it is to practice humility as a human.

Because it is so hard and because it is so essential, God assures us that if we do practice humility we will be rewarded. Proverbs 15:33 tells us that humility will lead to *glory* in God's eyes. Peter wrote that if we humble ourselves under God's mighty hand He will *exalt us* (1Peter 5:6-7). James 4:10 likewise tells us, "God resists the proud, but *gives grace* to the humble. Humble yourselves in the sight of God and He will *exalt* you (New King James Version)." Other passages hammer this message home:

- Isaiah 57:15 NKV-For the high and honored One Who lives forever, Whose name is Holy, says, "I live in the high and holy place. And I also live with those who are sorry for their sins and have turned from them and are not proud. I give new strength to the spirit of those without pride, and also to those whose hearts are sorry for their sins.
- Isaiah 66:2 NIV- These are the ones I look on with favor: those who are humble and contrite in spirit, and who tremble at my word.
- Proverbs 3:34-35 New Life Version- God makes fun of those who make fun of the truth but gives loving-favor to those who have no pride. Honor will be given to the wise, but shame will be given to fools.
- Proverbs 16:5 NLV- Everyone who is proud in heart is a shame to the Lord. For sure, that one will be punished.
- Proverbs 22:4 NLV- The reward for not having pride and having the fear of the Lord is riches, honor and life.
- Proverbs 29:23 NLV- A man's pride will bring him down, but he whose spirit is without pride will receive honor.
- James 4:6 MSG- It's common knowledge that "God goes against the willful proud; God gives grace to the willing humble."
- 1 Peter 5:6 NLT- So humble yourselves under the mighty power of God, and at the right time he will lift you up in honor.

So we understand yet another element of humility:

11. God *rewards* humility even as He *opposes* pride.

What does any of this mean? Will humility be rewarded only in heaven or will we be rewarded here on earth as well? If on earth, what will that reward involve? Will we be rewarded with prosperity? My answer to that is maybe (though that will never be the case if we expect to be rewarded for our humility with wealth). Certainly Mother Theresa was not rewarded with wealth though there is little question that she lived a life of humility. God may choose to reward certain people by making them prosperous or wealthy. On the other side of the coin, there are a great many people on earth who have tons of "gold" but not an ounce of humility, so prosperity is not necessarily (or likely) a reflection of one's humility. I guess my feeling is that if someone really wonders whether they are going to be rewarded on this earth with prosperity, then wealth still has too prominent a place on their altar. It's like the Sons of Zebedee wondering which of them will receive the seat closest to God in heaven. People wondering if they will be rewarded on earth for their humility are missing the point when it comes to humility.

I fully acknowledge my family is blessed, but I must also confess that I am seduced by the pleasure I imagine even more prosperity can bring. I yearn to once again own a boat. I'd like a camper, horses, money to travel, a cabin on a lake, a 4WD pickup truck, and a thousand other things. The list changes daily. Not all I desire is material. At times in my life I have greatly desired recognition and praise for who I am and what I have accomplished. Though I am greatly seduced by the types of rewards mentioned above, when I search my heart I know there are far greater rewards than material prosperity or recognition. There is, of course, the reward of salvation, but there is one earthly reward God offers yet so few of us ever experience: the Lord's peace. Jesus promised us that He would give us *His* peace, a peace different from the peace of this world. His peace is an inner peace toward the outer chaos of our world. It is a calmness that exists in our soul. The calmness that comes when a person begins to experience freedom from pride or arrogance. The calmness that comes when a person is able to accept God's plan for his life come what may. The relief from not having to defend your pride all the time. The calmness that comes with freedom from worry or anxiety. The warmth of being able to love yourself and from knowing that God loves you even though you sin. The feeling of release that accompanies freeing oneself from bitterness or the need to retaliate. The relief from being able to acknowledge your shortcomings, your losses, or your failures without becoming emotionally devastated. Freedom from the greed or envy that drives our pursuit of material things. The relief from being able to let go of the resentment for the life we don't have. The joy of being able to feel grateful for the life we have.

Christ's peace is not just a "gift," it is also a *reward* for a life of humility, obedience, and service. Christ's peace is an inner peace, but it will also manifest itself externally in the way others view us. Humble people are hard to rattle. They are slow to complain. They project contentment. They are not easily consumed by anxiety. There is a visible calmness in their day to day lives. Who wouldn't want to work with a person like this? Who wouldn't want to BE a person like this? I know that I will never experience this kind of peace fully while I am of this world, but I want that taste of what heaven will be like. I want my children to have it. I have seldom experienced this kind of peace because I am so crippled with excessive pride, because I have for so long lived a life fighting for that ton of gold without an ounce of humility. God make me good but not yet. God fix me, but don't break me down in the process.

It is important to me that anyone who reads this understands that I am at the beginning of a journey. This is not a journal of my past, a telling of what has worked for me. It is a guide for my future. I have written so far about commitment and humility. The challenge now is how we demonstrate this commitment and humility through the actions of our lives, and for the purpose of this book specifically through our actions as a public-school teacher. For those of you who are still wondering at this point whether I will ever get to the part where I suggest ways to honor God in your classroom, I'm afraid I have failed so far to make my point. We become the person God wants us to be by submitting ourselves to Him in humility, by making every effort to honor the commitment we made to Him, and by trusting Him to help us fill in our areas of weakness. *That* person will be the one who enters your classroom each morning, and it will be *that* same person who collaborates with or inspires peers, loves his wife, and teaches his own children to love and honor God. It really isn't a matter of inviting Christ to be present in my classroom. It is a matter of living a life where I keep my life open for Christ to work through me at all times so that by default He is automatically working through me the moment I stand before my students or my colleagues each day. I hope to provide examples of how this might look. Certainly it will manifest itself in a variety of ways. In some cases it might involve teaching a particular virtue. In most cases it will involve modeling one. In all instances, we hope and pray that our students, their parents, and our colleagues might catch a glimpse of Christ through us though we may never be able to say His name. This will only be possible if we clothe ourselves in humility. This humility should stand out, set us apart from the typical ways of the world. In us, people should recognize how we benefit from our humility so that it might appeal to them and lead them to pursue a closer relationship with God. What all this has to do with teaching is this: when you become the person *God* wants you to be, you will by pure default become the teacher *you* want to be. Or the air conditioning technician. Or the hotel chambermaid. Or the Senator from Ohio.

CHAPTER THREE

Faith

Faith is taking the first step even when you don't see the whole staircase.

Martin Luther King, Jr

Faith is a living, daring confidence in God's grace, so sure and certain that a man could stake his life on it a thousand times.

Martin Luther

Put GOD in charge of your work, then what you've planned will take place.

Proverbs 16:3 MSG

"Trying to do the Lord's work in your own strength is the most confusing, exhausting, and tedious of all work. But when you are filled with the Holy Spirit, then the ministry of Jesus just flows out of you."

Corrie Ten Boom

Very truly I tell you, whoever believes in me will do the works I have been doing, and they will do even greater things than these, because I am going to the Father. And I will do whatever you ask in my name, so that the Father may be glorified in the Son. You may ask me for anything in my name, and I will do it.

John 14:12-14 NLV

Foundational Concepts

- ✝ God desires for us to have absolute faith in His power and His promise.
- ✝ God's power flows through our faith.
- ✝ Doubt is a sin and therefore will be forgiven if we acknowledge it and repent.
- ✝ God rewards faith.

Central Questions

1. What effect can my faith have on my life and the life of others?
2. Will my doubts about God's power and promise lead me to lose my salvation?
3. How do I deal with the holes in my faith?

When she was younger, my daughter would walk up to me at random times and say two simple words: "trust fall." She would turn with her back to me, and when I signaled I was ready she would fall back into my arms. When we first started doing this, her survival instinct would force her foot backward in case I didn't catch her. Eventually she learned to trust that I would not drop her. She had faith in me. I have made a commitment. I have tried to humble myself before the Lord. Still I struggle day to day trying to honor that commitment and remain faithful. A large part of that is due to selfishness, wanting to live too much of my life on my own terms. But it is also a result of the struggles I have with my faith. When it comes to the things of this world, we are often able to "get by" with having a little faith in something or someone rather than having absolute faith in that thing or person. Innate in our fallen nature are the seeds of doubt, distrust, and skepticism. Because they are part of our nature, these seeds can take root and work their way into our relationship with God. On many occasions in the Old and New Testament, we are reminded that absolute faith in the power and promises of God is the standard in the same way that absolute commitment to God and absolute humility before God are. Many people look at faith as a "blind leap," something guided by an emotional need. I do not believe that is the way God intended it. The Bible clearly says that the infinite complexity, magnificence, and diversity of the Creation points to His infinite power. Likewise, the Word of God in the form of the living Bible provides us with the basis and the rationale for faith. If we believe that God created the universe and if we believe what is written in the Bible, how then could there be any doubt at all in God's power? God does not just desire for us to have complete and absolute faith in His promise and in His power, He expects it.

Therein lies the rub for us. The ability to have complete, sustained, absolute faith is completely alien to a fallen people. Doubt is part of being the sons of Adam. There are parts of the Bible I still struggle with. I know this to be true of many Christians. I *want* to accept all of the Bible, but the other knowledge I have bouncing around in my head often results in conflict with what I read in the Bible. In college I studied ancient history in addition to "life science." I have a relatively advanced knowledge of biology, ecology, and genetics. I spend a lot of time trying to reconcile the Bible with science and sometimes world history. In most cases, this is a relatively easy task. The historical accuracy of the Bible has withstood a great deal of scrutiny. But there are areas I find more challenging to reconcile. I sometimes find myself asking whether certain events in the Bible reflect historical fact or an analogy or metaphor. I struggle in particular with the first few chapters of Genesis. For example, I believe our all-powerful Creator God could have flooded the earth, but my knowledge of science causes me to question whether the flood happened the way it is written. I'm a scholar, so inconsistencies that appear when comparing Matthew, Mark, Luke, and John trouble me. I have studied ancient history and am aware of the similarities in certain ancient stories to the stories in the Old Testament. From before the time when Abraham was called by God and up until even today in some cultures, humanity has been steeped in mythology. I struggle with events in Genesis that are presented in a similar fashion to the mythological stories of other cultures. As a result of my studies in college, I became for a very long time something along the lines of an agnostic deist. I believed there was a higher power that set the universe in motion, but I felt that all the religions and associated myths were attempts for our finite minds to make sense of something that is far, far beyond our ability to understand. While my faith has come a long way since then, I cannot say that I no longer deal with doubt.

We each live this dilemma to one degree or another. We want to experience the power of God in our lives, but at the same time we have doubts about that power. God knows this about us. I have fewer doubts now than I had in the past for sure, but I know that I continue to harbor far too many. If God's goal is to make me perfect, then just a single doubt is one doubt too many. I believe the reason so many of us experience only a measure of God's enormous power in our lives is because we constantly maintain a measure of doubt in His power and promises. Or perhaps, if you are like me, you believe in God's power to change your life but you are afraid of the way He might do it. We want to change, but we want to do it on our own terms with as little discomfort as possible. Another problem is how and where our faith is displayed. Faith is not stage play. Like our commitment and our humility, it cannot manifest itself only in the presence of others. What God will be examining more closely is how our faith and commitment hold up when nobody else is around to see it. When we are all alone at night in front of our computer, can we refrain from looking at sites that dishonor God? When we walk out of the grocery store and notice that we forgot to put the items from the bottom of the buggy on the counter for the clerk to ring up, do we go back in and point out our mistake? When the Coke machine accidentally pops out two drinks instead of one, do we take steps to make sure we pay for the second one? If we find a $10.00 bill in the hallway of our school, do we take it to the office or pocket it and treat it as a windfall? When we have wronged someone in some way he or she is unaware of, do we still make amends toward that person?

There is never a time when God is not aware of how we live our lives. God desires our total commitment to Him. He expects us to lead a life of humility. He wants us to put our complete faith in him. We can fake a relationship with others. We can pretend to care when we don't. We can pretend to be someone's friend when we aren't. We can help someone in a way that we want others to think is out of Christian kindness but that is in reality an attempt to draw attention to our own generosity. Real motives are easily disguised behind a properly constructed façade. We cannot do this with God. Proverbs 5:21 reminds us that everything we do in full view of the Lord, and He will examine *all* that we do. God alone understands the levels of our integrity, the depth of our faith.

How often do we demonstrate our lack of faith by showing disdain toward any of God's rules? God is very specific about how we are to treat others, about how we are to demonstrate charity and not hoard our wealth, about the types of books we read and the websites we visit. Even if in the core of our being we agree with his rules, they rub us the wrong way. God has promised that *His* way will lead to peace and joy. Our lack of faith in that promise is evident in the ways we try to live life *our* way. Whether we doubt God's power completely or doubt His choice of methods, what it basically boils down to is that when God says "trust fall" to us, we balk. Our foot goes back. God's standard is absolute faith in Him. Anything less falls short of his expectations. It's not that God isn't pleased with us when we show faith in certain areas of our life. The Bible tells that God is pleased when we are making steps in the right direction. He shares in our small successes. It is important to remember that God knows the challenges we face. He knows because He is omnipotent, but He knows as well because of His life on earth in the human form of Jesus. Even Christ's disciples were concerned that they did not have enough faith to carry out God's directives---and they were right. But in Luke 17:6 Jesus tells them that sometimes the quality of the faith is more important than the quantity:

> You don't need more faith. There is no 'more' or 'less' in faith. If you have a bare kernel of faith, say the size of a poppy seed, you could say to this sycamore tree, 'Go jump in the lake,' and it would do it.

Luke 17:6 MSG

I have never known a human (or should I say a human who was not also God) who was able to successfully command a mountain to move or a tree to uproot and jump in a lake. Obviously, nobody but Jesus has ever had the kind of absolute faith that is required to move mountains. No, Jesus did not move a mountain. He turned a handful of fish into a several thousand, calmed a storm, walked on water, healed the sick, and raised the dead. That's enough to convince me that had he had the need to move a mountain, He could have. We are not capable of that degree of faith. If God only rewarded us for absolute faith at all times and in all things, we'd be doomed. I believe what the Bible shows us is that a kernel of absolute faith is more powerful than an orchard of faith watered by doubt.

Throughout the Old and New Testament we see the human race meandering through the Valley of Doubt. Imagine how differently things may have gone for the Israelites if they had had more faith in God's power and promise to lead them to victory over the giants of Canaan the first time they stood on the threshold of their promised land. Imagine how things might have turned out differently for Joshua and the Israelites had they continued to express the same lack of faith about God's power and promises. They had wandered the desert for forty years in large part because they doubted God's power and promise. When forty years had passed (long enough for the old generation of Israelites to be replaced by their children) the command finally came to cross the Jordan and take the land God had promised. The Jordan was swollen to great heights by annual flooding. The fortified cities were protected by large, well trained armies. Yet Joshua issued his directives, directives he had received from God, and *this time* the Israelites followed. If you are unfamiliar with the story, God stopped the flow of the river so that the Israelites could cross. When it came time to take the fortress city of Jericho, His command to the Israelites had to have sounded bizarre at the very least. They were not instructed to destroy the walls with battering rams or to breach the walls with ladders and ropes. They were not instructed to fight *at all*. They were instructed to march around the city once a day for six days, then on the seventh day march around the city seven times and have the priests blow trumpets and ram horns, after which the walls of Jericho would come tumbling down and the Israelite army could simply march right in. Why no arrows, no battering rams, no breaching the walls? Because the capture of Jericho was not meant to be an exercise in or a demonstration of military might. It was a test of obedience and of faith. Up until this point, the Israelites had never been a conquering people. It is doubtful that they had a military as well trained, as well equipped, and as experienced as the armies that protected the wealthy trade cities of Canaan. They were no more capable on their own of defeating the armies of Canaan than a little league baseball team would be of defeating a major league club. Their lack of power on their own is demonstrated later in the book of Joshua in the first battle against the people of Ai. In His anger against the Israelites for the lack of faith demonstrated by those who had defied God, God withdrew his support from the army of three thousand who went to attack Ai. They were wiped out.

The defeat of Jericho was meant to be a demonstration of the rewards of faith and of the power of God. There could be no doubt in the minds of any of the Israelites that it was not through *their* own power that Jericho was taken but through God's power and promise. Why had they trusted and followed Joshua? These were a people who had had a very strained relationship with Moses at times. More than once they had complained and questioned him. Moses had been a man of great faith, but the fact that his contemporaries Joshua and Caleb were allowed to enter the Promised Land while Moses was denied this privilege illustrated the reward of absolute faith. Moses was wishy washy at times. He was plagued by self-doubt (which in his case translated into God doubt) and at times overly concerned with public opinion. Joshua had been more stalwart in his faith. Because of Joshua's faith, God had stopped the flood of the Jordan and caused the walls of a mighty city to tumble to the ground. In any area of our lives where we have absolute faith in God's power or promise we will experience either His full power or His full peace with our circumstances. Conversely, in any area where we have even the slightest shadow of doubt, God is unlikely to reward us with His full power unless we admit our doubt to him and ask for His help to launder the doubt from our faith. This type of honesty is illustrated in Chapter 9 of Mark. Jesus is approached by a man who begs Him to cast a demon out of his son. Christ's disciples had already tried and failed. The man had obviously heard of Christ's ability to perform miracles, but having never witnessed them his doubt in Christ's ability showed clearly when he said, "*If* you can do anything, take pity on us and help us." Christ responded to the man's lack of faith by responding simply, "If you can? Everything is possible for one who believes." *Everything is possible* for one who has faith. The man desperately wanted to have absolute faith in Christ's power to heal, but he recognized and acknowledged to Christ that he could not shed his doubt. He humbled himself before Christ and begged him to help him overcome his disbelief. Christ demonstrated the full power of God by healing the boy even though the boy's father had doubt.

Mother Theresa once said, "Be faithful in the small things, for it is in them that your strength lies." Certainly in the battle for your soul, it is better to have some faith than none. Some doubt will not damn us providing we acknowledge this doubt and recognize that it is a sin. Like all sins, our doubt will be forgiven if we repent. Christ will reward faith, even a struggling faith that is not 100% pure. He shares in the joy of our small victories, though He is not satisfied by them. Remember, His goal is for us to be perfect. I have heard people say that it would be much easier for them to believe in Christ's power if they had witnessed His miracles in person. The Bible simply does not support that position. Doubt existed even in the people closest to Christ and examples of faith are demonstrated before Christ came to the earth. Abraham's righteousness was credited to his faith. God told Abram to pick up all his belongings and his extended family and go. At age seventy-five, Abram went. But even Abraham (God changed Abram's name to Abraham) had doubts from time to time, particularly when God told the elderly Abraham that he and his elderly, barren wife would bear a child. Even the stalwart of faith, Joshua, shows that his faith waivers at times. When his soldiers are defeated at Ai in the first battle, Joshua starts complaining to God and questioning why God ever brought them to this land if He was going to allow them to be defeated. Certainly God was not pleased with Joshua's complaints. He basically told Joshua to stop whining, suck it up, and stop trying to blame Him for something that resulted from the transgressions of the people Joshua was called to lead. Though he may have scolded these men, God did not abandon Abraham or Joshua for their doubt and He will not abandon us when we struggle with our own faith. On the contrary, God will help us to navigate through this doubt to belief if we ask, just as He did the man in Chapter 9 of Mark.

As we continue to progress through the Bible, we find examples of the rewards for faith over and over again. In 1 Kings, the prophet Elijah challenges the priests who worshipped Baal and Asherah to prove whose God was real. The task was to call fire down from heaven to light the wood that had been placed under a sacrificial bull. Four hundred Baal and four hundred Asherah priests prayed all day and slashed themselves until they bled. Elijah had apparently been sitting nearby witnessing the failed attempts of the priests. He even engaged in a bit of smack talk ("Shout louder!" he said. "Surely he is a god! Perhaps he is deep in thought, or busy, or traveling. Maybe he is sleeping and must be awakened.") Then came Elijah's turn. He had not even rebuilt the alter or laid out the wood yet so that nobody could accuse him of foul play. His faith in God was so great that he even had the wood doused with water three times. Then, with no dancing or chanting or slashing, Elijah offered a simple prayer to God. The Lord responded with fire from heaven.

In Christ's time, we see more examples of how people are rewarded for faith. As was the case in the Old Testament, sometimes the faith was absolute, other times we are allowed to see that a shadow of doubt exists in the person who is calling on the Lord's power. In the example of the Roman centurion, recall that he had humbled himself before Jesus and had had so much faith that Jesus would heal his servant that he told Him He didn't need to bother to walk all the way to the centurion's house. He believed that Christ could just say the word and the servant would be healed. A paralyzed man and his friends appeared before Christ and He was so moved by the friends' faith the man was healed. A woman who had experienced menstrual bleeding for twelve years believed that if she could just touch Christ's outer garment she would be healed. A blind man told Christ he believed He could heal him and his sight was restored. A Phoenician woman whose daughter was afflicted with a spirit humbled herself at Christ's feet and her daughter was healed without Christ ever seeing the girl. Does God always demand absolute, unfaltering faith before He will answer a prayer or a request? No. But you will notice that whenever a person demonstrated absolute faith in Christ's power, Christ *commended them for their faith* and let them know that it was according to their *faith* that they were healed. Later Jesus tells Jairus, the leader of a local synagogue, to have faith that He could heal Jairus' daughter. In fact, it was more than simply "healing" her. A messenger had reported that she had died while Jairus was seeking Jesus. Because of Jairus' faith, his daughter was resurrected.

During the early days of Christ's ministry, it is highly unlikely that anyone would have believed completely that He could heal them either because His reputation was not known or, ironically, because the person of Jesus up until His ministry was known. It is in this latter case where we see one of the most poignant examples of the power of faith and the consequences of a lack of faith. In His own hometown of Nazareth, people knew Jesus as the son of a carpenter. Perhaps many had even recalled that He was conceived out of wedlock. Nazareth was a town of little importance. In the opinion of most people from Nazareth and those who knew something about Nazareth, nothing fabulous ever happened there and nothing fabulous had or would ever come from there (I imagine Mary would have disagreed). From this passage, it seems clear that none of Christ's power had been demonstrated during His childhood years. They were abuzz about how "such a person" could talk the way he was talking. Some were so outraged at Jesus that they wanted to take him to the edge of a cliff and throw Him off! In their eyes, He lacked credibility. Few people from Nazareth had even a kernel of faith in Jesus, and because of this Jesus was unable to perform miracles except to heal a few people of (presumably) more minor illnesses. Although they may not have been issued in as cruel a manner, I imagine many of the people from Nazareth challenged Him with requests similar to the ones He had experienced when being tempted by Satan in the desert and again on the day of His death: if you have power and authority, then do [this.] Such requests were not honored by God through Christ because they were not accompanied by anything resembling faith.

Faith in and of itself is not necessarily powerful. The power is still God. What we have seen is how God's power flows through faith. Through faith in God's power and promises, it is clear that we can accomplish great things, but things that must ultimately be for the good of others and the glory of God. In John 14:12 (NIV), Christ tells His disciples, "Very truly I tell you, whoever believes in me will do the works I have been doing, and they will do *even greater things* than these, because I am going to the Father. And I will do whatever you ask in my name, so that the Father may be glorified in the Son." Christ did not mean that any of us would be able to do greater miracles than He did. He knew no other "man" could deal with the inner conflict born of original sin the way He was able to. By greater works, I believe Christ is referring to how His followers would lead billions of people to Him, something He did not have the opportunity to do during His short time on earth. One could argue that leading people to Christ, though perhaps not as impressive a feat as raising a person from the dead, is at least as important and perhaps more important than most of Christ's miracles. And consider the arena. Two thousand years ago, people witnessed Christ perform His miracles. He did miracles to demonstrate God's power and to reward faith. They experienced His power first hand. They had God with them in the flesh. Yet even then people struggled to believe in Christ. He was not the Messiah they had expected. Even though the ancient prophets had spoken of a savior just like Jesus, a complex mix of desires, memories, doubts, and disappointment, had made faith in Christ a difficult sell. Two generations after Christ's death when nobody was left alive that had been an actual witness to these miracles, faith took on a different dimension. Two thousand years later, we have a story handed down to us initially through oral tradition and then through ancient manuscripts. We live in a culture that in so many ways values the very opposite of what Christians should value. I believe Christ recognized that the further removed in time we become from His life on earth, the harder it may be for Christians to have faith. But before His death, Jesus reminds us in the last part of the passage that we now have something in heaven that even Jesus did not have: an advocate on our behalf. Someone we could be assured understood the challenges of our human nature because He had lived them. In addition, He promised He would be sending us "a helper." This helper, the Holy Spirit, and Christ's advocacy for us in heaven are what make us capable of those "even greater things" Jesus spoke of.

The examples of faith discussed above offer us snapshots into a moment in the lives of an ancient people. There is no way of knowing for sure how strong the faith of any of those people was in God's power and promise in other parts of their lives nor how strong their faith remained as they dealt with the challenges of life. They were no more capable than any of us of escaping the human condition. Even when we look at the track record of the people closest to Christ we can see that no one lived a life free from some shadow of doubt. Christ's own disciples were constantly plagued by doubt. At times, Christ's irritation with their childish behavior, lack of understanding, and lack of faith is visible. For example, when His disciplines woke an exhausted Jesus during a crossing of the Sea of Galilee because they were afraid they were going to sink and drown during a storm, Jesus rebuked them. In the account of this story in the Book of Mark, Jesus asks them, "Why are you so afraid? Do you still have no faith?" The disciples had witnessed Jesus perform a number of miracles at this point, yet they still had their doubts about His power. They had seen Him heal people of illnesses, but they had never witnessed Him command nature in such a way. Likewise, even after Christ had fed five thousand families with five loaves of bread and two fish, the disciples were terrified when they saw Him later walk to them across the water. After Christ's death, the disciples were dejected. Even though Jesus had made it crystal clear what kind of king He was and what kind He was not, the world ruled by Roman oppressors had not changed and there was clearly doubt among them whether Christ was who He had claimed to be. In their eyes, Christ was gone for good. Since they had initially fled, they may have been worried about whether they would be persecuted as well as followers of Jesus. Perhaps they would be outcasts in the eyes of their fellow Jews- those foolish people who were naïve enough to follow the most recent person to claim to be the Messiah. Though the disciple Thomas earned the reputation forever as "the doubter," Luke's account of Christ's first appearance to His disciples illustrates how persistent doubt continued to fester in all of them. They had heard from Mary Magdalene and two other women that Christ's tomb was empty and that He had appeared to them. The disciples did not initially believe them. They were, after all, "only" women. Peter's curiosity (rather than his faith) caused him to pay a visit to the tomb where he saw for himself that it was empty. Cleopas and his companions had also seen the risen Christ and reported it to the disciples (Christ had walked along the road and socialized all day with them). But when Christ appeared the first time to His disciples (minus Thomas), we learn from Luke how their doubt lingered even then:

> They were startled and frightened, thinking they saw a ghost. He said to them,"Why are you troubled, and why do doubts rise in your minds? Look at my hands and my feet. It is I myself! Touch me and see; a ghost does not have flesh and bones, as you see I have." When he had said this, he showed them his hands and feet.
>
> Luke 24:37-40 NIV

After seeing Christ's crucifixion wounds, their attitude changed from a pessimistic doubt to a "joyful" doubt: they thought it was too good to be true. Christ reminded them again that this is exactly what He had told them would happen, what the prophets had said would come to be. In a sense, he was returning to His old question, "Do you still have no faith?" I'm sure some people would defend the disciples by pointing out that they had yet to receive the Holy Spirit, so their doubt is understandable. I would point out simply that few people at this point had experienced the Holy Spirit and remind them that absolute faith in God had been demonstrated throughout the Old and New Testament prior to the arrival of the Holy Spirit. As I mentioned earlier, faith in the power and promise of God is not a "blind leap." In his letter to the Romans, Paul writes, "For since the creation of the world God's invisible qualities—his eternal power and divine nature—have been clearly seen, being understood from what has been made, so that people are without excuse" (Romans 1:20 NIV). In his letter to the Ephesians, Paul prayed that the members of the church of Ephesus not lose sight of the enormous power of God, the power that raised Christ from the dead and seated Him at His side in heaven.

I have confessed that I struggle with my commitment to God. I struggle with my humility. I struggle with my faith. I don't struggle as much with accepting God's power so much as His promise. I don't doubt He can fulfill His promise to fix me, but I'm afraid of what I might have to go through during this process. I know how much must be "fixed" in me in order for me to become a credible, effective representative for Jesus. But sinner that I am, I possess a healthy element of cowardice. I want to be stalwart as an example of God, but I would much prefer that He just snap His fingers and make me that way. I want God to fix me without pain, without breaking me, but I know in my heart that change seldom comes without pain. Just like God does not force us to love Him because it would be disingenuous, so too will He refuse to simply make us good. To make things even more challenging, God expects us to pray for things that honor Him even if it means praying for something we don't personally want to pray for. Dietrich Bonhoeffer, a Lutheran minister living in Nazi Germany once wrote, "If we are to pray aright, perhaps it is quite necessary that we pray contrary to our own heart. Not what we want to pray is important, but what God wants us to pray. The richness of the Word of God ought to determine our prayer, not the poverty of our heart." Like Bonhoeffer, Corrie Ten Boom wrote movingly about how she too had to call on God's strength and goodness to pray for those who had held her captive in a Nazi death camp, men and women who had partaken in the slaughter of millions of people including her beloved sister. Honoring a commitment is not easy. Living a life of humility is not easy. Having faith is not easy. We must never lose sight of the fact that, "With man this is not possible, but *with* God all things are possible" (Matthew 19:26 NIV).

In all honesty, my impurities are so prevalent and obvious in my character that God has no choice but to do invasive surgery to remove them. During basic training, my drill sergeants broke us down and then rebuilt us into something better. The process was horrible. The results, though, were admirable. I have experienced my fair share of pain and discomfort in my life, but I do recognize that in every instance I came out the other side a better person. I cannot in all honesty say that I experienced the same kind of growth and maturity as a result of being blessed. I have gained far more wisdom and gratitude as a result of my trials than I ever did as result of my success. God has a process for us. He has His way of doing things. Whether I like it or not, whether I *fear* it or not, I do believe His way is *the* way. I have needed and will continue to need God's hand in fixing me. That requires a greater faith than I have been able to muster in my life, and though I have certainly prayed for greater faith, God has surely discerned the hidden conditions I have attached to this request. Remaining as broken as I have been will inhibit my ability to honor God in my classroom or anywhere else, and so instead of making the blanket request for more faith, I focus on one aspect of that faith at a time. This seems to be a far more effective strategy. I may for a period of time, for example, focus on honoring God by serving my colleagues. Offering compliments or encouragement. Covering duties. Helping to shoulder their loads. Even something as simple as bringing in some muffins. Service can be intrinsically motivating. We know we are serving the Lord by serving others, but it also really "feels good" as well.

The holes in my faith also show when it comes to sharing the message of Christ. I admit that I am still often afraid at times to share the gospel with people who know me because, well, they know me. They have seen me in action and know the kind of life I have led. Those closest to me see me fall repeatedly in my walk. I have no doubt that many people would scoff at the notion of someone "like me" writing a book or manual on anything related to Christian living. I don't blame them at all and I cannot be offended by their doubt. More often than not I feel that same sentiment about myself. After all, aside from God who knows my shortcomings better than me? It took faith for me to embark on this endeavor, faith that God knew all the obstacles in my way and would work with me to overcome them. I needed to accomplish the goal of finishing this book for me to become more of the person God wants me to be. If anything good is to ever come from this process, it will be entirely a result of God working His way through me. I fully admit that I am *not* qualified to produce such a resource. I am *not* the most credible person. I do not have the right "history." But God chooses whom He will work through. I had a need and I felt a calling. No person has ever produced something that glorifies God without God feeding that person through the front end. I relied entirely on God to complete this task. Through this process I was plagued by self-doubt, had my mind scrambled about how to organize the information in this book, tried to write when I had children arguing or crying in the background. I wanted to quit and leave this task up to someone else. I loathed the idea of going through the standard "self-publishing" steps common for today's new authors. I could not afford to have the manuscript edited professionally, so the thought that teachers might be picking apart a host of grammatical errors caused further anxiety. The devil and my own fallen nature have worked against me at every turn. But the fact that I finished is proof that when I call on God, He will work through me.

When my faith falters, I turn to God to calm my panic and doubt about how someone like me could possibly live a life that honors Him, how I could possibly produce something as valuable as a guide book for teachers. When doubt rises to the surface, God reminds me how He has called into service some of the most unlikely characters to carry out His work. He chose a childless elderly man and his wife to be the founding patriarch of a chosen people. He chose the youngest of eight sons of a Judean herdsman to defeat a giant and become one of the greatest Hebrew kings. He made a young girl from a small town the Mother of God. I began to accept that if God could make something great out of the Christian persecutor Paul, the hated tax collector Matthew, and the arrogant Peter, He could make something worthwhile out of someone like me despite my long laundry list of sins.

I have also come to understand something that should have been obvious from the start: Christ is with me step for step on my walk. I lack the power to honor my commitment to Him with my own strength. I lack the ability to remain humble with my own strength. I lack the faith to trust in God's power and promise on my own. Wherever I am too weak to fulfill my commitment, I must call on His strength to help me. He is there to pick me up time and time again when I fall. His Word is there to encourage me and guide me. Fellow Christians are there to do the same. God may even choose to use non-believers to strengthen my faith. Not only do I not have to count on my *own* willpower to live a life that honors Christ, I am expressively told not to rely on such human weakness. We are not meant to. In his book of proverbs, King Solomon tells us,

> Trust God from the bottom of your heart; don't try to figure out everything on your own. Listen for God's voice in everything you do, everywhere you go; he's the one who will keep you on track. Don't assume that you know it all.
>
> Proverbs 3:5-12 MS

In his epistle to the Romans, Paul reminds us that when we try to do things on our own we are doing things through our sinful nature. "The sinful nature is always hostile to God. It never did obey God's laws, and it never will" (Romans 8:7 NLT). In Chapter 3 of his letter to the Galatians, Paul writes, "Anyone who tries to live by his own effort, apart from God, is doomed to failure" (Galatians 3:10 MSG).

God will provide us with the help we need to fulfill our commitment to Him, not through our own power but through His. He will help us as we struggle with our faith. He will never be satisfied completely until we are perfect. He will share in our joy at each small victory. He helps us to stop worrying about *how* we will succeed and from beating ourselves up when we don't. If we keep our minds, our eyes, and our hearts open, we can see how God is working every second of the day to help us honor our commitment, learn humility, strengthen our faith. We have God's promises in writing. Consider these passages:

- Psalms 37:5-6 NIV- Commit your way to the LORD; trust in him and he will do this: He will make your righteous reward shine like the dawn, your vindication like the noonday sun.
- Luke 11:9-10 NIV- So I say to you: Ask and it will be given to you; seek and you will find; knock and the door will be opened to you. For everyone who asks receives; the one who seeks finds; and to the one who knocks, the door will be opened.
- Proverbs 3:5-6 NIV- Trust in the Lord with all your heart and lean not on your own understanding; in all your ways submit to Him and He will make your paths straight.
- Galatians 3:9-10 MSG- So those now who live by faith are blessed along with Abraham, who lived by faith—this is no new doctrine! And that means that anyone who tries to live by his own effort, independent of God, is doomed to failure.
- Ephesians 3:20-21 MSG- God can do anything, you know—far more than you could ever imagine or guess or request in your wildest dreams! He does it not by pushing us around but by working within us, his Spirit deeply and gently within us.
- James 1:5-8 MSG- If you don't know what you're doing, pray to the Father. He loves to help. You'll get his help, and won't be condescended to when you ask for it. Ask boldly, believingly, without a second thought. People who "worry their prayers" are like wind-whipped waves. Don't think you're going to get anything from the Master that way, adrift at sea, keeping all your options open.

- Zephaniah 3:17 NLV- The Lord your God is with you, a Powerful One Who wins the battle. He will have much joy over you. With His love He will give you new life. He will have joy over you with loud singing.
- Psalms 32:8-9 NIV- I will instruct you and teach you in the way you should go; I will counsel you with my loving eye on you. Do not be like the horse or the mule, which have no understanding but must be controlled by bit and bridle or they will not come to you.
- 1 John 3:21 NIV- Dear friends, if our hearts do not condemn us, we have confidence before God and receive from him anything we ask, because we keep his commands and do what pleases him.
- Proverbs 119:33-34 NIV- Teach me, oh Lord, the way of your decrees, that I may follow it to the end. Give me understanding so that I may keep your law and obey it with all my heart. Direct me in the path of your commands, for there I find delight. Turn my heart toward your statutes and not toward selfish gain.

In the first three chapters, we looked at three elements of our relationship with God with the goal of understanding that the person that stands at the head of your classroom every day must be the same person in all aspects of his or her life. It is unreasonable to expect God's power to flow through you in your classroom or in your relationships with your colleagues unless you aim for Godly character in all aspects of your life. The commitment to honor God with our lives must include all aspects of our lives. We cannot turn the humility switch on when we cross the threshold of our workplace then flip it off on our way out. We must demonstrate our faith in God's power and promise from the moment we wake until the moment we fall asleep at night. Christ called us to be a "light in the darkness." Our classroom is not the only area of darkness in our lives. God abhors hypocrisy. Nothing damages His credibility more than our hypocrisy. We have the power to lead people to Him or drive people from Him. God's power is diminished when it is forced through a medium of hypocrisy. Satan's power, on the other hand, is magnified through hypocrisy. In order for the power of God to flow through you in your job as a teacher (or any other noble job for that manner), there can be no "on" and "off" switches to the different rooms in your life. The character you bring to your workplace is the same character that goes with you everywhere.

CHAPTER FOUR

Loving One Another with Godly Love

Love is a command, not just a feeling. Somehow, in the romantic world of music and theater we have made love to be what it is not. We have so mixed it with beauty and charm and sensuality and contact that we have robbed it of its higher call of cherishing and nurturing.

Ravi Zacharias

Darkness cannot drive out darkness; only light can do that.
Hate cannot drive out hate; only love can do that.

Dr. Martin Luther King, Jr

Let me give you a new command: Love one another. In the same way I loved you, you love one another. This is how everyone will recognize that you are my disciples—when they see the love you have for each other.

John 13:34-35 MSG

Now that you have purified yourselves by obeying the truth so that you have sincere love for each other, love one another deeply, from the heart. For you have been born again, not of perishable seed, but of imperishable, through the living and enduring word of God.

1 Peter 1:22-23 NIV

And now these three remain: faith, hope and love. But the greatest of these is love.

I Corinthians 13:13 NIV

Christian brother, you were chosen to be free. Be careful that you do not please your old selves by sinning because you are free. Live this free life by loving and helping others. You obey the whole Law when you do this one thing, "Love your neighbor as you love yourself." But if you hurt and make it hard for each other, watch out or you may be destroyed by each other.

Galatians 5:13-15 NLV

Love has a hem to her garment
That reaches the very dust.
It sweeps the stains from the streets and lanes,
And because it can, it must.

St. Fabiola

Love is saying, "I feel differently" when you really want to say, "You are wrong."
unknown author

My dear children, let's not just talk about love; let's practice real love. This is the only way we'll know we're living truly, living in God's reality.
1 John 3:18-20 MSG

Let love and faithfulness never leave you; bind them around your neck, write them on the tablet of your heart. Then you will win favor and a good name in the sight of God and man.
Proverbs 3:3-4 NIV

The rule for all of us is perfectly simple. Do not waste time bothering whether you 'love' your neighbor; act as if you did. As soon as we do this we find one of the great secrets. When you are behaving as if you loved someone, you will presently come to love him."
C.S. Lewis

Why is love for others called a debt? We are permanently in debt to Christ for the lavish love he poured out on us. The only way we can ever begin to repay this debt is by loving others in turn. Because Christ's love will always be infinitely greater than ours, we will always have the obligations to love our neighbors.
NIV Application Study Bible Commentary on Romans 13:8-10

Foundational Concepts

✝ God commands us to love one another. We do not get to select whom we will and whom we will not show love.

✝ Loving one another does not always mean you must respect the other person, agree with him or her, approve of his or her lifestyle, or even *like* the person. God knows that because of our sinful nature, we may not be able to *feel* love toward some people. In such cases, though, God still expects us to act in a loving way toward that person.

Central Questions

1. What does it really mean to love one another?
2. How can I demonstrate love for my students and colleagues?
3. How do I deal with people who are just plain difficult to love?

If there is one all-encompassing theme in the Bible it is the concept of love. Sixth century Bishop Fulgentius of Ruspe once wrote, "Christ made love the stairway that would enable all Christians to climb to heaven. Hold fast to love, therefore, in all sincerity, and give one another practical proof of it." Saint John of the Cross wrote to fellow Christians in the sixteenth century, "At the evening of life, you will be examined in love. Learn to love as God desires to be loved and abandon your own ways of acting."

Herein lays the rub. Two thousand years removed from the life of Christ and the teaching of His disciples and early apostles, "love" has become a very confusing and complicated concept for us to grasp. Both in the Bible and throughout history this command has led to countless discussions about what it means to "love" someone and which people are we expected to love. From the fourth chapter of 1 John, we are told that love is holy. It comes from God. God *is* love, and as such none of us can ever know God without understanding His love. Many of the authors of the books of the Bible wrote of love, but by piecing together various verses from 1 John we get a very clear picture of the relationship between God and love.

> For this is the message you heard from the beginning: We should love one another.
>
> 1 John 3:11 NIV

> Dear children, let's not merely say that we love each other; let us show the truth by our actions. Our actions will show that we belong to the truth, so we will be confident when we stand before God.
>
> I John 3:18-19 NLT

> My beloved friends, let us continue to love each other since love comes from God. Everyone who loves is born of God and experiences a relationship with God. The person who refuses to love doesn't know the first thing about God, because God is love—so you can't know him if you don't love.
>
> 1 John 4:7-10 MSG

> My dear, dear friends, if God loved us like this, we certainly ought to love each other. No one has seen God, ever. But if we love one another, God dwells deeply within us, and his love becomes complete in us—perfect love!
>
> 1 John 4:11-12 MSG

> God is love. When we take up permanent residence in a life of love, we live in God and God lives in us. This way, love has the run of the house, becomes at home and mature in us, so that we're free of worry on Judgment Day—our standing in the world is identical with Christ's
>
> 1 John 4:17 MSG

> If anyone boasts, "I love God," and goes right on hating his brother or sister, thinking nothing of it, he is a liar. If he won't love the person he can see, how can

he love the God he can't see? The command we have from Christ is blunt: Loving God includes loving people. You've got to love both

John 4:20-21 MSG

The greatest example of God's love, of course, is sending his Son to us ultimately so He could be sacrificed as redemption for our sins. Jesus was a living exemplar of love in the way He lived His life and treated others, in the way He spoke of love, and in the way He honored God, the Father with love. Love was a central theme in many of His lessons. The parables of the Prodigal Son, the Lost Sheep, and the Good Samaritan each help us to understand what love looks like. The story of the Prodigal Son demonstrates the power of loving forgiveness and the celebration of restoration. In this story, the father does not go looking for the son; the son returns on his own. The parable of the Lost Sheep demonstrates the love of God for each of us, and in this case the shepherd shows this love by leaving his flock to find one sheep that has become lost. In both parables, the love that is shown is toward members of the same family (or flock). What makes the parable of the Good Samaritan so powerful is that it demonstrates the way in which God expects us to love someone whom we may not even *like*, let alone love. Jesus does not command us to love only those who are closest to us. He tells us that we must love even our enemies. It is this command which I feel may be one of the most misunderstood commands in the Bible because most of us do not understand the difference between Godly love and worldly love. Perhaps we can understand God's command to love by looking more closely at the parable of the Good Samaritan.

> In reply Jesus said: "A man was going down from Jerusalem to Jericho, when he was attacked by robbers. They stripped him of his clothes, beat him and went away, leaving him half dead. A priest happened to be going down the same road, and when he saw the man, he passed by on the other side. So too, a Levite, when he came to the place and saw him, passed by on the other side. But a Samaritan, as he traveled, came where the man was; and when he saw him, he took pity on him. He went to him and bandaged his wounds, pouring on oil and wine. Then he put the man on his own donkey, brought him to an inn and took care of him. The next day he took out two denarii and gave them to the innkeeper. 'Look after him,' he said, 'and when I return, I will reimburse you for any extra expense you may have.' Which of these three do you think was a neighbor to the man who fell into the hands of robbers?' The expert in the law replied, "The one who had mercy on him." Jesus told him, "Go and do likewise."

Luke 10:30-37 NIV

Most adults in the U.S. have some understanding of the story of the Good Samaritan. They know that it involves one person helping another person whom they do not know. What many people don't understand or are unaware of is the history surrounding the relationship between the people of Samaria and the Jews. In the eyes of the Jewish people, Samaritans were detestable half-breeds who deserved nothing but contempt. This contempt toward the Samaritans would not have been something perpetuated through passive mumblings. It would have been open and at times aggressive. The Samaritans, therefore, would have been keenly aware of just how detestable they were in the eyes of the Jews. The Samaritans returned this sentiment with equal vitriol toward the Jews, whom they felt were arrogant hypocrites. Both groups felt the other had strayed from the true teachings of God. The tension between the Jews and Samaritans was so thick that Jews would often cross to the opposite side of the Jordan River in order to go around the region of Samaria rather than pass through it. A modern-day comparison of the type of relationship that existed between the Samaritans and the Jews is the relationship that exists between the more avid factions of the world's Shiite and Sunni Muslim population. This is where the true power of the story rests. The Samaritan provides assistance to a victim who detested him and whom he most likely detested while members of the victim's own community chose to look the other way. The Samaritan didn't just wrap the victim's wounds and move on or send someone else for help. He cleaned his wounds with his wine and oil, loaded him on his donkey, went out of his way to deliver him to an inn, paid for the first few days of his stay, even committed to paying the innkeeper more if the victim required further stay. The Samaritan may very well have disliked the injured man because of what he represented, but never-the-less he "loved" the man. This may seem like a contradiction if we are to think of love in the way it is represented in pop culture. This parable, however, is not meant to represent that kind of love but God's love.

When discussing love, Jesus used different words or phrases to represent different kinds of love, and through his lessons we learn that Godly love is most often an *action* rather than an emotion. In the ancient Greek translation of the New Testament, the word "philia" refers to friendship or brotherly love. The Greek word "eros" does not appear in the Bible but was used to refer to erotic or sensual love. The term "agape" refers to the deepest kind of love, Godly love. It does not involve sentimental notions of romantic love nor does it *require* any element of friendship. Agape refers to the character of God's love. Agape love is selfless, unconditional, and is associated with sacrifice. It is the love that compelled the Samaritan to provide the kind of assistance he did for a man who, for all intents and purposes, was his enemy. Jesus calls us to love people even if we don't actually "like" them. As a parent, I know what it is like to feel unconditional love for my children. As a Christian, I understand that however much I feel this deep love for my wife and children, it is infinitely incomparable to the degree in which God loves us unconditionally. But as a fallen man, I feel compelled to confess that there is almost no other person on earth whom I love unconditionally. If I am to be totally honest, I am regrettably stingy when it comes to loving others in a way that reflects a deep emotional attachment. I naturally love people who are easy or convenient to love. Fortunately for me and others like me (which is most people), God understands the nature of my sin. Only God can love perfectly. So what are we to make of Jesus' command in Matthew 5:46-47 (NIV):

> If you love those who love you, what reward will you get? Are not even the tax collectors doing that? And if you greet only your own people, what are you doing more than others? Do not even pagans do that? Be perfect, therefore, as your heavenly Father is perfect.

Over the course of our teaching careers we may have hundreds or even thousands of students pass through our doors, and many of them will not be easy to love. Some will be very difficult to even like. We are not perfect like God, so how then can we love these students perfectly?

When the Bible speaks of God's love for us we understand that it refers to the deep, passionate, personal, intimate relationship He has with us. But it also refers to the *acts* of loving us. Pope Gregory I wrote, "The proof of love is in the works. Where love exists, it works great things. But where love ceases to act, it ceases to exist." Godly love was clearly evident in the life of Jesus. For new Christians and for those outside our faith, then, it seems an incredibly tall order that we are to love others like Jesus loved us, to love others "perfectly." Truthfully, it is not just a tall order but an impossible order unless we understand what it means for us to "love one another." It is the understanding of love "the act" versus love "the emotion" that distinguishes the two. In as much as humility and commitment are actions, "to love others" may mean to *show love* or *act in a loving way* even when we don't *feel* love toward the person. William Arthur Ward wrote, "Love is more than a noun -- it is a verb; it is more than a feeling -- it is caring, sharing, helping, sacrificing." In 1 John 3:18 we read, "Dear children, let us not love with words or speech but with actions and in truth." If we were to show love only to those with whom we had a deep emotional commitment, none of Christ's mission for us on earth would be possible. In his first letter to the members of the church in Corinth, Paul wrote:

> If I have the gift of prophecy and can fathom all mysteries and all knowledge, and if I have a faith that can move mountains, but do not have love, I am nothing. If I give all I possess to the poor and give over my body to hardship that I may boast, but do not have love, I gain nothing.
>
> 1 Corinthians 13:2-3 NIV

The conversation that led Jesus to tell the parable of the Good Samaritan involved a man who wanted to know what he needed to do essentially to qualify for eternal life. Jesus directed the man to tell Him what God's law was pertaining to this, to which the man replied, "You must love the Lord your God with all your heart. You must love Him with all your soul. You must love Him with all your strength. You must love Him with all your mind. You must love your neighbor as you love yourself." When Jesus affirmed his statement, the man then wanted Jesus to define for him who his neighbor was. Perhaps he was looking for a loophole. Christ's parable of the Samaritan made it clear for this man and for us that our neighbor is the person in front of us at any given time regardless of our personally feelings toward or about that person. In Matthew 22:40 (NIV), Jesus went one step further by stating, *"All the law and the prophets hang on these two commandments."* In 1 Peter 4:8 (NIV), we are told, "Above all, love each other deeply, because love covers a multitude of sins." Martin Luther King, Jr. referred to the story of the Samaritan to illustrate the need for all people in our divided society to look at and treat each other in a different manner than that which had perpetuated through embedded racial discord. Dr. King wrote:

> The first question which the priest and the Levite asked was: "If I stop to help this man, what will happen to me?" But... the Good Samaritan reversed the question: "If I do not stop to help this man, what will happen to him?"

The people who should have provided assistance to the victim did not. Instead, a person who had been treated poorly by the victim's culture provided the help. As teachers I would argue that we face a similar situation every day. One inescapable reality of public education is that teachers cannot hand pick which students will walk through their doors at the beginning of each school year. Kids come with baggage, and some of them dump that baggage out in the middle of our classrooms. In the next chapter we will spend some time reviewing the challenges many of us face when it comes to showing love toward the most troubling or challenging students, but the preface to that is that regardless of how they act or perform in our class, God expects us to love them. Some of these students will exhaust the limits of your professional expertise. As Christians, though, the "limits" we have when it comes to treating them in a loving way continue even after our professional solutions are tapped out. Most of these children are in desperate need of support and guidance from "their own" people, but for some reason that support and guidance has been lacking. The question for us becomes, then, if "their own" people are unable or unwilling to help, who will? Our answer to this question will reveal a great deal about how we view our roles as a teacher and as a Christian in our secular classrooms. Where do the roles overlap and where do they diverge?

God expects us to act in a loving way toward everyone, even those whom we find it difficult to like. So, what then does "loving one another" look like? We have discussed that love is revealed in *action*. This action can involve something we say or do or something we don't say or do. Perhaps the clearest description of love is found in Paul's letter to the church in Corinth:

- Love is patient,
- Love is kind.
- It does not envy,
- It does not boast,
- It is not proud.
- It does not dishonor others,
- It is not self-seeking,
- It is not easily angered,
- It keeps no record of wrongs.
- Love does not delight in evil but rejoices with the truth.
- It always protects,
- Always trusts,
- Always hopes,
- Always perseveres.

Love is Patient

In his letter to the Galatians, the Apostle Paul identifies patience as one of nine fruits of the spirit:

> The fruit of the Spirit is love, joy, peace, **patience**, kindness, goodness, faithfulness, gentleness and self-control. Against such things there is no law.
> Galatians 5:22 NIV

These attributes or virtues often appear together in the Bible. In his letter to the Colossians, Paul wrote:

> So, as those who have been chosen of God, holy and beloved, put on a heart of compassion, kindness, humility, gentleness and **patience**; bearing with one another, and forgiving each other, whoever has a complaint against anyone; just as the Lord forgave you, so also should you.
>
> Colossians 3:12-13 NASB

The fruits of The Spirit refer to the Godly attributes that are reflected in a person who is allowing the Holy Spirit to work in his life. As a fruit of The Spirit, our patience is a direct reflection of our commitment to God. While the Bible teaches us not to judge one another, it does provide us with a way to assess the degree to which a person is truly committed to doing God's work on earth. In the Book of Matthew, we are told:

> You will know them by their fruits. Grapes are not gathered from thorn bushes nor figs from thistles, are they? So every good tree bears good fruit, but the bad tree bears bad fruit. A good tree cannot produce bad fruit, nor can a bad tree produce good fruit. Every tree that does not bear good fruit is cut down and thrown into the fire. So then, you will know them by their fruits.
>
> Matthew 7:16-20 NASB

In this case the passage is referring to identifying false prophets, but Galatians 5:22 makes it clear that the behavior of all Christians should be characterized by their fruit. In the Parable of the Sower, Jesus makes it clear that *living* His teachings rather than just *listening* to His teachings is the only way to produce a harvest: "And those are the ones on whom seed was sown on the good soil; and they hear the word and accept it and bear fruit, thirty, sixty, and a hundredfold" (Mark 4:20 NASB). Our fruits of The Spirit or lack of them will be the aspect of our ministry that will have the most influential effect on our students. We cannot talk with them about our Lord, so we must teach them about Him by the way we act toward them and others. Our actions define us as Christians. We do not act this way to *earn* salvation, we act because we have already received salvation. One of the most confusing concepts for new Christians to grasp is whether a person is saved by grace or by deeds. So much of the Bible talks about the acts of people that it is easy to understand why some people might think that a person's salvation if based on these acts. Mature Christians understand, however, that we are saved by God's grace alone when we accept Jesus as our Lord and Savior, and that our actions (our fruits) are a result of *being* saved not a means of *becoming* saved. Our fruits represent our commitment to God and our gratitude for His grace. They reflect our love for Him. The absence of fruits of The Spirit in our lives immediately casts doubt about how committed we really are to Christ, how grateful we are for His gifts, and how much we actually love Him. We show love for God in two primary ways: by putting our faith in Him and thanking Him for His many blessings and for his grace and by doing *what He has asked us to do*. In what other way could any of us establish ourselves as credible in His eyes, in the eyes of fellow Christians, and in the eyes of those who are looking at us from the other side of the glass but who know enough about our faith to have some idea of how we should act?

Consider this analogy. Suppose a person applies for a job as a middle school math teacher. During the interview, he talks at great length about his love for math and for his students. He states that he is committed to being the best math teacher possible. He talks a good game. When the interviewers call several of their old contacts at the man's current or past schools, however, they learn that the candidate never taught math at all, was frequently called out for talking to students in a demeaning manner, complained constantly about a whole host of things, was one of the last to arrive and the first to leave campus every day, taught straight from a textbook every day, never enrolled in optional professional development, made it clear he would not teach special needs students in his class, and bucked every new change related to curriculum, teaching models, teaming, or any other aspect aimed at school improvement. Furthermore, his attitude toward colleagues put him at odds with most of them. He was described as being selfish, arrogant, even condescending toward them. He had a reputation for talking about others behind their backs and for trying to stir up dissension among the ranks. How *credible* then are the claims he made during his interview? Only a fool would hire this man based on his claims alone. Our deeds, our fruit, determine our credibility.

That does not mean we need to be perfect in the production of each of these fruits. We are each at different stages in our walk with Jesus, and I for one remain a work in progress. When it comes to working with my students, I find that I have to focus on a few "fruits" at a time until the actions start to become my new second nature. Patience is one of the fruits I have struggled with the most to produce. I think it's fair for me to admit that the day patience was handed out in kindergarten I overslept and missed the bus. I am, by nature, a very impatient person. I don't like waiting for anything. I am absolutely baffled by people who have the patience to wait in line for hours or even days to get the newest version of a cell phone. To me, any notion of Hell must include something akin to a Black Friday line in which you wait ten hours in line only to learn that the item you waited for is sold out once you reach the head of the line. I lack patience when it comes to repeating my directives to my own children or students. I lack patience when my own children or my students haven't done what I asked them to do. I am impatient when it comes to my students getting off-task or goofing around. If I am fishing with a worm on a hook rather by casting and retrieving I have to have a book, some music, or a comfortable seat in which I can nap. Otherwise, waiting for a fish to bite will drive me crazy. I become very uncomfortable when I have to sit in seminars, conferences, or lectures. I am impatient when it comes to having to "learn" something "new" related to teaching when I feel like I already know it or that it doesn't really apply to me. I become impatient when one of my students does not perform up to my expectations for him or her. I could list all the areas of my life where my patience is tested, but it would be easier to simply admit that *whenever* patience is called for I am tested. When patience is called for I frequently become anxious, irritable, antsy, or quick-tempered. More often than I care to admit, the reaction time between the antecedent irritant and the puff of irritability can be measured in fractions of a second. These responses are in many cases a reflex. Patience as a parent and as a teacher is one of the things I pray hardest for because the repercussions of impatience are so counterproductive in both roles. So much of my success or failure as a parent, a husband, and a teacher depends upon the degree to which I manage my impatience.

Teachers have their patience tested daily. If you have been a teacher for more than a week, you know that there will be times when your patience will fail. Any parent knows how one child can test a parent's patience. Imagine, then, how your patience can be tested by working every day with over one hundred children, especially when these kids are middle-school tweens and teens. Many middle-school students are inherently programmed to test a teacher's patience. To us, this often seems intentional and we take it personal. When the smoke has cleared, though, it is hard for me to really believe that most students behave in a certain way "just to test my patience." Ironically, it is much easier for many of us to muster the patience to deal with people whom we realize are intentionally trying to "push our buttons." The truth is that most kids have a hundred different impulses competing for attention in their head at any one time, and most of what we see is a result of them dealing with these impulses.

When I pray to God for patience, I pray specifically sometimes for the self-control to be more patient. Self-control is another fruit of The Spirit, so I guess I'm actually praying for two fruits at once. Self-control is one of those fruits from which other fruits can spring. Unfortunately, I can think of few areas of my life where my *own* degree of self-control is now or will ever be substantial enough to ever accomplish anything truly meaningful or worthwhile. Whether it is patience, staying healthy, or resisting temptation, my self-control alone will not be sufficient for me to accomplish my goal. I rely a great deal on God blessing me with some of his infinite self-control to get me through most challenges. Likewise, God has the capacity for infinite patience, and His patience is not diminished when He sends some of His patience our way. I need God's power and strength. When our patience fails, we can call on Him for some of His.

I also pray that God will help me to understand *why* I am so impatient about certain things. It may be as simple as "I don't want to be here doing this. I'd rather be there doing that." Or, I become impatient because I don't really like a particular restaurant enough to wait an hour to be seated, but it is the one my in-laws wanted to go to. I believe the root of impatience with students for many of us is fear. For example, we are afraid if our students don't perform to a certain level or behave in a certain way we could lose our job and with that our ability to provide for our families. In some cases our impatience is due to resentment. We may feel like we are working harder for the students than the students are working for us or for themselves. Our job requires so much of our attention and time that we usually have less time than we desire to spend with our families. There are only so many hours in a day, and when we become tasked with even more to do we become impatient because it eats into what little time we already have to do something else other than work.

Sometimes we become impatient because we forget to examine a situation with a compassionate eye. Several times throughout the chapters of this book I emphasize that attributes such as humility, compassion, love, and even patience are *actions*. If they are not attributes that we possess naturally, we are still expected to act in a humble, compassionate, loving, and patient way toward others because God commands us to do so. I am well aware of the numerous factors that can affect a child's behavior and academic performance. Challenges can be related to puberty, family strife, poverty, abuse or neglect, a deployed parent, abandonment, loss of job or a home, death or family illness, peer pressure, low self-esteem or self-efficacy, bullying, bias, poor role models, to list a few. I cannot recall how many times I have lost my patience with a student or even my own children only to find out later that something personal to them was simmering under the surface causing the child's behavior or lackluster performance. In this case, I failed to demonstrate love by acting with patience and compassion. What makes this even more shameful is that I experienced a great deal of strife in my life as a child. Not only did I lack patience with the student, I failed to feel empathy though God has worked on me in a variety of ways throughout my life, I believe, for the express purpose of allowing me to experience empathy. I believe that a very large part of the trials God allows us to face is His way of helping us to develop empathy. Empathy is the only way we can truly understand another person's trials.

With over one hundred students on my team, I obviously don't have the luxury to stop and conference with every student on the spot to uncover underlying issues. But patience can mean that I give a child the benefit of the doubt until such a time when we can discuss privately what might be going on. This does not mean ignoring the problem, but how we deal with an immediate issue can make all the difference with that child and with others by proxy. Impatience can cause us to respond in a condescending tone that belittles or humiliates a child. The adverse effect of this interaction is amplified when the child is addressed this way in front of peers. We risk developing an image of ourselves not only in that student's eyes but in those of his peers as someone who is impatient and who is condescending toward students. Our reputation as a teacher can have huge implications when it comes to student success in our classroom. I live in the community where I teach and I frequently hear comments about the "sour fruit" produced by certain teachers in our district. Reputational bias can also affect us in the opposite direction. We usually have less patience with students who regularly test our patience. It is as though they have used up their allotment of patience, and nobody is going to come in to refill that cookie jar. The problem with this is that even if the child is making an effort to improve and goes for an extended period of time without testing our patience, as soon as he or she "messes up" we are on them as ardently and with as little patience as we had toward them when they were chronic offenders. We must allow these students to grow out of their reputation or risk having them throw their hands up in defeat thinking that no matter what they do it won't be enough for you (or anyone else).

Overcoming impatience has become particularly difficult for me because it is such a base impulse for me. It is a reflex, which by definition initially bypasses the thinking part of the brain and responds with immediate reaction. I'm sure there are deep-seated psychological or hereditary reasons behind my impatience, but it is much easier for me if I simply admit to God that it is a sin and ask Him for help to overcome this sin. I have prayed many long prayers about my impatience, but I've come to realize that God really doesn't need me to psychoanalyze every aspect of my sin. I believe that most of the time all God requires is that we acknowledge our sin, repent of it, and pray to Him for help. Furthermore, I think we need to be realistic in our requests. I have prayed that God would provide me with deep introspect about my impatience and point me toward an equally in-depth measure to "fix" this problem, but I understand how this is pointless in some ways. God doesn't "fix" the fact that we are fallen. If His approach was to "fix us," it would not have been necessary for Him to send Jesus to die for our sins. That being said, God is interested in us becoming more like Jesus. I believe He will help us by providing us with His strength while also helping us to develop our own fruits of the spirit.

All Christians should believe that God answers prayers. However, He does not answer all prayers or at least He may not answer them in a way we had wanted or expected. God knows best. I'm not sure that my prayers for deep introspect about my impatience have really ever been answered. Perhaps God does not see this as a worthwhile strategy for addressing my problem. Even if I understand the reasons behind my impatience, there is no assurance that enlightenment alone will improve my patience. Perhaps God understands that there really isn't enough available time in my life to spend intensively pursuing the path to master my impatience. Instead, God may speak to me with a relatively simple suggestion: "What if I could provide you with the ability to manage the impulse that leads you to lash out in impatience for *just two seconds?*" The human brain is capable of incredibly rapid processing. In the amount of time it takes to take a deep breath, we are capable of processing an impulse, our possible responses, and the consequences of those responses. So that is what God and are I are working on right now with regards to my patience: breathing. But there's a twist. Patience is one of those virtues that is best strengthened through trials. Christian evangelist Joyce Myers once said, "Patience is a fruit of the spirit that grows only under trial. It is useless to pray for patience. Well, actually I encourage you to pray for patience, but I'll tell you what you'll get: TRIALS!" So I understand that developing the ability to act with patience is certainly not an overnight thing. It takes patience to learn patience. Right now I'm simply trying to focus on breathing. When I feel the first tickle of impatience, I try to remember to take a deep breath. I'm not certain how often God is reminding me to breath and how much I am remembering on my own, but the results seem promising. Over the past few years I don't know that it would be accurate to say that I have *become* more patient. I am still the same impatient sinner. However, most of the time I am able to *demonstrate* more patience.

Additional Bible Quotes about Patience

- Proverbs 15:18 NIV- A hot-tempered man stirs up dissension, but a patient man calms a quarrel
- Ecclesiastes 7:8 NASB- The end of a matter is better than its beginning; **Patience** of spirit is better than haughtiness of spirit.
- (Ephesians 4:13 NASB- Therefore I, the prisoner of the Lord, implore you to walk in a manner worthy of the calling with which you have been called, with all humility and gentleness, with **patience**, showing tolerance for one another in love, being diligent to preserve the unity of the Spirit in the bond of peace.
- Colossians 3:12-13 NASB- So, as those who have been chosen of God, holy and beloved, put on a heart of compassion, kindness, humility, gentleness and **patience**; bearing with one another, and forgiving each other, whoever has a complaint against anyone; just as the Lord forgave you, so also should you.
- 1 Timothy 1:16 NASB- Yet for this reason I found mercy, so that in me as the foremost, Jesus Christ might demonstrate His perfect **patience** as an example for those who would believe in Him for eternal life.
- 2 Timothy 4:1-2 NASB- I solemnly charge *you* in the presence of God and of Christ Jesus, who is to judge the living and the dead, and by His appearing and His kingdom: preach the word; be ready in season *and* out of season; reprove, rebuke, exhort, with great **patience** and instruction.

Additional Quotes about Patience

- **Patience** and perseverance have a magical effect before which difficulties disappear and obstacles vanish (John Quincy Adams).
- **Patience** is the companion of wisdom (St. Augustine).
- **Patience** is also a form of action (Rodin).
- Experience has taught me this, that we undo ourselves by **impatience** (Michel de Montaigne).
- Have **patience** with all things, but chiefly have **patience** with yourself. Do not lose courage in considering your own imperfections, but instantly set about remedying them - every day begin the task anew (Saint Francis de Sales).
- **Patience** gives your spouse permission to be human. It understands that everyone fails. When a mistake is made, it chooses to give them more time that they deserve to correct it. It gives you the ability to hold on during the rough times in your relationship rather than bailing out under the pressure (Stephen Kendrick).
- Restlessness and **impatience** change nothing except our peace and joy. Peace does not dwell in outward things, but in the heart prepared to wait trustfully and quietly on Him who has all things safely in His hands (Elisabeth Elliot).
- Think of the **patience** God has had for you and let it resonate to others. If you want a more patient world, let patience be your motto (Steve Maroboli).
- The world gives us PLENTY of opportunities to strengthen our **patience**. While this truth can definitely be challenging, this is a good thing. **Patience** is a key that unlocks the door to a more fulfilling life. It is through a cultivation of **patience** that we become better parents, powerful teachers, great businessmen, good friends, and a live a happier life (Steve Maroboli).

Love is Kind

When I was considering kindness, I was curious about how different dictionaries defined it. Most sources include at least part of the definition as "the state or quality of being kind." As teachers, we don't like it when students define a word by using the word or a variant of it in the definition. Of the various sources I reviewed, the oft maligned Wikipedia offered one of the simplest and best definitions:

> **Kindness** is the act or the state of being kind, being marked by good and charitable behavior, pleasant disposition, and concern for others. It is known as a virtue and recognized as a value in many cultures and religions. Research has shown that acts of kindness do not only benefit receivers of the kind act, but also the giver, as a result of the release of neurotransmitters responsible for feelings of contentment and relaxation when such acts are committed.

As a life science teacher, I loved the little touch of adding the info about the release of neurotransmitters. Simply put, when we do kind things for others chemicals are released into our body that make us momentarily happy and relaxed. Being kind makes us feel good! Serving makes us feel good. Tell me there isn't a brilliant Creator God behind the universe!

Kindness is another fruit of The Spirit, one of the defining characteristics of God. God's kindness is referred to throughout the Bible. Psalms 116:5 and 145:17; Romans 2:4, 3:24, 11:5-6, and 11:22; 2 Corinthians 8:1 and 10:1; 1 Peter 2:3 and 5:10; Luke 6:35; Ephesians 2:7; and Titus 3:4-7 all speak of God's kindness. In Zechariah 7: 8-9, the Lord instructs the prophet to carry the message that His people are to "do what is right and be kind and show loving pity to one another." Just as it was His ultimate act of love, God's ultimate act of kindness was sending Christ in human form to be sacrificed for our sins. The kindness in this act was more than just the forgiveness of sins, it provided each of us with the means of achieving eternal life with God, something that would never have been possible to earn on our own. In the King James Version, kindness is sometimes referred to as "gentleness." Kindness and gentleness go hand in hand. If kindness is the act, gentleness is the manner in which the act is generally carried out. Saint Anthony Mary Claret wrote of gentleness, "No virtue is so attractiveness as gentleness. If you throw a little piece of bread into a pond the fish will come fearlessly up to your feet. But if you throw rocks, they will swim away and hide." Kindness is also often referred to in association with self-sacrifice, generosity, and compassion. In the Greek translations of the Bible, the word *chrestos* was sometimes used to represent kindness. It translates roughly as "good, useful, pleasant toward people, virtuous, benevolent." Another Greek word, *agathosune* was also sometimes used to refer to someone who is good-hearted, intrinsically kind to others. It is generally understood that kindness is *an act* of good will toward another with no *expectation* of reciprocity from the beneficiary. In 2 Peter 1:5-8 (NASB), brotherly kindness is presented as the chief component of Godly love:

> Now for this very reason also, applying all diligence, in your faith supply moral excellence, and in your moral excellence, knowledge, and in your knowledge, self-control, and in your self-control, perseverance, and in your perseverance, godliness, and in your godliness, brotherly **kindness**, and in your brotherly **kindness**, love. For if these qualities are yours and are increasing, they render you neither useless nor unfruitful in the true knowledge of our Lord Jesus Christ.

Kindness is demonstrated in a number of ways throughout the Bible. Rahab, at the risk of her own life, showed kindness to the Israelite spies sent by Joshua to scout the walled city of Jericho. Joseph showed kindness to his older brothers who many years before had sold him into slavery and reported to their father that he had been killed by a wild animal. In the Book of Joshua, Ruth shows legendary kindness and loyalty toward her mother-in-law, Naomi, as does Boaz toward the two women:

> See which part of the field they are harvesting, and then follow them. I have warned the young men not to treat you roughly. And when you are thirsty, help yourself to the water they have drawn from the well." Ruth fell at his feet and thanked him warmly. "What have I done to deserve such kindness?" she asked. "I am only a foreigner."

"Yes, I know," Boaz replied. "But I also know about everything you have done for your mother-in-law since the death of your husband. I have heard how you left your father and mother and your own land to live here among complete strangers.

Ruth 2:9-11 NLT

In Acts 9:36, a disciple named Tabitha (aka Dorcas) was recognized for continually showing great kindness toward others. When Paul and his shipmates are shipwrecked on Malta, Paul comments on the extraordinary kindness that was demonstrated toward them by the natives of Malta.

We learn the importance of kindness through the teachings of Jesus. In addition to his parables, Christ taught by using analogies that simplified His message. In Luke 11 (NIV), Jesus says,

Which of you fathers, if your son asks for a fish, will give him a snake instead? Or if he asks for an egg, will give him a scorpion? If you then, though you are evil, know how to give good gifts to your children, how much more will your Father in heaven give the Holy Spirit to those who ask him!

The Lord makes it clear that when we show kindness toward others, we are showing kindness toward Him.

For I was hungry and you gave me something to eat, I was thirsty and you gave me something to drink, I was a stranger and you invited me in, I needed clothes and you clothed me, I was sick and you looked after me, I was in prison and you came to visit me.'

Then the righteous will answer him, 'Lord, when did we see you hungry and feed you, or thirsty and give you something to drink? When did we see you a stranger and invite you in, or needing clothes and clothe you? When did we see you sick or in prison and go to visit you?'"

The King will reply, 'Truly I tell you, whatever you did for one of the least of these brothers and sisters of mine, you did for me.'

Matthew 25:35-40 NIV

Christ is not done with this example. In Matthew 25:45 (NIV) He also makes it very clear that *failing* to show kindness toward others is also a failure to show kindness toward Him:

He will answer them, 'I'm telling the solemn truth: Whenever you failed to do one of these things to someone who was being overlooked or ignored, that was me—you failed to do it to me.'

In similar fashion, James warns, "If you refuse to act kindly, you can hardly expect to be treated kindly" (James 2:13). The Bible also teaches us that while we should not expect reciprocity from the recipient of our kindness, God will reward us for it. In Luke 6:38, the Lord tells us, "Give, and it will be given to you. A good measure, pressed down, shaken together and running over, will be poured into your lap" (NIV). Several chapters later, we read:

> Then he turned to the host. "The next time you put on a dinner, don't just invite your friends and family and rich neighbors, the kind of people who will return the favor. Invite some people who never get invited out, the misfits from the wrong side of the tracks. You'll be—and experience—a blessing. They won't be able to return the favor, but the favor will be returned—oh, how it will be returned!—at the resurrection of God's people."
>
> Luke 14:12-14 MSG

However, if we are to receive God's full reward, our acts of kindness cannot be directed only at people of our choosing. This is something we must pay special attention to because regardless of what any teacher says, we do tend to have both favorites and students who rub us the wrong way. Kindness that honors God is impartial with respect to the recipients.

> My brothers and sisters, believers in our glorious Lord Jesus Christ must not show favoritism. Suppose a man comes into your meeting wearing a gold ring and fine clothes, and a poor man in filthy old clothes also comes in. If you show special attention to the man wearing fine clothes and say, "Here's a good seat for you," but say to the poor man, "You stand there" or "Sit on the floor by my feet," have you not discriminated among yourselves and become judges with evil thoughts?
>
> James 2:1-4 NIV

Taking it to an even higher level, kindness must be extended without discrimination even to those whom we may not like, respect, or appreciate. In fact, God tells us we must extend this kindness even to our enemies.

> Love your enemies! Do good to them. Lend to them without expecting to be repaid. Then your reward from heaven will be very great, and you will truly be acting as children of the Most High, for he is **kind** to those who are unthankful and wicked.
>
> Luke 6:35 NLT

In the second century as Christianity continued to spread throughout the Mediterranean, Clement of Alexandria, one of the most influential teachers and writers of the early church wrote:

> And don't judge who is worthy of your gift because you may be mistaken in your opinion. It is better in ignorance to do good to the undeserving, than to fail to serve the worthy by guarding against the unworthy. For by holding back and testing people for merit, you may neglect some that God loves.

In the late 1800s, Belgian priest Damien de Veuster served the lepers on the island of Molokai. Damien nursed their foul sores and rotting limbs, bathed them, and offered needed hugs to the lepers. He displayed no fear that he might contract the dreaded disease, and in fact the disease did end up claiming his life. Damien was only one of thousands upon thousands of Christians who have committed themselves to tending to the needs of the poor and afflicted both in developed areas of the world and in areas of the world where a person of forty years is considered an old man because so many die young from endemic disease. Perhaps millions of people around the world are familiar with the life of kindness and compassion characterized by Theresa of Calcutta, but even she would have acknowledged that for the thousands who lived similar lives this extreme level of kindness more often goes unrecognized and unheralded. Theresa did not become renowned for actions by celebrating them herself. Most of what she and others like her do is in complete obscurity from outsiders. Humans have an innate, sinful desire for recognition, and this desire very often becomes the motivation for acts of kindness.

It is hard for most of us to imagine having such tremendous humility that we could willingly choose a life such as Mother Theresa. Only a very small percentage of people have this kind of humility. There are different levels of need for kindness, and I do not think it is God's will that all of us follow the example of Damien or Theresa. That would leave voids in many other areas where different levels and acts of kindness are also desperately needed. But as kindness is a fundamental, inseparable component of love, each of us compelled to demonstrate kindness, praying all the while that our humility will increase and with it the exercise of kindness that requires greater and greater self-sacrifice.

As teachers, we have a multitude of opportunities to show kindness to our students, their parents, and to our colleagues every day. Kindness should start at your doorway every morning and between classes. Kindness begins when we establish a connection with our students that is not exclusively related to the schoolwork. We show interest in them as a person and develop a relationship where they feel valued even though they may not be the best or brightest student in the class. When they need fish, we don't offer them a snake. Simple acts of kindness are sometimes the most effective. Greeting children with a smile gets your class off to a good start and helps in building relationships. Kindness may involve a phone call or a note to a student or to her parents addressing something good the student has done. Most of the time as teachers, the notes we send and the calls we make are a result of something unpleasant involving a student. I keep a certain amount of money in my pocket each day for students who forget their lunch money. If a child doesn't have a pencil, I try to provide one without excessive fussing at him or her. It is, after all, just a pencil. I find at least two on my floor at the end of every day. Kindness can involve giving the students a break for the normal routine such as taking them outside for ten minutes for a breath of fresh air. Kindness can be shown by our willingness to listen to others when they need someone to talk to. It can be as simple as a kind or gentle statement to someone at the right time:

- Proverbs 12:25 NIV- Anxiety weighs down the heart, but a kind word cheers it up.
- Proverbs 15:1 NIV- A gentle answer turns away wrath, but a harsh word stirs up anger.

- Proverbs 15:23 MSG- Congenial conversation-what a pleasure! The right word at the right time-beautiful!
- Proverbs 16:24 NIV- Gracious words are a honeycomb, sweet to the soul and healing to the bones.

Nineteenth century theologian Frederic Ozanam wrote that,

> Help honors when, to the bread that nourishes, it adds the visit that consoles, advice that enlightens, the friendly handshake that lifts up flagging courage. It esteems the poor man when it treats him with respect, not only as an equal, but as a superior, since he is suffering what perhaps we are incapable of suffering.

Mother Theresa, whom we used above to illustrate a life of humility and kindness, also wrote about the importance of small acts of kindness:

> A mere smile, a short visit, the lighting of a lamp, writing a letter for a blind man, carrying a bucket of charcoal, reading the newspaper for someone—something small, very small—may, in fact, be our love of God in action.

Like all fruits of The Spirit, kindness may require sacrifice such as allocating some of our time to provide assistance to someone. A teacher's "to do" list is never done. It seems that as soon as we get a few things checked off, several more things are tacked on to the bottom of the list. It can seem overwhelming at times, particularly for new teachers, teachers with additional duties and responsibilities that are above or beyond what is normal, and for colleagues who are experiencing challenges of a professional or personal matter. If feels at times that operating in a state of being overwhelmed is normal for me, and when I am caught up in this pattern I have little to offer anyone else above the base requirements. Not everyone that needs help will ask either because of pride or because he or she knows how much everyone else has to do. In his letter to the Galatians, Paul tells us we should, "Carry each other's burdens, and in this way you will fulfill the law of Christ" (Galatians 6:2 NIV). Covering a duty or a class for someone, helping someone make copies, saying a kind word about someone to an administrator, recognizing people's effort, making lunch for your team, making meals for colleagues who have experienced some kind of family set-back or loss, bringing in a batch of homemade brownies during the more challenging weeks, and making the extra effort to help newcomers feel welcomed are but a few examples of how we can show kindness toward our colleagues. Many people are reluctant to ask for help because they feel they might inconvenience someone. We should not wait for people to ask for help. We can observe when there is a need and respond with kindness. Saint Thomas of Villanova once wrote,

> If you wish God to anticipate your wants, provide those of the indigent without waiting for them to ask you. Especially anticipate the needs of those who are ashamed to beg. To make them ask for alms is to make them buy it.

Helping someone in need may not be "convenient." At times it may be very difficult. Most of us have our own "to do" list that cascades from our desktop to the floor. We also must consider closely whether kindness may actually involve *not* providing someone with assistance. It is an unfortunate truth that some people take advantage of the kindness of others by manipulating the giver. Others become dependent upon the charity of others which can be crippling to the recipient in the long run. I do not think, though, that God intends any of us to be "all things to all people." We have to make decisions about who we can and will help and what resources we can and will commit to helping them. Trying to do too much can result in periods of burnout and even resentment which ultimately ends up not helping anyone.

Additional Passages on Kindness

- Philemon 1:4-7 NLT- I always thank my God when I pray for you, Philemon, because I keep hearing about your faith in the Lord Jesus and your love for all of God's people. And I am praying that you will put into action the generosity that comes from your faith as you understand and experience all the good things we have in Christ. Your love has given me much joy and comfort, my brother, **for your kindness has often refreshed the hearts of God's people (NLT).**

- Psalms 41:1 NLT- Oh, the joys of those who are **kind** to the poor! The Lord rescues them when they are in trouble).

- 2 Timothy 2:24 NLT- A servant of the Lord must not quarrel but must be **kind** to everyone, be able to teach, and be patient with difficult people (NLT).

- Ephesians 4:32 NIV- Be **kind** and compassionate to one another, forgiving each other, just as in Christ God forgave you.

- Romans 12:20-21 MSG- Our Scriptures tell us that if you see your enemy hungry, go buy that person lunch, or if he's thirsty, get him a drink. Your generosity will surprise him with **goodness**. Don't let evil get the best of you; get the best of evil by doing good.

- Colossians 3:12 NLT- Since God chose you to be the holy people he loves, you must clothe yourselves with tenderhearted mercy, **kindness**, humility, gentleness, and patience.

- 2 Corinthians 6:6 NLT- We prove ourselves by our purity, our understanding, our patience, our **kindness**, by the Holy Spirit within us, and by our sincere love.

- Romans 12:6-8 NLT- In his grace, God has given us different gifts for doing certain things well. So if God has given you the ability to prophesy, speak out with as much faith as God has given you. If your gift is serving others, serve them well. If you are a teacher, teach well. If your gift is to encourage others, be encouraging. If it is giving, give generously. If God has given you leadership ability, take the responsibility seriously. And if you have a gift for showing **kindness** to others, do it gladly.

- Proverbs 11:17 NLT- Your **kindness** will reward you, but your cruelty will destroy you.

- Proverbs 3:3-4 NLT- Never let loyalty and **kindness** leave you! Tie them around your neck as a reminder. Write them deep within your heart. Then you will find favor with both God and people, and you will earn a good reputation.

- James 2:12-13 MSG- Talk and act like a person expecting to be judged by the Rule that sets us free. For if you refuse to act kindly, you can hardly expect to be treated kindly. **Kind** mercy wins over harsh judgment every time.
- Proverbs 3:27-28 MSG- Never walk away from someone who deserves help; your hand is God's hand for that person. Don't tell your neighbor "Maybe some other time" or "Try me tomorrow" when the money's right there in your pocket.
- Proverbs 21: 13 NIV- Whoever shuts their ears to the cry of the poor will also cry out and not be answered.
- Acts 20: 35 NIV- In everything I did, I showed you that by this kind of hard work we must help the weak, remembering the words the Lord Jesus himself said: 'It is more blessed to give than to receive.'

Additional Quotes on Kindness

- Do all the good you can by all the means you can in all the places you can at all the times you can to all the people you can as long as ever you can (John Wesley).
- **Kindness** is in our power, even when fondness is not (Samuel Johnson).
- You cannot do a **kindness** too soon, for you never know how soon it will be too late (Ralph Waldo Emerson).
- Too often we underestimate the power of a touch, a smile, a kind word, a listening ear, an honest compliment, or the smallest **act of caring**, all of which have the potential to turn a life around (Leo Buscaglia).
- **Kind** hearts are the gardens,
  Kind thoughts are the roots,
  Kind words are the blossoms,
  Kind deeds are the fruits.
  (19th century rhyme used in primary schools)
- Because that's what **kindness** is. It's not doing something for someone else because they can't, but because you can (Andrew Iskander).
- Extend **mercy** toward others, so that there can be no one in need whom you meet without helping. Just consider how much we ourselves are in need of **mercy**. For what hope is there for us if God should withdraw his **mercy** from us (Vincent De Paul)?
- Each day look for every possible opportunity to do a **kindness** for those you do not like. After examining yourself on this matter every morning, decide what you are going to do, and do it faithfully with **kindness** and humility (John Baptiste De La Salle).
- The school of Christ is the school of **charity**. On the last day, when the great general examination takes place, there will be no question at all on the text of Aristotle, the aphorisms of Hippocrates, of the paragraphs of Justinian. Charity will be the whole syllabus (St. Robert Bellarmine).
- Spread loving **kindness** everywhere you go. Be the living expression of God's **kindness**. **Kindness** in your face. **Kindness** in your eyes. **Kindness** in your smile. **Kindness** in your warm greeting (Mother Theresa).

Love Does Not Envy

Envy was a serious enough sin that it made it in the Big Ten. The Tenth Commandment tells us, "You shall not covet your neighbor's house. You shall not covet your neighbor's wife, or his male or female servant, his ox or donkey, or anything that belongs to your neighbor" (Exodus: 20:17 NIV). We don't use the word "covet" in our modern vernacular. To us it is "envy." Sometimes we use the word "jealousy" synonymously, but the two really aren't the same. Envy is jealousy on steroids. The Bible tells us, "Envy rots the bones" (Proverbs 14:30 NIV). Jealousy may be used to refer to our feelings when we see our neighbor's new 4WD pickup truck and wish we could afford one of our own instead of driving our fifteen-year-old Honda. It may also be used to refer to the feelings we have when we see our spouse talking to a very handsome colleague. Envy goes way beyond this. Envy carries with it a deeper enmity. We don't just wish we had our own 4WD pickup truck *like* the neighbor's, we feel we should have been in the position to purchase one instead of him because we are somehow more worthy of it. We aren't just jealous because the neighbor's wife is prettier and wittier (in our mind) than our own, we desire her as our own. This bitterness and animosity is an abomination to God on so many levels. First and foremost it tells God that we are unsatisfied with the blessings He has bestowed on us. Secondly, envy almost always leads us down the road of other sins such as embezzlement, selling drugs, sabotage, or adultery. Envy led Cain to murder his brother. It led Joseph's brothers to sell him into slavery and lie that he had been killed. The "presidents and princes" of Babylon became so envious toward Daniel because he was in the king's favor that they conspired to get him killed. In Acts, the Jewish leaders become envious of the crowds that were drawn to Paul and Barnabas and plotted to get them expelled from the town. We can see the other sins considered together with envy in Romans 1:29-31 (NIV):

> They have become filled with every kind of wickedness, evil, greed and depravity. They are **full of envy**, murder, strife, deceit and malice. They are gossips, slanderers, God-haters, insolent, arrogant and boastful; they invent ways of doing evil; they disobey their parents; they have no understanding, no fidelity, no love, no mercy.

It's hard for us to imagine feeling this kind of envy toward our students. It is more likely that we are going to feel this kind of envy toward our colleagues. The people who seem to be the most respected, who have the boss's ear, who receive recognition or praise. A few years ago I took a trip down Envy Lane and from this God taught me a very valuable lesson. Every year, teachers are asked to nominate a colleague for Teacher of the Year (TOTY). That particular year I really thought it was my time. I had served on the Leadership Committee, had been the Department Head for the Science Department, had been chosen to create benchmark tests for the district, was mentoring two colleagues, was developing most of the materials we used in our grade level science department and my students had done exceptionally well on state standardized test for many years. We received the congratulatory list of TOTY nominees on a Friday. My name was not on it. In past years, I understood why I had not been nominated. However, I had made a number of changes in the way I conducted myself and I felt certain I deserved a nomination. In fact, I expected to be nominated. I felt *entitled*. I was surprised, then hurt, then downright angry. I stormed off that afternoon without a word to anyone other than a veiled, sarcastic e-mail to my department and my protégés about not being appreciated. I stewed all evening about it. I withdrew from my family and pouted but would not tell anyone why. God worked on me hard that night. My anger and envy toward my colleagues slowly began to transform into disappointment and anger toward myself. I began to realize I was being selfish, resentful, and envious. I began to understand and accept that I had not deserved to be recognized by such an honor, not because I had not done all the things I had mentioned, but because I had not done everything as a teacher that I had committed to God that I would do. I was not humble enough to earn such an honor. It was a long night, but the wound was entirely self-inflicted.

The next morning I still had a mixture of emotions running through me. I went back and forth between envy, resentment, embarrassment, and humility. About noon on Saturday, a phone call from the school principal brought this inner battle to a screeching halt. He sounded a bit unsettled, asked me how my day was going so far. I thought I had done something to offend someone, my e-mail perhaps, and I was being called to get slapped on the wrist. Then he came out with it. A colleague in our science department whom I had worked with for eight years had passed away unexpectedly in the early hours of that morning. He was in his early fifties, and it came as a tremendous shock to us. Needless to say, that phone call prompted a major change in my attitude. My life had once again been put into perspective for me. I had glorified myself, had come to feel entitled, and when I felt slighted, had allowed myself to deteriorate into a state of envy and resentment. A few years later, I would find my own levels of anxiety and health risks spiraling out of control and his death in part reminded me that I needed to calm down and let things go. It is impossible for me to see now how I could have been focused on honoring God when so much of my attention was consumed by worries about whether my colleagues would notice my efforts and honor me.

On Monday, I confessed my sins to my two protégés who had felt the sting of my sarcastic e-mail the most. They were both apologetic. They had missed the deadline for getting their nomination in. I feel to this day that something else more powerful was at work. It was not God's will that I be recognized. I explained to them that I was not disappointed with them, and that the right person, a very hard working and excellent teacher, had earned the honor. Further, I shared with them (both Christians) my sincere belief that God had not moved anyone to nominate me because I had not honored the commitments to Him with regards to my job. I was not humble enough to earn such a reward. I don't know what criteria, if any, God may have had for anyone else for them to be blessed by such an honor, but I know what criteria He has for me. God knew the darkness of my heart. Prior to giving my work over to Christ several years ago, I had a great desire for recognition and perhaps even admiration from my peers. I wanted to be the best and I wanted people to know I was the best. I carried a great deal of envy, pride, and resentment toward others and toward my profession for a host of reasons. I was superficially nice, but internally I was burning with all the consuming fire that comes with pride and resentment. Such sinful behavior had eaten away at me to the point where I was ready to leave the profession. I didn't feel "appreciated enough." I still struggle with some of those feelings from time to time, but prior to that fateful day I thought I had finally begun to develop genuine humility. After that weekend, I felt like a recovering alcoholic who had been dry for years but then tied one on when he found out his ex was getting remarried. Envy, pride, and resentment will always be in my "house," but I felt they had been mostly regulated to the basement. That week I dusted them off and put them back on the mantel for a while. Sin ruled. As I have said previously, I remain a work in progress. I did end up being recognized as the TOTY and went on to win one state and four national teaching awards. A description of how that affected me is covered in the epilogue to this book. It was not what I nor what most others would have suspected. In short, it tore me to pieces emotionally, spiritually, and physically.

We are told in the Bible to let others praise us with their comments. But it also says we should show kindness to others by patting them on the back every now and then. As an act of kindness, how often do any of us "brag up" our colleagues? How often do we unofficially recognize and applaud those whom we know are working hard or who are living as a Godly example? How often does our "gossip" focus on a good aspect of a person? Why are we so stingy when it comes to paying compliments to our colleagues? In a word, envy. If we are not receiving compliments ourselves, we often withhold them from others. We feel like if anyone deserves a compliment, it is us, and if we aren't getting any then certainly we are not going to pay compliments to others. This behavior is certainly not what God expects from us. When I am not so wrapped up in my own issues, I try to make it a point to "brag up" colleagues whom I see doing something admirable. I bring this attention to their supervisors but have never told any of them that I did so. That way, there can be no misunderstanding that I am trying to look magnanimous in their eyes or that I am expecting some kind of reciprocity. I am simply doing what the Bible says we can and should do. When I am caught up in my own selfishness, I think it is safe to say that on a few occasions I have thrown some people under the bus. We are all human, and humans have an innate desire for recognition. But we need to understand this is part of our fallen nature rather than our divine nature. Nothing is hidden from God, so He sees all that we do *and* he has the greater advantage of knowing the motivation for our actions. It is okay to be recognized and to feel good about being recognized, but being recognized by other people cannot be our driving goal. We want people to see us living a Godly example, to be the lamp in the darkness, but this is for the purpose of glorifying God and leading people to Him. It is also Godly behavior to pay a compliment to a person for his or her Godly behavior, for his or her hard work, for his or her willingness to tackle a duty that nobody else wanted.

Passages on Envy

- Galatians 5:21 NIV- The acts of the flesh are obvious: sexual immorality, impurity and debauchery; idolatry and witchcraft; hatred, discord, jealousy, fits of rage, selfish ambition, dissensions, factions **and envy**; drunkenness, orgies, and the like. I warn you, as I did before, that those who live like this will not inherit the kingdom of God.
- James 4:1-3 NIV- What causes fights and quarrels among you? Don't they come from your desires that battle within you? You desire but do not have, so you kill. You **covet** but you cannot get what you want, so you quarrel and fight. You do not have because you do not ask God. When you ask, you do not receive, because you ask with wrong motives, that you may spend what you get on your pleasures.
- 1 Peter 2:1-3 NIV- Therefore, rid yourselves of all malice and all deceit, hypocrisy, **envy**, and slander of every kind. Like newborn babies, crave pure spiritual milk, so that by it you may grow up in your salvation, now that you have tasted that the Lord is good.

- James 3:13-16 NIV- Who is wise and understanding among you? Let them show it by their good life, by deeds done in the humility that comes from wisdom. But if you harbor **bitter envy** and selfish ambition in your hearts, do not boast about it or deny the truth. Such "wisdom" does not come down from heaven but is earthly, unspiritual, demonic. For where you have **envy** and selfish ambition, there you find disorder and every evil practice.
- Titus 3:3-5 NIV- At one time we too were foolish, disobedient, deceived and enslaved by all kinds of passions and pleasures. We lived in malice and **envy**, being hated and hating one another. But when the kindness and love of God our Savior appeared, he saved us, not because of righteous things we had done, but because of his mercy.
- Romans 13:13 NKJV- Let us walk properly, as in the day, not in revelry and drunkenness, not in lewdness and lust, not in strife and **envy**.
- Proverbs14:30 NIV- A heart at peace gives life to the body, but **envy** rots the bones.

Additional Quotes on Envy

- The **envious** man thinks that if his neighbor breaks a leg, he will be able to walk better himself. (Helmut Shoeck).
- When men are full of **envy** they disparage everything, whether it be good or bad (Tacitus).
- It is in the character of very few men to honor without **envy** a friend who has prospered. (Aeschylus)
- **Envy** is a littleness of soul, which cannot see beyond a certain point, and if it does not occupy the whole space feels itself excluded (William Hazlitt).
- God's truth judges created things out of love, and Satan's truth judges them out of **envy** and hatred (Dietrich Bonhoeffer).
- **Envy** is like a fly that passes all the body's sounder parts, and dwells upon the sores (Arthur Chapman).

Love does not boast, is not proud, is not self-seeking, does not dishonor others, and keeps no record of wrongs.

Chapter Two discussed humility in depth. Boasting, acting in a prideful manner, considering ourselves better or more deserving than others (arrogance or conceit), taking care of our own desires ahead of the needs of others, making ourselves stand out or look good at the expense of others, gossiping, gloating over the misfortunes of others, and keeping track of the injustices or wrongdoings leveled against you (real or perceived) are all actions inconsistent with humility.

Passages Related to Humility

- Romans 12: 3-5 NIV- For by the grace given me I say to every one of you: Do not think of yourself more highly than you ought, but rather think of yourself with sober judgment, in accordance with the faith God has distributed to each of you. For just as each of us has one body with many members, and these members do not all have the same function, so in Christ we, though many, form one body, and each member belongs to all the others.

- James 4:16 ESV- As it is, you boast in your arrogance. All such boasting is evil.
- Psalms 94:4 ESV- They pour out their arrogant words; all the evildoers boast.
- 1 Corinthians 10:12 ESV- Not that we dare to classify or compare ourselves with some of those who are commending themselves. But when they measure themselves by one another and compare themselves with one another, they are without understanding.
- James 3:5 ESV- So also the tongue is a small member, yet it boasts of great things. How great a forest is set ablaze by such a small fire!
- 2 Corinthians 11:30 ESV- If I must boast, I will boast of the things that show my weakness.
- Isaiah 10:15 ESV- Shall the axe boast over him who hews with it, or the saw magnify itself against him who wields it? As if a rod should wield him who lifts it, or as if a staff should lift him who is not wood!
- Romans 3:27 NIV- Where, then, is boasting? It is excluded. Because of what law? The law that requires works? No, because of the law that requires faith.
- Psalms 17:10 ESV- They close their hearts to pity; with their mouths they speak arrogantly.
- 1 Samuel 2:3 ESV- Talk no more so very proudly, let not arrogance come from your mouth; for the Lord is a God of knowledge, and by him actions are weighed.
- Romans 12:3 ESV- For by the grace given to me I say to everyone among you not to think of himself more highly than he ought to think, but to think with sober judgment, each according to the measure of faith that God has assigned.
- Proverbs 8:13 ESV- The fear of the Lord is hatred of evil. Pride and arrogance and the way of evil and perverted speech I hate.
- Isaiah 13:11 ESV- I will punish the world for its evil, and the wicked for their iniquity; I will put an end to the pomp of the arrogant, and lay low the pompous pride of the ruthless.
- Proverbs 27:2 ESV- Let another praise you, and not your own mouth; a stranger, and not your own lips.
- Romans 12: 9-10 MSG- Love from the center of who you are; don't fake it. Run for dear life from evil; hold on for dear life to good. Be good friends who love deeply; practice playing second fiddle.
- Philippians 2:3-4 NIV- Do nothing out of selfish ambition or vain conceit. Rather, in humility value others above yourselves, not looking to your own interests but each of you to the interests of the others.
- Proverbs 24: 17-18 NLV- Do not be full of joy when the one who hates you falls. Do not let your heart be glad when he trips. The Lord will see it and will not be pleased, and He will turn away His anger from him.
- Ecclesiastes 7:21-22 MSG- Don't eavesdrop on the conversation of others. What if the gossip's about you and you'd rather not hear it? You've done that a few times, haven't you- said things behind someone's back you wouldn't say to his face.

Love is Not Easily Angered

Anger is an incredibly complicated emotion. It has different faces and a myriad of underlying causes. Anger in and of itself is almost never a primary emotion. It is an emotion that follows another: disappointment, jealousy, envy, embarrassment, annoyance, fear, shame, pride, grief, or one of many other primary emotions. Anger can manifest itself in a number of ways. I struggle with a quick temper. Imagine sitting near a campfire. My quick temper is like the "pops" the fire produces when small bubbles of sap explode. The pop sends a few sparks upward, but the duration of the event is short-lived. The coals of the fire are analogous to another, deeper, potentially more dangerous type of anger: an underlying anger that constantly burns and consumes whatever it comes in contact with. I have a quick temper, but I battle to keep from becoming an angry person because I have experienced first-hand how easy becoming an angry person was for me and how utterly miserable it was for me and others to live in that state. Though I don't always act like it, I do recognize I have far more than I need and certainly far more then I deserve. I realize how unbelievably blessed I am. I am grateful for my many blessings. But in me is the potential to become an angry person. This tendency was built into me at a very young age. An angry person carries his anger with him all the time. Sometimes the coals are baking beneath the surface, but these coals are so hot that any fuel added immediately goes up in flames. This type of anger can be deeply destructive to the person with the anger and to those around him. Anger is not always "bad." It is not always a sin. In fact, as Jesus showed when he upset the tables of the money-changers defiling the temple anger can be righteous. Anger can serve a productive purpose, but like the flames it can produce it can also be destructive.

I see a good bit of anger in my workplace, most of which is directed at policy or what we see as exceptionally high and, to some people, unrealistic expectations and unfunded mandates. Some of these expectations and mandates originate at the school level, many at a much higher level. Many teachers will not admit that they are angry or may not even realize the depth of their anger particularly when asked by someone in a supervisory position. They may be unwilling to express their anger at something that is happening in the workplace to the supervisor for fear of reprisal or of being perceived as weak. Instead, they express their anger to members of their team and department. The result is that many surveys on workplace moral may reflect a much higher rating then what may be accurate. Perhaps the worst type of work climate to work in is one where dissatisfaction is festering beneath the surface but where nobody dares to share this dissatisfaction with the administration. Some districts may have a reputation for not really being attentive to what the teachers think or how they feel. Others may have an "open door policy" where teachers are encouraged to express their concerns, but ultimately these concerns are seldom taken into consideration when decisions are made that affect the teachers. If this is the case, I would caution my fellow teachers about automatically assuming their voices were not heard because their concerns were not valued. It may be that there are mandates at play that come from the district, state, or even national level that do not allow for flexibility or input.

If I am to be honest, I would have to say that I have not worked in many systems where teachers have a strong presence in the decisions that are made regarding policy and procedures. It is easy to get fixated on this and become bitter, but the Bible clearly tells us that we are to do our work without complaint and strife as though for the Lord and not for men. Years of experience in our profession can either foster cynicism or resilience depending upon how we view and deal with the challenges we face. I have some very strong feelings about the educational system in our country and not all of them bring me to a warm, fuzzy place. After nearly thirty years, I often find myself battling the weariness that comes with fighting the good fight for this long. It is often hard to sustain the passion that is needed to be an effective public-school teacher. Given the particulars of my personality, my life history, and my genetic predispositions, it has not been my experience that contentment is as simple as making a choice to be content. But the Bible commands us to act at times contrary to how we feel if we are to be the light in the darkness. This does not mean that we pretend we are not angry when we are angry or pretend we are happy when we are not. It means that we act in a way that reflects the light of Christ regardless of the internal strife or external pressure that is upon us. I do not know this for certain, but I would find it hard to believe that someone like Mother Theresa was free from either internal strife nor external pressure, nor do I believe that she loved doing all the things she did in her service to the people of India. All jobs have the potential to cause us internal strife or exert tremendous external pressure. The challenge is to remember what Paul told the people of Colossus: do your job as though for Christ and not for men. We treat others in a loving way even if we don't even like a person. We refrain from yelling or belittling others regardless of how angry we feel inside. We do what is expected of us without constant complaint.

Not all anger, of course, is work related although I have found that many people who are constantly angry at work express a lot of anger about aspects of their lives outside of the workplace. Some people are just plain angry about their lives, and that anger does not get checked at the front door of the school. Mostly, teachers are angry at all the different things they are expected to do in our profession. I get that. Though I am not at this point in my life an angry person, for years I was an angry teacher. The air in the sail of sinful anger is quite often resentment. Resentment because the job we thought we signed up for is not the job we are expected to do. Pre-service training and even student-teaching do little to prepare prospective teachers for the actual rigors of the profession, which is why many new teachers leave the profession within a few years. Resentment that the nature of our job has changed so that we can no longer do the things the way we used to. Resentment because doing our job *well* requires so much more time than the standard eight-hour work day. Resentment as we see the autonomy we once had or thought we would have gradually stripped away. In more challenging schools, resentment because of the way we are allowed to be treated by our students or resentment toward being blamed for all that is wrong with the students. Resentment that our hourly salary by comparison is lower than other professions. I had taught over twenty-three years and had a graduate degree before I ever crossed the $30 per hour mark-and that is if I actually worked only 190 days and a forty-hour week which is laughable. My real hourly salary is considerably lower. Resentment because we do not feel appreciated by the students, the community, our nation. Resentment toward all the educational laws and mandates that are created by people who have never worked as educators. I have felt resentment toward each of these, and it led to more resentment. It nibbled away at my soul. We must, if we are to survive and prosper in this profession, be driven by a desire to serve our students, their families, our administration, our community, and our profession even when we feel our dignity is constantly under attack. We must focus on what is right and good about what we do rather than what is wrong with it. We need to focus on the fact that we are serving God with our work, we are doing this for Him. If we are doing this for Him, then it should make us feel a sense of satisfaction that we are doing this for Him despite the multitude of challenges that have successfully driven millions of teachers from our profession. We are fighting the good fight.

We as Christians are the light. We must do better. A house divided against itself cannot stand, and a house divided is often what we see among our colleagues. The house divided is weakened. Working in an environment with people who are constantly negative or angry about something is one of the most draining aspects of our jobs. Angry people complain incessantly, and very often their anger spreads to others who then begin complaining incessantly as well. They frequently take their anger out on others, whether it is colleagues, leaders, or students. One of the hardest things for me deal with is listening to teachers who constantly bash students. I am all for legitimate debate, expression of concerns, and I recognize the cathartic benefits of a little venting from time to time, but being surrounded by negativity has the effect of sucking the life out of me. I cannot imagine that it does not do the same to the students. I understand that students can be challenging, but there is no justification for any teacher to spew derogatory personal comments about students. I have worked with teachers who seem to have very little to say good about any of their students. They bash students, the parents of the students, other teachers. Their bashing is usually very personal, targeting aspects about the child's appearance, hygiene, clothing, intelligence, personality, etc. It puzzles me how people who seem to have such disdain for students would choose such a career! Our job is incredibly difficult but being angry and complaining constantly will do nothing to make our jobs easier. On the contrary, when the well becomes tainted all who drink from it suffer. It becomes even more of a problem when others around these people jump on the bashing bandwagon. Confronting these people usually does very little good. Their anger and their lack of humility floods them with an imposing sense of self-righteousness. It should be impossible for a person to maintain such a disposition and be a highly effective teacher and a follower of Christ. God expects us to look for the best in people. He expects us to seek and find the best in our students, their parents, our colleagues, our leaders. The only chance we have of influencing people like this is by winning them over by our example. In Chapter Six, we will discuss the importance of serving as an example for students and colleagues.

Passages Related to Sinful Anger

- Ephesians 4:26-27 NIV- In your anger do not sin: Do not let the sun go down while you are still **angry**, and do not give the devil a foothold.
- Proverbs 26:20-22 ESV- For lack of wood the fire goes out, and where there is no whisperer, quarreling ceases. As charcoal to hot embers and wood to fire, so is a quarrelsome man for kindling strife. The words of a whisperer are like delicious morsels; they go down into the inner parts of the body.
- Ephesians 4:31 NLT- Get rid of all bitterness, rage and **anger**, brawling and slander, along with every form of malice.
- Proverbs 14: 17 NIV- He who has a **quick temper** acts in a foolish way, and a man who makes sinful plans is hated.

- Proverbs 14:29 NLT- People with understanding control their **anger**; a hot temper shows great foolishness.
- Proverbs 15:1 NIV- A gentle answer turns away wrath, but a harsh word stirs up **anger**.
- Proverbs 15:18 NLT- A hot-tempered person starts fights; a cool-tempered person stops them.
- Proverbs 19:11 NLV- A man's understanding makes him slow to anger. It is to his honor to forgive and forget a wrong done to him (NLV).
- Proverbs 22:24-25 MSG- Don't hang out with **angry** people; don't keep company with hotheads. Bad temper is contagious— don't get infected.
- Proverbs 29:22 NLV- A man of anger starts fights, and a man with a bad temper is full of wrong-doing.
- Proverbs 30:33 NLV- Shaking milk makes butter, and hitting the nose brings blood. So fighting comes because of anger.
- Colossians 3:7-8 NIV- You used to walk in these ways, in the life you once lived. But now you must also rid yourselves of all such things as these: **anger**, rage, malice, slander, and filthy language from your lips.
- Ecclesiastes 7:9 MSG- Don't be quick to fly off the handle. **Anger** boomerangs. You can spot a fool by the lumps on his head.
- Psalms 37:8-9 NLV- Stop being **angry**. Turn away from fighting. Do not trouble yourself. It leads only to wrong-doing. For those who do wrong will be cut off. But those who wait for the Lord will be given the earth.
- Ecclesiastes 7:9 NLV- Do not be quick in spirit to be **angry.** For anger is in the heart of fools.
- James 1:19-20 NLT- Understand this, my dear brothers and sisters: You must all be quick to listen, slow to speak, and slow to get **angry**. Human **anger** does not produce the righteousness God desires.

Love Keeps No Record of Wrongs

Imagine how our faith would be different if God kept a record of our wrongdoings so that, even though we asked for and received forgiveness for past sins, He brought them up and threw them in our face every time we made a mistake. We understand that we will all have to give an accounting of our lives when we are before God in Heaven, however, that is not the same as saying that He is going to hold all our sins against us. The Bible tells us that we repent of our sins, we are forgiven. Because of our faith, the death of Christ on the cross wipes out our transgressions. Through His sacrifice, He is able to present us as blameless before God, the Father. Simply put, God doesn't hold a grudge toward those who have truly accepted Christ as their Lord and Savior. He doesn't hold our past transgressions against us. I believe that our accounting will focus more on the things we *didn't* do, things we *should* have done rather than a review of all the sins for which we have been forgiven. In our role as teacher, we will be tested by ample opportunities to develop a grudge toward a student, his or her parents, a colleague, or an administrator. We may be greatly influenced by a student's "record of wrongdoings." We may find ourselves acting in an unfavorable manner toward a particular student simply because his parents are difficult to deal with even though the child is not. We may even act in an unfair way toward a student whose older sibling made our job exceedingly difficult even though this younger sibling does not. More likely it is our tendency to hold a grudge toward a current student who has offended us by being disruptive, disrespectful, dishonest, apathetic, or unproductive.

From the perspective of teaching and maintaining proper discipline, there are ways that chronic misconduct must be dealt with. However, the attitude with which we dispense our discipline should not reflect hostility or vindictiveness toward the student. It is possible to discipline with love, and I would argue that this is the far more effective means of discipline. Proverbs 17:9 (NIV) tells us, "whoever would foster love covers over an offense, but whoever repeats the matter separates close friends." This doesn't mean that we should not address problem behavior, it simply means that once we have addressed it we shouldn't keep throwing it back up in the student's face. Isolated incidents and chronic behavior are addressed differently, however, as Christians we must be concerned ultimately with building a person up. If we knock down some of the walls, it is always with the intention of building them back stronger and better. If our attitude towards a child whom we are disciplining projects vindictiveness or belittling rather than a genuine concern for them becoming a better person, we will most likely inspire an equal measure of vindictiveness from them toward us and perhaps others. As teachers, we can be compassionate and forgiving without being tolerant of inappropriate or counterproductive behavior. As we are forgiven, so too must we forgive.

Love Protects

To protect something means that we try to prevent any harm coming to the thing or the person. Understanding the concept of how love protects is more challenging than understanding the other characteristics of love Paul mentions. I love my children very much and I want to protect them from harm, but I know I will never be able to protect them from all things that may harm them. The other complication is that there can be a danger in being too protective. Obsessing over an object of interest can cause us to allocate much more time and energy to the protection of that object than the object warrants. When it comes to our own children and our students, we know that mistakes are an invaluable component of learning and character building. When we protect the ones we love, we try our best to steer them in the right direction, but when they choose another path that leads them to make bad choices we also protect them by our own response. Fallen people make mistakes-lots of them. To me, love protects by showing people that we will continue to love them even when they make mistakes. In 1 Peter 4:8 we are told that "love covers over a multitude of sin."

Every parent and every teacher knows the golden rule of discipline: *Never discipline when you are angry.* Impulsive, quick-tempered, impatient people like me really, *really* struggle with this. It is one of the worst things I do as a parent and as a teacher. It breaks my heart when I think of how many times I have broken my own son's or daughter's hearts by letting my temper and impatience get the best of me. Apologies help, but after a while apologies have a tendency to lose their effectiveness. When our own children or students make mistakes, love does not protect if it includes yelling or screaming at them, telling them over and over again, "I told you so!" Love does not include belittling comments. Love does not take pleasure in seeing the person suffer from his or her mistakes, nor does love protect if we maintain a sanctimonious, holier-than-though attitude. In my case, I have found that I need to remind myself that love does not protect when you are intent on "putting someone in their place" when other alternatives were available. As all of us are sinners, all of us should be able to empathize with the pain we often go through when we make mistakes. Love protects by not belittling a person and robbing him of his dignity.

Love does not protect when we go from person to person and gossip about a person's mistakes, our perception of their shortcomings, or failures. We do love to gossip. The juicier the gossip, the quicker we want to share it with someone else. Gossip does not show love because it does not protect. It is also hypocritical. The Bible explicitly warns us about slander and gossip:

- Leviticus 19:16 ESV- You shall not go around as a slanderer among your people, and you shall not stand up against the life of your neighbor: I am the LORD.
- Proverbs 10:18 NIV- Whoever conceals hatred with lying lips and spreads slander is a fool.
- Proverbs 11:13 NLT- A gossip goes around telling secrets, but those who are trustworthy can keep a confidence.
- Proverbs 20:19 NLV- He who goes about talking to hurt people makes secrets known. So do not be with those who talk about others.

When people make mistakes, love protects when we show compassion toward the person. Love protects when we help the person process his or her mistake in a nonjudgmental way with the aim of helping them to learn from it. Love protects when we help the sinner to consider what he or she can do to decrease the likelihood of his or her making the same mistake again and again. Love protects when we are able to help the person see things through another perspective. Love protects when it provides compassion rather than judgment for people who are struggling with their sin. And yes, love protects when it disciplines, but so many of us do such a poor job in making that love evident in our discipline. Christ disciplined his followers, often with gentle compassion, sometimes firmly, but always in a manner that they were able to understand the purpose for his discipline and in a way that his love was apparent. So what of those people who are convinced that they did not sin or do not care if they sinned, who appear to feel no remorse for their actions? Remember that you are the lamp of God's love. We are told not to "light a lamp and put it under a basket, but on the lampstand, and it gives light to all who are in the house" (Matthew 5:15). Who knows what influence your example might have on those who live apart from God? Almost certainly you will have no positive effect if you respond to indifference with indifference.

Love Always Trusts

The translation of the Greek word for trust in this case according to some scholars means to "trust in" or "believe in" something or someone. I have heard students time and time again over the years say that the best teachers they had, the ones they liked the most, the teachers who seemed to care the most about the students, and the ones that made the greatest impact on them were the teachers these kids felt *believed in them*. This is always something great to hear from any student, but it is particularly meaningful when the statement is made by a child who was struggling, who really didn't demonstrate that there was much for us to believe in, and who absolutely did not believe in himself or herself. Self-esteem refers to a person's overall feeling about his worth. Self-efficacy refers to a person's belief about his or her ability to accomplish something or deal with challenges. In our role as teachers and as Christians we have the responsibility to foster both. Love believes in finding the goodness in people. Love believes in people by not automatically assuming a person has done something bad despite his reputation for misconduct until we have all the facts. Believing in someone also means that we must not always be suspicious of their motives, though as a middle school teacher I have learned when it comes to tweens there is great wisdom in the old saying, "Trust everyone, but cut the cards."

Love Always Hopes

Hope goes hand-in-hand with believing in a person. Not only does love try to see the best in people, it also hopes for the best for people. We use the word "hope" a lot, but I don't think we always express Godly hope. In the Bible, the word "hope" sometimes translates to "hopefully trusts or believes in." In Thayer's Greek lexicon, the Greek word *epidzo* can also mean, "to wait for salvation with joy and full confidence." When we hope for people, then, hope is not loving if it is offered begrudgingly or insincerely. When a student burns out a teacher and is changed to another teacher's class, we often say to the parents, "I hope he is able to be more successful for that teacher than he was for me." But often we don't *really* mean it as much as we should. In fact, if the student does better for another teacher, then one might reasonably question whether the problem was really more with the original teacher than the student. When we hope for people, there must be sincerity and a sense of purity in that hope. And even though the translation "to wait for salvation with joy and full confidence" is in the context of salvation, I would argue that when we hope in a loving way there is also, if not joy, a great measure of good will in our hope. In addition, if we are to hope in a loving way, in a way that appeals to the Lord as a petition for that person, then we should "hopefully trust or believe in," have confidence, that our hopes for that person will be answered by God.

Love Always Perseveres

Relationships don't fail because love fails. Relationships fail because people fail to continue loving. Throughout this whole chapter, love is described as an act, the act of treating people in a loving way. I cannot imagine any circumstance where, if a person is able to consistently act in a loving way toward another person, both the giver and recipient will not benefit. The problem is, it is perilously easy to fall away from the practice of treating a person in a loving way. I recently gave a survey to my students to get some idea of how I was doing as a teacher. When I examined the results I was troubled to see that 12% of my 112 students felt like I did not care about them. Some of the respondents were probably students who received a disproportionate amount of disciplinary measures because of behavior issues. Many of them interpret discipline as not caring. But that would only explain a few students. I did some honest self-reflection and realized it was an entirely accurate reflection of my relationship with students. I had very good relationships with the majority of students because we engaged in conversations that extended beyond the lesson. I joked with some kids and not others. Some kids had nicknames, but most did not. I already had relationships with over twenty families because I taught older siblings, sometimes all the older siblings. But when I stopped to assess my interactions, I could easily identify a number of students with whom I did not engage in the same manner as I did others. I was not consciously excluding them. I simply did not give them the same degree of attention as I did many other students, and as a middle school student that translates into feelings that I did not care about them.

Had that been my only failure, it would have been an easier fix. But there was more: I also had to admit that there really were students I cared for more than I did other students. That is the mark of a sinner and we all have it. We don't usually admit that we have favorites in our classroom, but we do. As a follower of Christ there should be no difference in the way we treat those whom we favor and those with whom we do not feel as deep an attachment. We are, of course, also pushed in the wrong direction by more than just our own sinful nature. Because love is the cornerstone of Christ's ministry, Satan and his followers will throw up whatever obstacles they can to slow or even stop the flow of love from one person to another. They will place other things in our lives that divert our attention from loving a person or group of people. They will manipulate our own sinful biases and desires. Satan knows that loving others is an act that requires intentionality because it does not come naturally to us to act toward *all* people in a loving way. Satan is a powerful, supernatural being. He is more powerful than us. But he is not more powerful than God, and God will keep love flowing if we petition Him. It is too great a challenge for most of us to be intentional and persistent in treating others in a loving way without God's assistance. Love cannot persevere without God's help. We were originally wired that way-in God's image- but that changed with the fall of man. Our best attempts to be intentional and persistent in our love are usually toward our spouses and our own children, but even toward them we often fail to act in a loving way. The more challenging it is to treat certain people in a loving way, the more relentless we need to be in petitioning God for His assistance. We must see love through, allow it to persevere. This is particularly important when dealing with some of our most troubled students. Many of them have faced abuse or abandonment. If you begin to show them that you care for them, they will test you over and over again to make you prove it. With them, if our love fails to persevere, if they break us, then we confirm to them that caring about or loving others is a fruitless endeavor and they may carry that attitude into every relationship they have throughout their lives. God commands us to love one another. Paul makes it very clear that loving others is not a part-time job. Love *always* protects. Love *always* trusts. Love *always* hopes. Love *always* perseveres. There it is again: that one word in a passage that defines the statement. If we miss the word "always," when we read the passage, we miss just how important these things are to God. Even people who choose to live a life apart from God or who do not believe in God at all still understand that more good things will happen in this world through the acts of people treating others in a loving way than will ever happen in the absence of love.

Understanding the Line

It shouldn't come as a surprise to any public-school teacher that loving my students almost never involves talking to my students about God. Jesus says we are to obey the earthly laws, and the separation of church and state forbids the teaching of religious beliefs in public schools. I have known teachers who are ardent Christians and who believe it is worth the risk talking to students about God in school. My feeling about this is that God is not served if that person is reprimanded and eventually fired for violating this law. God needs good Christian role models at the head of the classroom. The only exception I make is if I am speaking personally to a student whose parents I know to be members of my church or who I know to be active in a church of their own. Some parents in my church expect other Christians to offer their children, my students, Christian guidance in school and I will honor that. Even here I proceed with caution. The conversation is usually brief, something perhaps even in passing. I certainly do not take time away from instruction or my planning period to hold lengthy conversations about my faith.

I want my faith to be evident in the relationships I try to develop with my students. As part of building a relationship with my students, I make an effort to learn more about them. I ask about their parents, their siblings, their last baseball game, how drama rehearsals are going, etc. There would be no reason for me not to ask about church events as they are just as much a part of many of their lives as those other activities. In truth, I am not sure whether this violates the separation of church and state any more than I understand whether wearing a "Jesus fish" tie does. If a student asks me why I seem to care so much about kids, I have no reservations telling them it is because of my faith. I have no problem briefly explaining that my faith calls for me to exercise a certain value like compassion. I understand though, that I cannot elaborate much more. As a teacher in a public school, I feel certain I would not be able to invite them to my church to learn more about my faith. I have spoken at greater length to parents and feel more comfortable inviting them if they express a desire to learn more, but when it comes to students, rather than me inviting them I encourage other students whom I see in church to extend invitations to their peers. Even here, we must be particularly careful about referring *specific* students to whom they might extend an invitation. In that case, it would still be an invitation from me and may still violate school law. I do wish I could speak to certain students about our faith in more detail. I have known many students over the years whom I think desperately needed to learn about God's love and the hope that exists in Christ. Ultimately, I believe God understands the legal limitations we have and I trust that my contribution toward leading a child to Him is a step in a sequence of events. In Philippians 1:6 (NIV), Paul tells us, "He who began a good work in you will carry it on to completion until the day of Christ Jesus." In this case, though Paul is writing mostly about completing the good work that is taking place in our own person, it stands to reason that where those "good works" affect others God will also see those works through to fruition. If I am able to light that spark in a child, I trust that God will put someone else in his or her life that will lead him or her through the next step. It is the *way we show love* that can put children on the path toward Christ. I have learned through my own experience that there are two sets of guidelines, two sets of expectations that exist in our careers as teachers. Inevitably each of us will come to the line where our teaching duties end. If this line is adjacent to the line where our duties as a person saved by the grace of a loving God end as well, I would argue we have greatly misunderstood our calling.

CHAPTER FIVE

Tough (to) Love

What do you think? If a man owns a hundred sheep, and one of them wanders away, will he not leave the ninety-nine on the hills and go to look for the one that wandered off? And if he finds it, truly I tell you, he is happier about that one sheep than about the ninety-nine that did not wander off.

In the same way your Father in heaven is not willing that any of these little ones should perish.

Matthew 18:12-14 NIV

If you love those who love you, what credit is that to you? Even sinners love those who love them.

And if you do good to those who are good to you, what credit is that to you? Even sinners do that.

Luke 6:32-33 NIV

Then Jesus said to his host, "When you give a luncheon or dinner, do not invite your friends, your brothers or sisters, your relatives, or your rich neighbors; if you do, they may invite you back and so you will be repaid. But when you give a banquet, invite the poor, the crippled, the lame, the blind, and you will be blessed. Although they cannot repay you, you will be repaid at the resurrection of the righteous.

Luke 14:12-14 NIV

My dear friends, don't let public opinion influence how you live out our glorious, Christ-originated faith. If a man enters your church wearing an expensive suit, and a street person wearing rags comes in right after him, and you say to the man in the suit, "Sit here, sir; this is the best seat in the house!" and either ignore the street person or say, "Better sit here in the back row," haven't you segregated God's children and proved that you are judges who can't be trusted?

James 2:1-4 MSG

On hearing this, Jesus said, "It is not the healthy who need a doctor, but the sick. But go and learn what this means: 'I desire mercy, not sacrifice.' For I have not come to call the righteous, but sinners."

Matthew 9:12-13 NIV

When we seek to discover the best in others, we somehow bring out the best in ourselves.

William Arthur Ward

The real black, diabolical Pride, comes when you look down on others so much that you do not care what they think of you. Of course, it is very right, and often our duty, not to care what people think of us, if we do so for the right reason; namely because we care so incomparably more what God thinks."

C.S. Lewis

Foundational Concepts

- ✝ The students who are the hardest to love are often the ones who need our love the most.
- ✝ God expects us to act in a loving way toward all students regardless of how they behave or approach their education.
- ✝ When discipline is necessary, God expects us to be compassionate even when we must be firm.
- ✝ We may be that one person god has chosen to make the greatest difference in changing a lost child's life for the better.

Central Questions

1. How do we love students (or colleagues) whose behavior makes them very difficult to even like?
2. What are some of the challenges we face trying to reach today's students?
3. How do we discipline in a loving way?
4. How do we build relationships with our students?

Oh, These Kids Today

Teachers take a beating in the national press. If one were to believe the articles about our national educational system, inadequate teachers are the cause of the decline of the American educational system. Rather than argue that premise, I will simply submit my firm belief that while the American education system certainly has its problems, the primary root of these problems is not inadequate teaching in most cases. It's tough on teachers to constantly take one on the chin like this because we know just how hard we work and understand the nature of the challenge we face better than those who make educational policy or write articles about us. It does not put us in the frame of mind to act in a loving way toward those whom we encounter in our profession. Our immediate defense is to turn the spotlight on other causes like poor parenting, apathetic students, senseless policies, etc.

When we allow the frustration of the public floggings to build up, often our go-to target for blame is the students. It's these kids today. They don't value education. Right? I'm not sure. Is it really that our kids don't value education as much as kids did thirty years ago? I think it would be very difficult to measure how much the majority of students value their education today compared to how much students thirty years ago valued their education. If we are to approach the challenges of the changing student dynamics strategically, I think we need to start by taking an honest look at some of the more measurable and observable characteristics of our students compared to students ten, twenty, or thirty years ago. But we need to be cautious about the motivation for our comparison. We shouldn't be examining the characteristics of today's students for the purpose of pointing blame at anyone. Nor should we build up such a case against them that we somehow justify feelings of resentment toward them. Understanding the nature of a child is strategic. It is necessary for us to reach a child, hook the child, and possibly change the child's life. The more we understand them, the more easily it is for us to make a connection with them. The better the connection, the easier it will be for us to act toward them in a loving way. Kids need to feel a connection with us for them to behave in a more positive manner toward us, but we also need to establish a connection with the child so that we can find it easier to act toward them in a loving way. I would caution that I am going to be discussing some trends I see in the overall youth population, but that is not to say there aren't loads of truly magnificent students passing through our education system every year. I have had no shortage of these students and if truth be told during much of my time as a teacher the great students (which is not just an academic measure) have far outnumbered the students who struggle with some of the issues we will cover in this section of the book.

Teachers now are dealing with what has been referred to as the Millennial generation. For some teachers, it can be challenging to behave in a loving way toward our "Millennial" students. But during my early teaching years it was Generation X that some teachers would argue opened the gates of Hades. My generation was the leading edge of Generation X. We are the grandchildren of the "Greatest Generation." That generation learned to make do with little during the Great Depression. They died by the thousands fighting evil in Europe. When the war was over, the United States entered a period of prosperity. This prosperity landed in the laps of the children of the Greatest Generation, the "Baby Boomers." The Boomers gave birth to Generation X, and if we are to use the 1983 landmark report from the National Committee on Excellence, it was this generation that ushered in the era where our educational system went off the rails. Despite the fact that GenX is the primary driving force behind much of the technology we have come to know and love, PCs, Video Games, DVDs, flash drives, tablets, smart phones, etc., this generation has frequently been portrayed as listless, directionless, apathetic, even lazy. Whether one personally believes their technological creations have advanced our society overall is a topic of great debate, but we cannot discount their innovation and vision. They advanced technology more in twenty years than any other generations did in ten thousand years. I don't disagree that children today are, in many ways, just like children of previous generations. However, as our culture and society have changed dramatically, it would be silly to assert that children have not changed in some dramatic ways as well. Again, though, when we examine how students have changed it should be for the purpose of understanding them from a strategic standpoint. The following are my own observations and are based on my experiences working with children over a period of nearly thirty years

1. Kids today are allowed too much of the wrong kind of freedom. That may sound like an ironic statement given that at the age of six or seven, it would not be uncommon for me to be sixty feet up in a tree, playing deep in the woods behind my house, or hopping on bikes with my friends to go play on the slippery granite ledges of coastal Maine. With no direct parental supervision. That was our life, but today I would never allow that freedom to my son. I am talking about different freedoms held by today's youth. I understand that our country was founded on the basis of freedom (though obviously it was not applied to all humans at first), but I think there is such a thing as too much freedom particularly in the hands of people who are not mature enough to handle that freedom. The Bible states that we are free to do anything but not everything is beneficial. Many kids today are accustomed to doing more or less whatever they want. This plays out in the educational setting in a number of different ways. Educational experts will tell you that one of the keys to success with students today is allowing them a degree of freedom when it comes to the types of activities and projects they do, but in truth the system we have is not set up to allow much of this type of learning. I teach over one hundred students every day. That's a lot of different activities and projects I would have to accommodate and that requires time I generally do not have. In the past several years we have lost increasing amounts of instructional time preparing students for "The State Test" at the end of the year by giving a multitude of standardized tests throughout the year. Covering the required curriculum in the time leading up to the test requires us to maintain a very tight pacing guide with little room for in-depth exploration of many important topics. Kids who are accustomed to freedom outside of school can become very anxious or apathetic when they are constrained to a tight curriculum that does not allow them the opportunity to explore and create. And then, of course, the freedom (in their eyes) to behave in the manner they see as acceptable often leads to discipline issues.

2. Too many children and youth receive too little supervision. This is not always a result of "bad" parenting. When I was a young child, my mother usually knew *where* I was and generally what I was doing even if she wasn't right there with us. For the first ten years of her marriage, she was primarily a stay-at-home mom. After the divorce, my mother was forced to work two and sometimes three jobs just to pay the rent and put food on the table. She worked to meet our needs. Fulfilling our "wants" was seldom something we were able to consider. My father, one of the hardest working men I have ever known and in many ways a kind and generous man, was also an alcoholic. I do not know how much money he provided for our upbringing after the divorce, but the fact that my mother had to work so much suggests that it wasn't much. I imagine it was more a result of money squandered than money intentionally withheld. My mother became the primary provider after the divorce. As a result, she had a much more difficult time supervising my siblings and me. Friends and neighbors helped out, but it's not the same.

Consequently, my siblings and I at times became involved in behavior that was self-destructive to us and sometimes to others. Our individual "wants" have also increased. We have become an increasingly more materialistic culture. The drive to have "more" means that our work consumes more of our family time. I see this in myself at times. I have a tendency to be a workaholic though in my case it never ends up in more money. I know my family suffers from this at times, if not from a supervisory standpoint than at the very least from the standpoint of bonding. As a result, the number of students who fall in the "inadequately supervised" category has drastically increased. Children who are inadequately supervised often do not adjust well to the structure of a supervised setting. To complicate issues, we now have to deal with the consequences that can arise when we are unable to supervise what our children are viewing online.

3. There are far more things competing for their attention. When I was a child, we had three channels of t.v. and no computers. Today's kids are totally wired up. They are so technologically savvy, so ensconced in a world where technology rules, I would never consider trying to teach without incorporating technology into my instruction. But it has also had some adverse impacts on human behavior. Hundreds of channels of television to choose from. On-demand movies. Music players that can fit neatly in their pockets. Cell phones. Video games. Texting rather than face-to-face communication. As a parent, I understand how challenging it is to try to supervise a child who has access to the Internet and the ability to send and receive text messages. Technology is greatly improved our lives in many ways, but in some manifestations it has stolen the attention of our children. And then there is the change in the dynamics of sports! Sports are no longer a seasonal thing. Some students are part of travel teams that play all year round, sometimes traveling hundreds of miles on weekends. With all these other things to choose from, sitting down to study, do homework, talk to their parents about their day, and go to church may seem like completely humdrum alternatives. Most children lack the ability of forward thinking. They have a hard time relating how what they do now will relate to their future. As a result, many prioritize what they will do by the amount of immediate gratification it will provide or by some imagined and usually unrealistic belief about where certain behaviors or obsessions will lead them. Kids have always been this way, I'm sure. I cannot say that kids today have any more or less "self-discipline" than they did when I first started teaching twenty plus years ago. Clearly they have a bunch more things to distract them and clearly they have a much, much more difficult time delaying gratification because they live in a world of instant gratification. In their defense, we adults are not much better. We have much of the same technology and the same addiction to it, and it is our exploding credit card debt as a nation that is the greatest example of our inability to delay gratification.

4. Many do not seem to have had instilled in them as strong a work ethic as kids I knew or taught years ago. I grew up on Mount Desert Island along the coast of Maine. Acadia National Park was literally minutes from my doorstep. The main industries were commercial fishing, forestry, and tourism. As early as age eight, I would rise just after sunrise to shovel the snow from people's walkways or rake leaves for fifty cents. In middle school, I got up at 5:00 a.m. to deliver newspapers. We collected aluminum cans

to earn money for recycling. Not every job earned us money. During the summer, we often helped my grandfather by stacking hay. He didn't have a hay bailer, so we loaded the hay onto the wagon and then into the hay loft one pitchfork load at a time. The older boys were the pitchfork operators. The younger boys were responsible for tucking the hay tightly in the loft. Starting at the age of twelve, I worked on the lobster boat with my father. That was true of most fishermen kids as it was the children of farmers and woodsmen in northern Maine. In the winters, we worked in the woods with our father who maintained the property of a number of wealthy summer cottage owners. When I was in high school, nearly everyone aged fifteen and older worked during the summer. There were hundreds of jobs at restaurants and gift shops found on our island to be filled, and most were filled by local high school students. Even the kids from the wealthier families worked. Today if you go to Bar Harbor you will notice that many of the shops and restaurants are manned by young men and women from foreign countries. Beginning about fifteen or twenty years ago, it became so difficult to recruit local kids to work that the many businesses had to turn to these foreign sources. From my discussions with several of these workers, I learned that most come on a six to nine-month work visa. Many work on Mount Desert Island from June to about October, save their money, then once the tourist season winds down they use the remainder of their time to travel throughout the U.S. I do understand that in some small towns or rural areas, there aren't a whole lot of jobs for high school students. I also understand that in the troubled economy of our recent "Great Recession" many of the jobs that were previously filled by students are now filled by adults who cannot find employment elsewhere. But this trend began long before the economy tanked, and I cannot help but think it is more a reflection of changes in our culture than in our economy.

5. In the U.S. today, just by the sheer presence of communicative technology, American children are exposed to more ungodly behavior in a week than past generations were exposed to in a year. I would caution against hearkening back to "the good old days" when children were taught values because not all the values they were taught were Christ-like then either. The development of our identity as an American culture has followed a myriad of paths, some of which were paved in the deepest, darkest layers of subjugation, prejudice, and oppression. But let's be honest: at no time in recent history has a culture been so bombarded by messages that are in direct opposition to traditional Christian beliefs. When I was in high school, I would visit my great grandmother and we would watch *Little House on the Prairie*. Sure, there were other shows like *Dallas* that people were drawn to because of the gratuitously atrocious behavior of some of the characters. But we also had shows like *Little House* where the core values of the characters were love, hard work, respect for others, and personal accountability. I was so distraught when allegations of sexual impropriety surfaced against Bill Cosby. *The Cosby* Show, though it did not specifically mention God, was so rich in many of the same values that made *Little House* and *The Waltons* so appealing. As a result of the court findings against Mr. Cosby, a permanent stain may remain forever on that show and that saddens. Nobody used these series as a kind of "teaching tool" for me. I watched *Little House* because I enjoyed spending time with my great-grandmother but as an adult I can see the inherent

value of the series. With hundreds of channels to choose from today, how many shows like that can we find? Certainly there are some, but I learned the hard way that even shows on "children's channels" needed to be closely scrutinized before allowing my daughter to watch them. In one very popular show for young girls one of the characters was dishonest, manipulative, disrespectful towards adults, selfish, and just plain mean at times. The problem for me as a parent and Christian is that instead of using this character to demonstrate the adverse consequences of this behavior, the behavior was used to promote how endearing she was to viewers. Her antics were accompanied by laugh tracks. In this same show and in others like it, I was appalled at how the shows portrayed teachers as incompetent, bumbling idiots who were "out to get" the students all the time. Needless to say, I no longer allowed my daughter to watch those shows and I take the time to screen the other "children's" shows before I allow my children to watch them. Movies can also be problematic. One of the most popular book and movies series in the past few years was built on a premise of kids killing other kids in a competition! Advocates of the movie argue that there are important values and morals children can learn from. I would argue that the same values could be modeled in a different context.

Even "news" shows and talk radio are oftentimes laced with such a vitriolic, judgmental, and often childish tone and language that the message leaves a terribly sour taste in our mouths even if we agree with their arguments or conclusions. I was listening to one conservative talk show host one day while driving home as he espoused Christian values and complained about the degradation of our society. A while later he and his sidekick starting ridiculing Monica Lewinsky and even referred to her as "that fat chick." My twelve-year-old daughter was in the car with me. She heard that. Not only was the discussion fueled with sinful judgment, it was just plain cruel. This was by no means an isolated incident. Just the other day I listened as another talk show host mocked a person with a lisp. Social media because it is regulated so weakly or not at all is even worse.

In addition to this, our news media has become more sensationalized, focusing on the seediest and darkest aspects of our human nature. Politicians sling mud and talk about each other in the most demeaning of ways as they continually refuse to work together. We are living in an era where even the President of the United States is making sarcastic and deeply offensive remarks about a woman's behavior while on her monthly cycle, how women can be controlled if you grab them by the privates (though he did not use that term), dismissing former POWs as not worthy of his attention because he "prefers people who don't get caught," mocking people with disabilities, equally dismissing impoverished countries, and sending out a flurry of tweets that might as well have been written by an intoxicated teenage frat boy. If my students behaved toward each other like our elected leaders in Washington they would be suspended from school.

As each generation passes, the "new normal" is several more steps away from God. No doubt our culture's slide away from morality is seen by millions of Americans as "progress." A divorce rate of 50% is normal. Rampant promiscuity is normal. Living together outside of marriage is not only normal but is in many cases recommended. Fewer people give these things much thought anymore. Same sex marriage is now the land of the law. Among increasing subgroups of citizens, religious freedom is respected only as long as it does not contradict certain cultural values. In the "new normal," Christian bakers are fighting for the right to honor their faith by choosing not to support same-sex unions. God's guidance on how to influence our children hasn't changed for several thousand years, but the challenge of raising children with Christian values in this culture has increased dramatically. What we need to understand as parents is that we are part of the problem. In reality, however pious we may believe ourselves to be compared to "other people," we have slid away from God along with the culture we live in. We watch the shows that contain immoral behavior and tell ourselves that it is ok as long as our kids are not in the room. We set the example when it comes to the accumulation of material goods. We increasingly put work ahead of family and our duty to our church. Our kids do not just witness sinful behavior in the media. They witness it *every day* in *our* behavior, and I would argue that since we have a more personal relationship with them our sinful behavior has a much greater effect on them than anything they might see on t.v. or hear on the radio.

6. Too many children have been indoctrinated into a culture of entitlement and dependency. I have read in a number of sources that somewhere between 45-49% of Americans now receive some sort of government assistance. Since the inception of our country, one's work ethic was a matter of family pride. Americans took pride in not being dependent upon others to provide them with the things they needed to survive. In agrarian areas, children were up early helping to take care of the animals or do other chores before going off to school for the day. Charity was offered willingly to those who needed a hand up, but those who expected something for nothing were not well received. The Bible clearly supports the idea that we are expected to work, contribute, make an effort to provide for ourselves and our family, and not take advantage of or manipulate charity. In most circumstances, charity should be a temporary solution. Unfortunately, in many areas of America a culture of dependency has developed and has been handed down from generation to generation. Too many people know that the government will provide them with nearly free housing, food, health care, additional money for their child's public education, additional money for each child born out of wedlock to parents who were already unable to provide for the children they had, and apparently now even cell phones in some areas. It is a system that is easy to beat.

In the 1970s and 80s, I knew of very few parents who were manipulating the system. Those who did receive assistance saw it as a short-term solution. I am sure today there are many hard-working parents who, though hard-working, are unable at the end of the month to make ends meet. I am grateful that our system of government has a way to provide some help. My issue is with the millions who take advantage of this system, manipulate it, and adopt it as their lifestyle. I have taught hundreds and hundreds of their children. These children often do not understand the importance of a strong work ethic, of self-reliance. They are apathetic toward education because they do not see it as necessary in the long run. Each lives in a home that has the basic amenities- running water and electricity. They have food daily. Many have transportation. And if my experience is any indication, a great many have high quality cell phones, cable t.v., the latest form of portable music players, expensive basketball shoes, expensive cell phones, and a fully stocked name-brand wardrobe. This lifestyle of hand-outs vs. a hand-up is all some of them have ever known.

OK, so I'm guessing that some of you read that last paragraph were ready to throw down with me. How dare I be so judgmental! First, I would respond that most of my observations are based on data, others on personal experience. But no matter. Addressing the issue of poverty in the U.S. is a mine field, so I want to make sure to clarify that not all or even most low-income families have an attitude of entitlement. Many are what we refer to as "working poor," which is what my family was. This is not an indictment of all people who receive charity or government assistance and I certainly do not want to seem insensitive to families who struggle with poverty. I also understand that of the 45% receiving government assistance, many are elderly. I am intimately sensitive to the condition of poverty. I grew up poor (by American standards). There are a lot of holes in my memory about my childhood, but I seem to recall drinking powdered milk on occasion. My mother received food stamps for one year following the divorce and we moved to subsidized housing when I was in high school. As I got older, I felt the stigma of poverty.

In the U.S., we tend to have a very biased view toward the poor. When we consider the poor living in a third world country most Americans will attribute their poverty to a lack of opportunity, corrupt leaders, or some other external factor. In other words, something outside of the control of the impoverished person. In our "Land of Opportunity" we tend to feel that a person is poor because of his own actions. That may be true for some people in some cases. Certainly laziness exists. Our welfare system can be and is manipulated by people who feel entitled or who have been a part of the welfare state for generations and know little else. Feeling "entitled" is a sin that is certainly not restricted to this particular sub-group of the poor. All of us at times struggle with feelings of entitlement. Admittedly it is difficult for many of us not to automatically assume the worst of the poor. We live in a materialistic society that has conditioned us to respond this way. My family's poverty was due to a number of factors, but neither laziness nor a sense of entitlement played any role. We should also not automatically assume that the academic struggles of a student from a low-income family are a result of apathy toward education in the home. My mother, a member of the "working poor," valued our education, but working two jobs often seven days per week left very little time for her to be as involved in our education as she wanted or needed to be.

Even if a family is poor because of the behavior of a parent or parents, the child should *never* suffer at anyone's hands for his or her parent's actions. Many teachers reading this might think they would never think differently of a child due to his family's socioeconomic status. I have heard far too many comments about "poor white trash," welfare kids, oversized "Goodwill" clothes or "high water" pants, personal hygiene, etc. to accept that this is not one of the areas where some teachers struggle. As a teacher and as a parent with children in public schools I am ashamed to admit that I become concerned when I know housing for lower income families is becoming more available in my school's attendance area. I know of very few teachers who do not feel some concern. It changes the dynamics of the class. It is not inherently discriminatory to recognize the effects of poverty on cognitive development and behavior. Study after study have supported the fact that family income is one of the most significant factors contributing to a child's academic achievement. The correlation between relative poverty and academic success is perhaps the best supported public education data available for American students. A significant percentage of School Improvement Plans have goals that specifically target raising achievement levels of students from lower socioeconomic households. That does not mean that every child from an impoverished home will do poorly in school, but the data for the effects of socioeconomic "status" are irrefutable. In America, we spend tens of billions of dollars each year trying to bridge the achievement gap for students from lower income homes. To complicate things even more, data seems to also support that students from low-income families have higher rates of misconduct. Even students from impoverished homes who have high cognitive abilities often struggle in school. Many of these students are the primary caregivers for younger siblings in the evening, leaving little to no time for studying. Many work after school to help supplement family income. Many do not have a place in the home where they can study or do their homework without constant distractions. There are dozens of explanations for lower achievement and higher rates of misconduct in students from low-income homes. The challenge for us is to accept these as "explanations" rather than as "excuses." The former will allow us to strategically and compassionately approach the significant challenges of teaching this population of students. The latter attitude will allow us to write these children off.

You may not be someone who comments on a child's personal hygiene or dress or who refers to an unruly child as "poor white trash." But how much do you truly address the legitimate challenges associated with students from lower-income homes? If you are constantly complaining about their "laziness," their lack of self-discipline, their conduct, their attendance, their low ability level, or any other aspect then you may be complaining about aspects of this child that are directly related to growing up in a low-income home. It is one thing to understand this, another to allow it to be a source of resentment. If you allow yourself to become resentful toward that child or his or her family because of the sometimes considerable extra effort it takes to teach that child or manage that child's behavior, then I would respectfully suggest that you consider whether that attitude is actually a form of discrimination. I would not care to guess how many times throughout my career I have dishonored the Lord because of my discrimination toward others. It is both ironic and sad that I grew up poor and yet have caught myself discriminating against low-income families, not by outwardly speaking or treating them as though they were lesser humans but rather by stubbornly refusing to accept the effects of poverty on their educational experience. How completely unfair to them.

I was fortunate. There was only one instance in all my school years where I felt that particular sting of discrimination from a teacher. Our community built some low-income housing on the outside of town in the late 1970s. One of my teachers lived on the same street as this housing development. I sat in class one day listening to him rant about how these homes would be filled with hoodlums and cause his property values and quality of life to suffer. I already knew that my family would be moving into one of these homes. In fact, we ended up moving into the house directly across the street from him. It hurt to hear what he had to say, and surely he should have used more discretion. But I cannot judge him now that I have been guilty of at least feeling the same way. In fact, he was a good teacher. And while I certainly don't condone his actions, he understood the reality of what often happens when subsidized housing is provided in an area. The people living in the length of the street across from him were by no means "hoodlums." Nearly all were single mothers with young children. All of them worked at least one job. But fast forward thirty-five years and one will see that many of his concerns became reality. The abundance of data related to welfare dependence and crime associated with low-income housing is compelling, and my old housing development has not escaped that. In the case of students who have grown up in families who feel entitled to free assistance, you may be a person who helps them to understand the strength and fulfillment that results from self-reliance (in this context- I'm not suggesting the type of self-reliance where one lives apart from God) and a strong work ethic if those attributes are truly missing from their household.

I have worked in schools where the poverty level was near 80% and in schools where the poverty level was 15%. I have never worked in a school that had no students from low income families and I would guess that for the majority of teachers these students will be in nearly every class. I have also never worked in a school where most of the classes did not have some students whose cognitive skills were well below most of the other students in the class because of other underlying factors such as a learning disability. You want to really test your mettle as a teacher, really serve God in your teaching? Work with kids outside the norm. Kids with emotional or behavior disorders. Kids with severe or profound intellectual impairments or physical impairments. Dedicate yourself to helping students with significant learning struggles succeed in a "regular" classroom. A deep passion for working with struggling learners is a true gift from God and a rare one. I *thought* I had that as a gift and I did in some ways, but it turns out I am not as gifted in that area as I once thought, at least not in ways that are as effective in settings different from the ones I was accustomed to as a self-contained teacher for students with behavior disorders or as a behavioral specialist.

I worked with struggling students for many years because that is apparently where God needed me and I had a great deal of "relative" success because of other gifts He gave me. Most of the time, however, I was not their "teacher of record." My name was not at the top of the report card nor on the report when the state scores came back. I did not realize how much that mattered until I became the teacher of record in a "regular" classroom. It was in this capacity that I realized I lacked the gift and the deep conviction to work with students with significant reading and math deficits *in the regular classroom* as the *teacher of record,* tasked with trying to bring these students' scores closer to "average." To compound matters, in my case this was almost always without classroom assistance from a co-teacher or a paraprofessional. In many schools, the budget allows for math and ELA teachers to have co-teachers or paraprofessional support while science and social studies teachers operate under the "consultative" model: no help in the class and sometimes very little if any real help at all. The struggling students get extra help in math and ELA, go out to remedial classes during the day, but somehow do not require that same level of help in the two classes with the most complex vocabulary and reading passages. Another peculiarity of our educational system. In a "regular" classroom as the teacher of record my passion as a teacher is intellectual discussion and engaging in real-world issues rather than reading and mathematics remediation. I began as a high school teacher. I learned as a "regular" middle school classroom teacher that I am not passionate about sitting on the side with a small group of middle school students working on basic reading or math skills which is odd because that is precisely what I spent a great deal of time on in my self-contained classroom and even as a behavioral specialist. Kids who are struggling learners often misbehave to divert attention from the fact that they can't read as well as the other students in the class and sometimes even misbehave in an attempt to be removed from class which to them is a hostile environment. Working on reading skills was a behavioral intervention.

I care about these students and I want them to succeed. Unfortunately, I am not as effective at basic reading or mathematics remediation or differentiation as I would like to be because my training has included few strategies in this area, I apparently do not have *these* skills as a gift from God, and my passions as a teacher are not well-matched to their needs. In order to help these students I must act in a way that is contrary to what I would like to do at times and remember that it is on those with the highest needs that God wants us to direct our greatest effort. Students with cognitive delays and students with emotional or behavior disorders (discussed at length in an upcoming section) are our "lost sheep." The Bible tells us that it is not the healthy who need the doctor but those who are ill. All students deserve our best effort, and if their needs do not align with our needs or preferences as a *teacher*, then as a *Christian* it is our needs that must become secondary. It is up to us to find a way to help them succeed. We need to help them celebrate the little victories which may or may not be the same as those of their classroom peers. It is, for sure, a balancing act, trying to meet the needs of a heterogenous class with a wide range of cognitive levels. Lacking the skills and the passion to teach remedial reading and math as I do, I believe it would be impossible for me to help these students without God's constant intervention.

To end this section, I would like to make it clear that I recognize stay-at-home parents work as hard or harder than many people who have jobs outside the home. Taking care of a home is a job, and sometimes it is the only viable option for one of the parents. This was the case in our family up until the divorce. After the divorce the exact opposite was the case. My mother had no option but to work outside the house. We knew all our neighbors, many of whom were also single mothers, and every one of them worked.

Understanding and Dealing with Challenging Student Behavior

There is a big difference between explaining behavior and excusing behavior. There is also a big difference between forgiving a person for his or her trespasses and condoning the trespass. Acts of misconduct must be addressed. Proverbs 12:1 (MSG) tells us, "If you love learning, you love the discipline that goes with it— how shortsighted to refuse correction!" Later in chapter 19, verse 1, we are told to, "Discipline your children, for in that there is hope; do not be a willing party to their death." The Bible gives clear guidance on how to discipline in a Godly way. For starters, our discipline should not be judgmental. Our Lord provides very clear guidance against judging others:

> But if you think that leaves you on the high ground where you can point your finger at others, think again. Every time you criticize someone, you condemn yourself. It takes one to know one. Judgmental criticism of others is a well-known way of escaping detection in your own crimes and misdemeanors. But God isn't so easily diverted. He sees right through all such smoke screens and holds you to what you've done. You didn't think, did you, that just by pointing

your finger at others you would distract God from seeing all your misdoings and from coming down on you hard? Or did you think that because he's such a nice God, he'd let you off the hook? Better think this one through from the beginning. God is kind, but he's not soft. In kindness he takes us firmly by the hand and leads us into a radical life-change.

Romans 2:1-4 MSG

Godly discipline is never impulsive. Children do not want to be disciplined in our anger any more than we want God to discipline us in His anger. "Discipline me, Lord- but only in due measure; not in your anger, or you will reduce me to nothing" (Jeremiah 10:24 NIV). The way we discipline our child can help to build them up or reduce them to nothing. Godly discipline is thoughtful, considerate, compassionate, and loving. Paul asks us in 1 Corinthians 4:21 (MSG), "So how should I prepare to come to you? As a severe disciplinarian who makes you toe the mark? Or as a good friend and counselor who wants to share heart-to-heart with you? You decide." This approach allows us to focus the attention on the behavior rather than the person. We shouldn't expect our own children or students to enjoy being disciplined, but as they become wise (if we discipline them in a Godly way) it will bear fruit. Consider Hebrews 12:11 (NIV) which says, "No discipline seems pleasant at the time, but painful. Later on, however, it produces a harvest of righteousness and peace for those who have been trained by it." We need to learn to persevere when it comes to seeing the fruit of our discipline with the most challenging students. Often the behavior will become much worse before it gets better. Tough kids need to test our resolve to see for themselves whether we are truly invested in them or not. Many are accustomed to having people give up on them and they are determined to see whether we are going to do the same. The person who sticks it out and perseveres will stand the best chance of changing that child's life. "If the ax is dull and its edge unsharpened, more strength is needed, but skill will bring success" (Ecclesiastes 10:10).

With experience and more importantly with God's guidance I have learned to be less presumptuous about student behavior. Many of these students are dealing with a crushed spirit. Proverbs 18:14 (MSG) tells us, "A healthy spirit conquers adversity, but what can you do when the spirit is crushed?" Many times I have been humbled when, after criticizing unmotivated students, I was offered a look into their lives where I could see very clearly where some of the problems originate. A glimpse behind the curtain of a child's life can reveal a lot about how a child behaves at any given time. A parent deployed to a war zone. Divorce. Stress in the home due to a parent losing a job or even their home. A new baby that keeps everybody up at night. Physical abuse. Sexual abuse. Emotional Abuse. A parent addicted to alcohol or drugs. Loud neighbors partying the night away. Being bullied. Living in the shadow of a superstar older sibling. Fighting parents. PTSD. Gunshots ringing out in the neighborhood at night. Not feeling as attractive as other kids. Not being as athletic. These are not "excuses." They are perfectly legitimate explanations for why a child might not be performing well in school or in other areas of his or her life. Kids are of this world just as we are, and being less cognitively, physiologically, and emotionally mature are less prepared to deal with its challenges. These kinds of issues are equally or more devastating to them as problems such as divorce, losing a job, being passed over for a promotion, being abused by a spouse, infidelity, having the car die when there is no money to replace it, finding out our teenage child is pregnant, having a spouse deployed in a war zone, and other "adult stressors" are to us. As someone who has struggle with anxiety most of my adult life, I can testify that anxiety can bring anyone to his knees.

As teachers, we need to attempt to understand what is going on behind the curtain, and sometimes even if we are not able to determine exactly what is affecting a child's performance, we need to extend to that child the benefit of the doubt. Kids may be willing to share that their parents are getting divorced or that they have a parent serving in Afghanistan, but very few are willing to share their secret of being sexually or physically abused. I have worked with a number of students whom I know to have been sexually abused by a parent, another relative, or an older sibling. I have worked with children whose parents allowed them to be a sex toy for their friends at parties and others who prostituted their young children out to pay for their own drug addiction. One student I worked with used to watch his mother through a hole in his wall as a parade of lovers would be secreted into their home while the father was away at work. On several occasions, the child overheard heated parental arguments where his mother admitted to his father that the child was not his but the child of a secret lover. I have worked with children who have witnessed their father beat their mother. My sister bears the scars of seeing my father physically abuse my mother. She remembers those instances whereas I do not even though at times I was huddling next to her in our bedroom as the abuse was taking place. I have learned about far too many similar instances, yet I am convinced that what I actually learned barely scratches the surface. What if I did not have my sister to tell me what I witnessed and repressed? How would I understand that some of the anxiety I struggle with might be PTSD? The point is, there is almost always an explanation for a child's behavioral issues or lack of productivity. We can discipline in a compassionate manner, and when we do, I believe the child benefits far more from both the discipline and from the love shown to them.

My own life could be a study in duplicity. There were certainly happy things about my childhood that kept me sane. I lived in a beautiful part of America, had great friends, was active in athletics, was relatively "popular," and attended great schools with great teachers. On paper, though, I met nearly every criterion of an "at-risk" student. One parent was a high school graduate, the other was forced to drop out of high school to take care of his younger siblings when his father ran off with another woman. From the age of eight I lived in a single parent household. My father was an alcoholic and at times an abusive husband. As I already shared, after the divorce, we became even more impoverished than we had been so my mother was forced to work two jobs. An unsupervised youth from such a background seldom seeks the path of righteousness. I grew up in a small town, so I'm sure that many people who knew me also knew my father was an alcoholic, that I received free lunch, that for a period of time during my childhood we lived in subsidized housing, and that in high school I lived for a time in a tiny trailer with no running water for a year until we moved into a bigger trailer with its own issues. We all know what types of thoughts we have about people who live in trailers or trailer parks. We are sinfully stereotypical and judgmental. It was no different back then. I was ashamed and tried to overcompensate for it. I walked a dangerously fine line as a teenager. I engaged in behavior that was self-destructive, reckless, and irresponsible. I was a house of cards. Statistically speaking, I was destined for an adult life far less rewarding and fulfilling than the one God has given me. But now I see that my life was part of God's plan. He had no intention of letting the difficulties of my childhood go to waste. To protect me through this process, He also put people in my life that kept me from falling over the cliff. Some were relatives. During my younger years, my great aunt Nita and Uncle Perly, my great grandmother Verna, my mother's sister "Aunty Rita" and her husband Art all fit this bill. Others were the parents of one of my friends. The Reverend George Price and his wife, Harriet, sheltered me through some very tumultuos high school years. I participated in athletics year-round from middle school through high school. Neither of my parents came to more than a few events throughout this entire time. My junior year, I was a member of a 4X400 meter relay team that won first place in our division for the state. I had no family members in attendance, but after I had run my leg of the race Phil Brown, my science teacher at the time, came up to me, grabbed my shoulders and yelled enthusiastically, "You short-legged little thing (not the actual term he used)! You held the lead! You held the lead!" Phil was there primarily to see his daughter, a state champion herself. But her events had been over for some time. The mile relay was the last event of every meet. Phil stayed until the end. I doubt he would remember that day. I don't remember a lot of specific events from my childhood, but that I remember well. Some of these people were Christians. Others not so much. Some were teachers. These people treated me in a loving way. God used these experiences and these people to shape me for a higher purpose. As a result of my own childhood, I am able to understand and empathize with children, teens, and young adults who are going through rough times of their own- and that has been invaluable to me in my career. It is entirely possible that God has or will put YOU in a particular child's life because you are the only person in that child's life that can make the difference with regards to his future.

But I forget. Oh, how I forget. I get caught up in the whirlwind of public education and at times I fail to consider the reason why a particular child may be acting in a particular way. Sometimes I feel so overloaded with the burden of all that is expected of me as a teacher that I feel like I cannot find or make the time for compassion. I want the problem to go away or hope somebody else will do something about it. I become frustrated and angry at students whom I feel are not giving their "best effort" without taking a moment to find out what might be going on behind the scenes. I hate it when I see a child (or anyone else for that matter) manipulating other students or teachers, especially when they are manipulating for attention. I forget to ask, though, what about them is so broken that they feel the need to manipulate? I forget to treat them in a loving way. When our love for a person is based on a deep emotional attachment we can't "forget" to love them. We can and do, however, forget to treat even these people in a loving way. How much more easily, then, do we forget to act in a loving way toward those in our lives with whom we do not have such a deep, emotional attachment or worse, for whom we find it a challenge to even *like*? Are all students likable? I would have to so no. My own mother told me on a couple of occasions when I was testing the boundaries of youth, "I love you, but I don't like you very much right now." Some students are so inconsiderate, selfish, disrespectful, unmotivated, spoiled, and mean to others (even the teacher) that they are just plain unlikable. But are they *lovable*? If we truly love God, the answer must be "yes." We must still try our very best to treat them in a loving way regardless of whether we feel they deserve it or not because that is what Jesus commands us to do. I am quite certain that I do not deserve the kind of love I receive from God, but I receive it anyway. Christ gave to us a gift we did not deserve. We do not deserve His grace, yet He offers it to us. That is what grace is all about. Like Christ, we must show love toward everyone regardless of whether we feel they deserve it. Few of these types of children will ever change if the important or influential adults in their lives act as unloving toward them as the child does toward the adults.

Treating people in a loving way does not mean that we "pretend" to love people, or that we tell them we love them when in truth we do not feel love for them. Such an expression would be insincere. In Romans 12:9, the Apostle Paul reminds us, "Love must be sincere." Kids can be masters at identifying whether a person is sincere or not. Even when they are not old enough to understand the concept, little warning bells sound in their heads. Tweens and teens are masters at detecting insincerity and hypocrisy. One of the most important and effective things a teacher can do is establish a relationship, a connection with his or her students. Many students will distrust your sincerity and will test your interest in and commitment to them. Most kids will respond positively to you when you *act* in a loving way toward them and when you take the time and show an interest in making a connection with them. These students will generally work harder for you and will be more open to your correction. They will trust you more and be less fearful about opening themselves up to you. "There is no fear in love. Perfect love puts fear out of our hearts. People have fear when they are afraid of being punished. The man who is afraid does not have perfect love" (1 John 4:18 NLV).

In Chapter 10 of John, Christ tells the parable of the Good Shepherd. In this parable, Christ is the Good Shepherd. However, the example is one that is applicable to our relationship with students. Are we a shepherd to our students or are we overlords? Does a loving and trusting relationship exist between us and our students or not? Verse 4 says, "When he (the shepherd) puts forth all his own, he goes ahead of them, and the sheep follow him because they know his voice." This isn't meant to suggest that our students follow us blindly and thoughtlessly like zombies. Rather, they come to us because they know they are cared for, valued, and that we will look after them. A shepherd is a comfort to his flock. Teachers who do not have a loving and trusting relationship with their students do not instill that kind of comfort in their students. Without this kind of connection, these teachers are far less capable and perhaps willing to love and care for students who are struggling emotionally, behaviorally, socially, or academically. Jesus says in John 10:11 (NIV), "The good shepherd lays down His life for the sheep." In contrast, Jesus continues in John 10:12-13 (NASB) by saying, "The hired hand, and not the shepherd, who is the owner of the sheep, sees the wolf coming and leaves the sheep and flees, and the wolf snatches them and scatters them." The "hired hand" could symbolize the teacher who does not have a shepherd-like relationship with their students. The lives of our students are full of wolves. They may be full of hired hands who have fled to look out for their own interests. We may be the only "shepherd" that some kids know.

So what about those students who you just can't seem to connect with either because of issues with your own feelings or theirs? Ideally, God wants us to love others sincerely, but when we find this too difficult He still expects us to treat people in a loving way. You will most likely never come to love a person whom you are pretending to love. You may, however, come to love some of the most difficult people in your life through the process of treating them in a loving way. Every teacher knows what a challenge this can be with some students (or colleagues for that matter). During a parent conference, Johnny says he always gets in trouble because the teacher dislikes him. Johnny may be wrong about *why* he is getting in trouble, but he may be correct about the latter part of his statement. We speak in politically correct terms in parent conferences when we say "I don't dislike Johnny. I dislike his behavior." For parents who are reading this here's an eye opener from the vault of honesty and full disclosure: if your Johnny is rude, disrespectful, uncooperative, disruptive, and mean to others, it is highly likely that we dislike both Johnny and his behavior. We can't tell you that because it would be hurtful and unproductive and because we are supposed to project the unrealistic expectation that teachers are superhumans who are capable of liking all of their students. Also, it might damage the self-esteem of your poorly behaved child. The *reason* we don't like a particular child, though, may be as much a representation of our own character flaw as it is the child's. Sometimes we see ourselves as a hired hand when it comes to dealing with Johnny rather than a shepherd. It's the nature of being fallen. Let's take it one step beyond pure ugly: how many of us would be willing to admit that at least part of the reason we don't like certain students is not so much because of their conduct, but because we harbor some degree of bias toward them because of their race, religion, or socioeconomic standard. The child is from "poor white trash" stock. The child's parents are wealthy and the child drives a much nicer car than we do. We suspect a student may be gay. He or she doesn't speak English fluently or speak using proper grammar. People have very, very differing criteria for determining whom they like and dislike. "Likability" can be a legitimate response to unlikable behavior, but it can also be a result of deeply rooted, sinful thoughts or beliefs on our behalf. The implications for a follower of Christ are particularly perilous because God makes it clear the scales we use to measure others will be the same scale He uses to measure and judge us. I believe this is a main reason why God did not include "likability" as one of the criteria for loving one another.

Loving the "Tough to Love"

Perhaps nowhere is our love, guidance, and attention needed more than for those students who tax every bit of our patience in just about every way possible. Students who act out constantly in order to gain the attention of their peers. Students who seem to put forth little to no effort when it comes to doing their schoolwork. Students who bully others. Students who insist on engaging in horseplay the second you turn your back. Let's face it, not only do we find it difficult to like these children, at times these are the students we begin to resent the most. In our minds, they make our job more difficult. They "steal" time from the more serious students. They eat up large chunks of our attention that we feel could be used in a more productive manner. Sometimes they challenge our authority or make us "look bad" in front of our colleagues or our supervisors. They can make us feel inadequate. Quite often we perceive little assistance from their parents, or worse yet, their parents may heap all the blame for their child's struggles in school on the teacher. These are the students that gray our hair, raise our blood pressure, age us prematurely, keep us up at night, send us to our physician for a refill of our anxiety or depression meds. These are the kids we wish were "somebody else's problem." These are the kids we feel don't deserve to be in a regular classroom. In a very real sense, they are "the enemy."

What we fail to recognize or remember, though, is that from a heavenly perspective these are the very types of students who need our guidance the most and whom God desires most for us to embrace. In Luke 5:31 (NIV), Christ reminds us "It is not the healthy who need a doctor, but the sick." In Chapter 6, verses 32-33 (NLT), He continues, "If you love only those who love you, why should you get credit for that? Even sinners love those who love them! And if you do good only to those who do good to you, why should you get credit? Even sinners do that much!"

These children are not in our lives by accident. We recall Matthew 18:12-13 (NIV) and remember they are among those to whom Jesus was specifically referring in the parable of the lost sheep:

> What do you think? If a man owns a hundred sheep, and one of them wanders away, will he not leave the ninety-nine on the hills and go to look for the one that wandered off? And if he finds it, truly I tell you, he is happier about that one sheep than about the ninety-nine that did not wander off. In the same way your Father in heaven is not willing that any of these little ones should perish.

God understands how great a challenge it is for us to show love toward people whose actions cause us great discomfort. But He has a different way of looking at it. In God's eyes, the very challenge of these people is a test of our faith and our resolve. The more faithful we are, the more determined we are to honor God regardless of our circumstances and the more likely it will be that such people will bring out the best of us rather than the worst. In his sermon on the mount, Jesus said,

> You're familiar with the old written law, 'Love your friend,' and its unwritten companion, 'Hate your enemy.' I'm challenging that. I'm telling you to love your enemies. Let them bring out the best in you, not the worst. When someone gives you a hard time, respond with the energies of prayer, for then you are working out of your true selves, your God-created selves. This is what God does. He gives his best—the sun to warm and the rain to nourish—to everyone, regardless: the good and bad, the nice and nasty. If all you do is love the lovable, do you expect a bonus? Anybody can do that. If you simply say hello to those who greet you, do you expect a medal? Any run-of-the-mill sinner does that.
>
> Matthew 5:43-47 MSG

I admit that I don't pray for God to send me tough kids every year, though perhaps I should. I guess part of me feels that after nearly thirty years I have had my quota of problem children filled. But I have to admit that when I was successful at making a connection with some of these tough students I learned a whole lot about myself and teaching through the process. When I failed to make a connection despite trying, I also learned from it. When I failed to make a connection because I wrote the child off I learned a whole lot about myself as well though it was certainly not something to be proud of. Through these students rather than those who are much easier to teach comes our opportunity to build our Godly character through adversity. God knows that a lack of adversity leads to complacency, and so throughout our lives we are taught to expect, no *welcome* adversity. There is no path to God that does not include trials. These students provide not just the opportunity to test and improve our skills as teachers but the opportunity to demonstrate our gratitude for God's grace and our trust for Him by not completely coming apart when things are not going as well for us as we'd like. I understand the stress that comes with teaching these students. I spent many years working almost exclusively with troubled students. I believe that God has provided me with the skill, knowledge, and personal and professional experience to be a very effective teacher. Yet I would have to admit that I have succeeded far too often in allowing these students to bring out the absolute worst in me which subsequently led me to bring out the absolute worst in them. The turning point for me came only a few short years ago when I realized that I was looking at these kids through the eyes of a tapped-out teacher rather than looking at them through God's eyes. I had become too consumed with how these students would affect my scores on the end of the year standardized test. I knew there were other ways I could help them, but I resented how much additional time and effort it would take. When it came to kids who had discipline problems, problems with their work ethic, and delayed or underdeveloped skills as a result of them, I was stuck in the mindset that someone else was responsible for breaking them so someone else should step up and fix the problem. I have felt more times than I wish to admit that certain students don't deserve my extra effort or attention. I have secretly wished certain students would move away. And while I do not believe I have done so myself, I have seen teachers set up students to elicit behavior from them that resulted in suspension.

My struggle to demonstrate love toward these students was a result of my own selfishness, but I believe it is also rooted in fear and doubt. A significant part of our ongoing evaluation is based on how well our students score on standardized tests. The people at the higher levels who look at our data don't know and most likely don't care how many students we have on our roll with cognitive or academic delays, how many have social or emotional problems, disabilities that adversely affect their performance, troubled home lives, who are learning English, who move several times a year, have parents who are unable to provide enough support and supervision because they are working long hours and more than one job just to survive, or who come from homes where education is not valued. Schools are taxed with fixing the problem regardless of its origin. I think it is absolutely necessary to have standards for teachers and will admit that far too many ineffective teachers are allowed to remain at their posts because of ridiculous tenure policies that no other corporation in America would tolerate. But evaluating success solely based on a set of empirical data trivializes the nature of the task we face and the students we serve. I believe the turning point in every great teacher's career is that point where (s)he finally collapses under the weight of the task and throws in the towel or when instead (s)he accepts the nature of the beast and endeavors to persevere. For Christians, this means embracing the challenge God has set before us.

If we are to honor Christ in our teaching, we must start by seeing these challenging students from His perspective rather than our own. We must stop withholding that extra measure of attention from these students because "it is not part of my job description" as a teacher. You may be right. It may not be part of your job description to act a particular way or do a particular thing for a student. But in this case, we really aren't talking about your job description. We're not talking about the contract you have with the school board. We are talking about the commitment you made to God. You are a teacher, but you are also a shepherd. If you are to live a life that honors God, you cannot exclude the people with whom you spend the better part of each day. If you believe that being a teacher is your calling from God, then you must also accept that it is one of the primary settings in your life where you must model the traits of Christ and thus directly or indirectly lead others to Him. We cannot allow disdain or hatred to build in our hearts toward anyone, even those who tax our every nerve. The Lord tells us

> Whoever claims to love God yet hates a brother or sister is a liar. For whoever does not love their brother and sister, whom they have seen, cannot love God, whom they have not seen. And he has given us this command: Anyone who loves God must also love their brother and sister.
>
> 1 John 4:20-21 NIV

God loves everyone, but He is particularly protective of children. What kind of father would he be were that not the case? Jesus indicates this a number of times in his ministry. He warns us, "Be sure you do not hate one of these little children. I tell you, they have angels who are always looking into the face of My Father in heaven" (Matthew 18:10 NLV).

Still, we may feel that it is beyond our ability to show love toward certain students. In this instance, we must pray for God's strength. It is worth recalling Dietrich Bonhoeffer's quote from Chapter Four:

> If we are to pray aright, perhaps it is quite necessary that we pray contrary to our own heart. Not what we want to pray is important, but what God wants us to pray. The richness of the Word of God ought to determine our prayer, not the poverty of our heart.

We must always have in mind the impact we can have on this child. Our calling is about making an impact. The apostle Paul reminds us, "Do not work only for your own good. Think of what you can do for others" (1 Corinthians 10:24 NLV).

The deeper a child has fallen into a well, the more grateful he may be toward the person who goes through the intense struggle to rescue him. While I would hope we would make a positive impact on the lives of all our students, the students who are the most "lost" stand to benefit the most if we can reach them. In Luke 7:41—43 (NIV), Jesus tells Simon a parable about two debtors to demonstrate this principle:

> Two people owed money to a certain moneylender. One owed him five hundred denarii, and the other fifty. Neither of them had the money to pay him back, so he forgave the debts of both. Now which of them will love him more? Simon replied, "I suppose the one who had the bigger debt forgiven." "You have judged correctly," Jesus said.

Does this mean that this child will turn everything around that year and meet all the criteria for your class including passing the end of the year state test? Maybe. Maybe not. Chances are you are not going to feel the full depth of your impact on that child while he or she is still with you. The seeds you plant take time to grow. It may be that they don't fully germinate until years later. As for scores, I can't say that we should not be concerned about scores because they carry so much weight when it comes to evaluating the effectiveness of a student, a class, a school, a district, a state, and even our nation. Scores can be predictive of future success, but so can a host of other attributes that are never measured. Ultimately, scores on a test matter little to God. It is some of the "other" attributes that concern God more. He is far more interested in the character of your students. That being said, I do believe God respects the job you are being asked to do and understands how your success will be measured by the world. *If* being a teacher is the calling God has led you to, I cannot imagine that He would not help you to experience success if you repeatedly called on Him to be with you at all times in your classroom. A few short years ago I was so burned out that I was ready to find another profession. I was resentful that the measure of our success as teachers boiled down almost entirely to standardized test scores. I was resentful about a lot of other things at that time as well. My dilemma was that I had been teaching so long that I was not certain I could do anything else. I felt like I needed to leave teaching while I was still young enough to find another career but God had not opened any other doors for me. I began to actively look at job listings in hopes that something would jump out at me. Nothing did. This cycle of burnout happens to a lot of teachers. It comes and it goes. Sometimes a change of grade level or even subject is enough to perk us up. At the twenty-seven year mark I am feeling the restlessness to move on to something different. I am not on board with the changes that are taking place in our middle school or perhaps in middle schools in general, but I expect my mind will come back around to what I learned those years ago. During that crisis, I began to realize that being a teacher was my *calling* and sensed that God had always meant for this job to serve a higher purpose than teaching science or social studies. I began the process of handing myself over to God for Him to use me as His instrument through my job as a teacher. Although I don't remember my actual words, in essence my prayer went like this:

> Lord, I want to be your instrument in my job. I believe you made me to be a teacher, but until now I have misunderstood the most important part of this calling. My calling is to teach these students, but more importantly it is to lead them to You. Since I cannot do so directly, I pray that you help me to do so indirectly by the life I lead. Lord, I will love my students, your children. I will try to model your love in my interactions with them and with my colleagues. But Lord, I cannot do this when I am constantly stressed out about standardized test scores, changes in curriculum, an increasing work load, larger class sizes, new mandates, and all the other complications associated with this job. This burden, Lord, I need you to take. With your help and guidance, I will try to teach as hard as I can for as long as I can. I will try to love them as you love us. I'll let you worry about the score.

I did not start believing the scores of my students were unimportant, however, I also did not believe they would drop as a result of my no longer worrying (as much) about them. On the contrary, I had faith that God would take care of the scores. And for the most part He did. For the next four years, I experienced a great deal of satisfaction as a teacher. I was working on this book and the book was working on me at the same time. I finished the initial draft of the book during the summer of 2014. When I was selected as our Teacher of the Year, I openly gave credit to God in front of my colleagues and explained to them that since turning my work over to God I no longer experienced workplace stress. I was riding high. I put the copy of my book in the drawer in my classroom with the intention of returning to it to keep my light bright. It just sat there collecting dust. The process of writing the book gave me strength. I guess I figured that strength would simply continue. I was terribly, horribly wrong. A few months into the school year, the principles I had put to paper over a course of four years were forgotten and I began to spiral downward. Over the course of the next few years, overwhelmed by an old adversary, I experienced a crippling level of anxiety and a new chronic health condition that resulted in two trips to the ER. Genetic predispositions play a large role in my depression and anxiety, but my complacency toward living out what God had intended for me after empowering me to write this book unraveled the strings that prevented those illnesses from ripping me apart. The Devil doubled down on me. This period of struggle for me is explained more in depth in the epilogue.

Showing Love Does Not Mean Being a Pushover

I have known many teachers whom the kids adored but whom they had very little respect for as a teacher. Comments about such teachers might sound like, "Oh, I didn't learn anything in her class, but she let us get away with whatever we wanted to do. She was really cool." So I see the dangers of being entirely too rigid and being entirely too lax as being equally ineffective both from an academic standpoint and for building character in students. Children must learn the importance of discipline, and that is impossible without consequences. Scripture tells us to fear God, but also to love Him deeply. We don't want our students to fear *us* (well, maybe middle school students a bit), but we do want them to understand and fear the consequences of misconduct, sloth, etc. I think it's important to distinguish that a fear of God does not imply cowering in the corner, being put constantly on edge, or being traumatized. It means understanding we are accountable to God. We cannot violate God's "rules" without consequences. Students need to "fear" the consequences of their behavior in the sense that they need to understand and respect them enough that they are inclined to behave in one way rather than another. We are not told to fear God because He is a tyrant. God loves us deeply and wants us to spend eternity with Him, but we can't do that unless we are willing to accept His discipline. We need to discipline our students, but we need to do so in a loving way and, if possible, a way in which students recognize our intent is not to break them down but to build them up. I have already confessed that this is an area where I struggle greatly because of my quick temper. Students must understand there is a line and that if that line is crossed in a way that interferes with the health and welfare of other students consequences will follow.

If the student demonstrates repeatedly that he or she will not toe that line, I do believe that student should be removed from the class until he or she is able to respect the rights of others. Unfortunately, we don't have a whole lot of options. In-school suspension and even out-of-school suspension are not a deterrent for many students and they have the added disadvantage of resulting in that student falling further behind in learning. When that happens it becomes our responsibility to find the time to catch that child up. We don't have that time built into our schedules. It does not exist. It becomes something we must do after school on our own time which is even more problematic if a teacher is the only one in the room with a problem student.

I am a firm believer in alternative classrooms but not ones that are based on intimidation or that are minimally staffed and do not have the materials to provide the student with a quality education. Unfortunately, from a budgeting perspective that is exactly what most alternative classrooms for students with conduct issues look like. I believe teachers of alternative programs for students with chronic behavior issues should receive additional supplements and that each child in the program should be involved in counseling while he or she is in the program and then during the transition back into the standard classroom. I believe that alternative classes are a last resort, but that does not mean I agree that a child should be allowed to run roughshod over a classroom for half a school year while one method after another is tried. That simply reinforces the sense of power the student feels he or she has from being able to essentially control the atmosphere of the learning environment. The key to any alternative program is that it must operate on compassion rather than on intimidation, but that does not mean there are not firm boundaries, expectations, and immediate consequences for undesirable behavior. I sometimes joke that my success with students is that I treat them with the "right combination of love and intimidation," but by intimidation what I really mean is that I want my students to understand that words and behaviors have consequences-good and bad- and that I will follow through with a consequence if it is necessary. I want them to fear bad consequences to a degree though not so much that they develop habits of lying about behavior to avoid consequences. I try to build a relationship with my students so they know I care about them as a person not just as a student, that I care about them becoming "better" people, and that I care about helping them to build skills for a more fulfilling and rewarding future.

I try to deal with the discipline on my own whenever possible rather than refer a student to the office. I also try to work it out with the student before I get his or her parent involved. I want them to know that I am invested in them and that I have confidence we can work most things out on our own. Common sense also has to be a factor in discipline and this includes knowing when to pick your battles. I don't think I am lax with my discipline, however, I would rather employ a number of strategies to address discipline on my own before turning the issue over to administration. Yes, some kids will see warnings or mini-conferences with me as "getting off scot free." Some kids insist on learning the hard way, pushing things to the limit until I have no choice but to do a referral. As Mark Twain once wrote, "A man who carries a cat by the tail learns something he can learn in no other way." I know a lot of my colleagues might disagree with me but I think it is important to be well-liked by students though not at the expense of discipline. You can have your cake and eat it too. I don't think it's important to be popular with students because it is a good way to get your ego stroked. Wanting to be popular with the kids is strategic and, I would argue, Godly if it is for the right reasons and if it doesn't compromise their learning. If my students like me then I am more likely to get the best out of them. Let's face it, many kids are not intrinsically motivated. They do well in school to please mom and dad or to get mom and dad off their back. When they are very young they try to do well to please their teacher but that fades as they get older. It doesn't have to. Your praise as a teacher can be an enormously powerful motivator. Whether your praise matters to your students has a lot to do with the relationship you build with them. Are you just their teacher for an hour a day or do you take the time to get to know them on a more personal basis. Do you show them that you care about them as a person? If a kid feels like you are interested in or invested in him or her as a person as well as a student, (s)he will more often than not give you their best effort. Enthusiasm for students results in enthusiasm for your class even if the subject you teach is not necessarily the child's favorite. If you show love toward them, which includes disciplining them in a loving way, your class will be a place where students want to be.

When we have this kind of relationship with our students, we can have an impact outside our class as well. I don't talk to my students about my class only. If I see they are not working up to their potential in another class, I will speak to them about it. I talk to them about their behavior in other classes. I let them know that I expect them to behave as well for the other teachers as they do for me even if they think the other teacher is "mean" or "unfair." If I didn't have a personal relationship with them, if they didn't believe that I cared about them as a person, such a conversation would probably be a waste of time. Developing a loving connection with students is much more challenging if you limit your conversations and interactions only to the curriculum and only to the classroom. Most students appreciate it when you show an interest in their lives outside the classroom. A number of years ago, my daughter's teacher showed up at her drama performance. Not only did she come, she brought her husband with her and flowers for my daughter. I cannot begin to tell you how much that meant to my daughter. She already thought her teacher hung the moon. After that, I believe she thought she had hung the stars as well. That same teacher was later recognized by her peers as the Teacher of the Year for her school and I am certain the way she shows love for her students played a large part in receiving that honor.

I also enjoy attending my students' sporting events or performances. I am not the least bit interested in nor do I understand the sport of soccer, but I try to attend at least one soccer game a year if I have current or former students playing. We are sometimes required to attend PTSO events where the chorus and band performs, but I would go even if we weren't required because I know it means a great deal to my students when I am there to watch them. I enjoy living in the town where I work, and I think it only improves my teaching. No matter where I go, I run into one of my students, former students, or their parents. I enjoy speaking with them, catching up. It is rewarding to see how that connection with them continues as time passes. The enthusiasm they show when they see me is very gratifying. All the hard work seems more worthwhile when a parent tells you, "he actually enjoys coming to school now because of your class," or "she talks about you all the time." Of course that was not always the case. I have had students who struggled in my class, who did not find it enjoyable. But even with most of them the conversation in public years later is amicable and pleasant. It affirms for me that while I may not have been the best teacher at times, I certainly made a favorable impression upon them. It suggests to me that I did at least a fair job of acting in a loving way toward them.

So I say unapologetically that I want my students to like me, trust me, value their relationships with me. If they like me for the right reasons, then it stands they will usually try harder for me. If they try harder for me, then usually they do better. If they do better, then they will probably enjoy school more. If they enjoy school more, then there is a better chance they will do better overall in school. If they do better overall in school, more doors will be open to them as adults. Also, if they like me, trust me, and value our relationship, they will be more open to my guidance and counsel when it comes to developing their character. All of this becomes possible when you commit to treating your students in a loving way regardless of how they initially treat you. We are the lamp. Our light should show the character of God for all to see. If we love in a Godly way and our colleagues see how enthusiastic, well-behaved, and productive most of our students are for us, then perhaps they will be inspired to follow our example. In a setting where we cannot talk about God, we can only lead people to a live-saving relationship with God by the example of our lives. If we are able to light that spark, God will lead those we have influenced to the next step toward their salvation.

CHAPTER SIX

The Lamp

No one lights a lamp, then hides it in a drawer. It's put on a lamp stand so those entering the room have light to see where they're going. Your eye is a lamp, lighting up your whole body.

If you live wide-eyed in wonder and belief, your body fills up with light. If you live squinty-eyed in greed and distrust, your body is a dank cellar. Keep your eyes open, your lamp burning, so you don't get musty and murky. Keep your life as well-lighted as your best-lighted room.

Luke 11:33-36 MSG

I have a serious concern to bring up with you, my friends, using the authority of Jesus, our Master. I'll put it as urgently as I can: You must get along with each other. You must learn to be considerate of one another, cultivating a life in common.

1 Corinthians 1:10 MSG

Whatever happens, conduct yourselves in a manner worthy of the gospel of Christ.

Philippians 1:27 NIV

Don't copy the behavior and customs of this world, but let God transform you into a new person by changing the way you think. Then you will learn to know God's will for you, which is good and pleasing and perfect.

Romans 12:2 NLT

Do not withhold good from those who deserve it when it's in your power to help them. If you can help your neighbor now, don't say, "Come back tomorrow, and then I'll help you."

Proverbs 3:27-28 NLT

Two are better than one because they have a good return for their labor. For if either of them falls, the one will lift up his companion.

But woe to the one who falls when there is not another to lift him up.

Ecclesiastes 4:9-10 NIV

Live an exemplary life among the natives so that your actions will refute their prejudices. Then they'll be won over to God's side and be there to join in the celebration when he arrives.

1 Peter 2:12 MSG

You show and make obvious that you are a letter from Christ delivered by us, not written with ink but with [the] Spirit of [the] living God, not on tablets of stone but on tablets of human hearts.

Corinthians 3:3 Amplified Bible

Could a greater miracle take place than for us to look through each other's eyes for an instant?

Henry David Thoreau

Let us always meet each other with a smile, for the smile is the beginning of love.

Mother Theresa

Preach the Gospel at all times, and when necessary use words.

St. Francis of Assisi

Do all the good you can by all the means you can in all the places you can at all the times you can to all the people you can as long as ever you can.

John Wesley

Foundational Concepts

- ✝ Though none of us is without sin, people should be able to see a reflection of Christ in the way we live our lives.
- ✝ Hypocrisy not only damages our own credibility but our Lord's as well.

Central Questions

1. What does Christian integrity look like?
2. Do people see a glimpse of Jesus in me?

Avoid Hypocrisy

It is said that when asked one time, Mahatma Gandhi responded, "I like your Jesus, I do not like your Christians. Your Christians are so unlike your Christ." Though we know we are expected to "Follow God's example, therefore, as dearly loved children and walk in the way of love, just as Christ loved us and gave himself up for us as a fragrant offering and sacrifice to God" (Ephesians 5:1-2 NIV), it's not difficult to understand Gandhi's point when we consider how easily and readily we violate this counsel, even toward those who share our faith. Some people dislike Christianity because Christian beliefs are inconvenient to their particular lifestyles. Some people, though, come to hate Christians because Christians showed hate toward them first. We love to assume the moral high ground because, well, we are Christians by God! We do this at times in our job as teachers toward students, their families, toward colleagues. We act toward them in ways that alienate them even if we are not aware that we are doing it, and alienated students and parents find it hard to partner with us in the success of the child. We can be such busybodies! Listen to the scuttlebutt when teachers learn that a high school girl is pregnant. Listen to some of us talk about mothers who have multiple children out of wedlock from a number of different fathers. How do we talk about people who seem to take advantage of the welfare system? Listen to how we gossip about someone who has had an affair or who is going through divorce. What about our judgmental whispers when we learn that one of our students has "two daddies." If we *feel* this way, I would argue that it would be impossible for us to completely hide these feelings from our students and their families. Our sinful attitude will come through in subtle ways. They will pick up on it. This is contrary to what we are taught in the Bible. In his second letter to the Church at Corinth, the Apostle Paul wrote:

> Because of this decision we don't evaluate people by what they have or how they look. We looked at the Messiah that way once and got it all wrong, as you know. We certainly don't look at him that way anymore. Now we look inside, and what we see is that anyone united with the Messiah gets a fresh start, is created new.
>
> 2 Corinthians 5:16-20 MSG

James, the brother of Jesus adds:

> Listen, dear friends. isn't it clear by now that God operates quite differently? He chose the world's down-and-out as the kingdom's first citizens, with full rights and privileges. This kingdom is promised to anyone who loves God. And here you are abusing these same citizens!
>
> James 2:5-6 MSG

In verses 8-11, James continues

> You do well when you complete the Royal Rule of the Scriptures: "Love others as you love yourself." But if you play up to these so-called important people, you go against the Rule and stand convicted by it. You can't pick and choose in these things, specializing in keeping one or two things in God's law and ignoring others.

When Christians expose our biases toward others, we have the potential to confuse our colleagues and our students as much as the media does. Even atheists hold Christians to a higher standard. We *should* be held to a higher standard because *we are expected not to reflect the beliefs of this world* but those of the Kingdom of God. Acting judgmental and vindictive toward God's children is a sin. And while I believe "sin is sin" and we should not be concerned with ranking them, given how many times hypocrisy is mentioned in the Bible I think it would be wise to consider it when we are engaging in the act. Sin cannot conquer sin. Only love can conquer sin. We will encounter students (and parents and colleagues for that matter) in our work who lie, slander, gossip, steal, sabotage, cheat, take advantage of people, put their own needs above others, bully, ignore, and so on. We will encounter many who have beliefs that are very different from that of a mature Christian. Is this kind of behavior more prevalent than it was in the past? Perhaps. But is that even relevant? The Lord calls us to treat each of these people in a loving way. Furthermore, each one of us at times will lie, slander, gossip, steal, sabotage, cheat, take advantage of people, put our needs above others, bully, ignore, and so on. The Bible tells us God uses the same measure to judge us that we use to judge others. When Christians behave badly, we don't just damage our own credibility; we damage Christ's credibility and interfere with His mission on earth for us and for others.

On the other hand, Proverbs 16:7 (NASB) tells us, "When a man's ways are pleasing to the Lord, he makes even his enemies be at peace with him." Christ certainly doesn't need us to make believing in Him any more difficult than it is for the eighty percent of the earth's population that believes in another god or gods or no god at all. He was a hard sell even in His own days on earth. Even many of those who witnessed His miracles were skeptical that Christ was the Messiah. We are supposed to be the living example of Christ on earth. In 1 Peter 2:12 (MSG) we are told, "Live an exemplary life among the natives so that your actions will refute their prejudices. Then they'll be won over to God's side and be there to join in the celebration when he arrives." In his letter to the church in Corinth, the apostle Paul writes, "Your very lives are a letter that anyone can read by just looking at you. Christ himself wrote it—not with ink, but with God's living Spirit; not chiseled into stone, but carved into human lives—and we publish it" (2 Corinthians 3:3 MSG). People should be able to get to know Christ and *seek* Him through our example. In 2 Corinthians 5:20 we are told that we are, "Christ's ambassadors, *as though God were making His appeal through us* (my emphasis)." In Matthew 5:14-16 (NLV), Jesus tells us that we are to be a light in the darkness:

> You are the light of the world. You cannot hide a city that is on a mountain. Men do not light a lamp and put it under a basket. They put it on a table so it gives light to all in the house. Let your light shine in front of men. Then they will see the good things you do and will honor your Father Who is in heaven.

We have already learned about the fruits of The Spirit from Paul's letter to the Galatians: "The fruit of the spirit is love, joy, peace, forbearance, kindness, goodness, faithfulness, gentleness and self- control" (Galatians 5:22-23). The Bible tells us that we will be recognized by the "fruit" we bear:

> A good tree cannot have bad fruit. A bad tree cannot have good fruit. For every tree is known by its own fruit. Men do not gather figs from thorns. They do not

gather grapes from thistles. Good comes from a good man because of the riches he has in his heart. Sin comes from a sinful man because of the sin he has in his heart. The mouth speaks of what the heart is full of.

Luke 6:43-45 NLV

We are told that we must, "clothe [ourselves] with compassion, kindness, humility, gentleness, and patience" (Colossians 3:12). Philippians 4:5 says, "Let your gentleness be evident to all. The Lord is near." The question we must ask ourselves is *do people see these traits in us*? And as an indicator of integrity, is this what we look like when there is *no* audience? Paul counsels his protégé, Timothy, to "Teach believers with your life: by word, by demeanor, by love, by faith, by *integrity*" (1 Timothy 4:12 MSG). Living with integrity means that you walk the walk. It is the opposite of hypocrisy. To say God is irritated by hypocrisy is an understatement of Biblical proportions. Hypocrisy is a Kingdom killer. When a Christian is trying to lead a person to Christ, the first thing he or she does shouldn't be handing the person a Bible and telling them to read it and get back to him. We may share the Word with them, but ultimately it is our conduct that will intrigue people and compel them to learn more or turn them off from our faith –perhaps forever! We cannot expect to influence people and lead them to Christ if we don't practice what we preach. James 3:2 reminds us that we all stumble. As I mentioned in the introduction to this book, I stumble often. I admit that I frequently act in a hypocritical manner, but I recognize this about myself and I respond by asking for God's forgiveness and for Him to help me behave less like this so that I may bring more glory to Him. I can and do try to make amends for my hypocrisy by further acknowledging it to my students or colleagues.

The more dangerous type of hypocrisy, I think, is when people behave in such a manner and either don't realize they are acting like a hypocrite or they realize and don't care. Some people may feel that their hypocritical behavior is righteous and justified. The main problem Jesus had with the Jewish Pharisees was that they taught the law and rigorously tried to hold people to it, but they didn't always adhere to it themselves. Warnings against hypocrisy are found throughout the Bible. Some of Christ's most well-known analogies address hypocrisy. For example:

> Why do you look at the speck of sawdust in your brother's eye and pay no attention to the plank in your own eye? How can you say to your brother, 'Brother, let me take the speck out of your eye,' when you yourself fail to see the plank in your own eye? You hypocrite, first take the plank out of your eye, and then you will see clearly to remove the speck from your brother's eye

Luke 6:41-42 NIV

Earlier in Chapter Two of this book, we saw how the parable of the tax collector and the Pharisee in Luke 18:10-14 was used by Jesus to illustrate hypocrisy. In Chapter 8 of John, Christ comes across a group of men about to stone a woman accused of adultery. When the men asked His thoughts about what they were doing, Jesus drew something in the dirt and said to the men, "Let any one of you who is without sin be the first to throw a stone at her" (verse 7). A lot of people have speculated about what Jesus wrote in the dirt. I tend to agree with those who think he wrote something that revealed the sins of the men to them. Whatever it was, it was enough to send the men away without another word. In 1 John 1:8-10 (NIV) we are warned, "If we claim to be without sin, we deceive ourselves and the truth is not in us. If we confess our sins, he is faithful and just and will forgive us our sins and purify us from all unrighteousness. If we claim we have not sinned, we make him out to be a liar and his word is not in us." Sin is sin, but when the Bible addresses a particular sin over and over again, we should infer from it that we should pay particular attention to how often that sin is reflected in our words and actions.

The opposite of hypocrisy is integrity. Integrity is essential in the life of a Christian. Integrity means that we try to maintain our walk in all aspects of our lives whether in the presence of others or on our own. It means our conduct is consistent. Our integrity should be visible to others, and it cannot be a façade. A person with genuine integrity will behave in a God honoring manner whether someone is watching or not. We live in a world that is connected by a complex network of media and communication technology. Sooner or later what we think we are doing in private will see the light of day. One's integrity must be valued and protected. A reputation for integrity is something a person builds over a lifetime but can lose in an instant. Our degree of integrity, our ability to walk the walk, will do more to win people over to Christ than any sermon a person might hear. It's important to emphasize this point again: most people don't learn about Jesus at first by reading the Bible. Most people learn about Jesus by seeing His light shine from mature Christians who serve God with integrity. 2 Corinthians 6:3-4 (NLV), Paul warns us to, "live in such a way that no one will stumble because of us, and no one will find fault with our ministry. In everything we do, we show that we are true ministers of God. We patiently endure troubles and hardships and calamities of every kind." If our example has the result of casting doubt about God's love and promise, then surely we cannot say that we are honoring God's purpose for us on earth. I have no doubt that on the day of my accounting one of the first issues that will be addressed by the Lord is the number of people I led to Him. I may not know the exact answer to that, but He will, and I certainly don't want my Lord, the Lord who commanded me to lead others to Him, to show me an empty slate. I especially don't want to see a list of people whom I turned away from making the choice to follow Christ because they observed me in the midst of my struggle to live my life in a way that honors the Lord.

Serving a living example of God's character is a continual work in progress for most of us. In the introduction to this book, I admitted that I was a hypocrite. I am certainly not proud of it, but I recognize that I am not alone. Moses, David, Peter, Paul-each acknowledged his hypocrisy at certain points in his lives. If you are still alive on this planet, you too will succumb to your own hypocrisy from time to time. It may be in public, but then again it may be where only God can see you. For those of us like me who have developed a reputation over a lifetime for ungodly behavior, we face the added challenge of changing people's perception of us. Paul faced that challenge, as did Matthew and a number of other Biblical giants. It took seeing Paul persecuted, beaten, imprisoned, and executed before many people trusted his credibility. It is not likely that I will have to demonstrate my commitment to God in the face of death or imprisonment, so I would argue that people like me have a much longer "row to hoe" when it comes to changing people's perceptions of us.

It is not always "new" Christians that cause the most problems. One of the most bitter, slanderous, and degrading teachers I recall was a person who claimed to have been a Christian all her life and who was active in her church. You may be saying to yourself, "Well, if she acted that way then she was certainly not a *sincere* Christian." That's your wisdom speaking. Not everybody has the wisdom to distinguish those who are trying their best to be true to the calling from those who simply wear the badge. If a person calls him or herself a Christian, then in the eyes of many people he or she is a Christian, and if that is the example for them of our faith I do not blame them for not wanting to be a part of it! We also need to keep in mind that there are consequences for this kind of behavior. In Psalm 7:14-16 (NLV), we are told, "See how the sinful man thinks up sins and plans trouble and lies start growing inside him. He has dug out a deep hole and has fallen into the hole he has dug. The trouble he makes will return to him. When he hurts others it will come down on his own head". On the other hand, the Bible also provides us with guidance that will allow us to show compassion toward people who are bitter. In Psalm 73:21-22 (NIV), Asaph writes, "When my heart was grieved and my spirit embittered, I was senseless and ignorant; I was a brute beat before you." It is highly unlikely that we will be able to thwart bitterness with bitterness. Nor can you lead a bitter person to a relationship with Jesus by simply avoiding or ignoring them. I'm not suggesting that you act as their counselor. I'm suggesting that each of us understand and accept that if the root of a person's bitterness is a grieving heart, then only compassion and love can help them to change.

As Christians, we must make it our aim to develop Godly wisdom over the course of our journey with Christ. Wisdom promotes self-control and Godly thinking. Wisdom allows us to analyze whatever circumstances we are facing from Christ's perspective. Wisdom allows us to understand the short and long-term consequences of behavior. Wisdom can help us to battle our hypocrisy. Wisdom provides us the knowledge and skills to offer effective counsel to those who are in need. In his second letter to Timothy, Paul writes, "Preach the word; be prepared in season and out of season; correct, rebuke, and encourage---with great patience and careful instruction" (2 Timothy 4:2 NLT). Wisdom fosters patience and acceptance of trials as part of god's plan. Wisdom enables us to accept less so that others may have more. Wisdom enables us to act in a manner that may be contrary to the sinful thoughts that tempt us. Wisdom strengthens our trust in God and our belief in His promises. But wisdom is not gained by the simple flick of a switch. It takes a great deal of prayer, time, study, conversation with mature Christians, and observing mature Christians at work. Proverbs 22: 29 (MSG) counsels us to, "Observe people who are good at their work---skilled workers are always in demand and admired; they don't take a back seat to anyone." Though Solomon is referring to occupational workers, the same concept applies to those wishing to develop Godly wisdom. In James 3:13-18 (MSG) we are told what godly wisdom looks like:

> Do you want to be counted wise, to build a reputation for wisdom? Here's what you do: Live well, live wisely, live humbly. It's the way you live, not the way you talk, that counts. Mean-spirited ambition isn't wisdom. Boasting that you are wise isn't wisdom. Twisting the truth to make yourselves sound wise isn't wisdom. It's the furthest thing from wisdom—it's animal cunning, devilish conniving. Whenever you're trying to look better than others or get the better of others, things fall apart and everyone ends up at the others' throats. Real wisdom, God's wisdom, begins with a holy life and is characterized by getting

along with others. It is gentle and reasonable, overflowing with mercy and blessings, not hot one day and cold the next, not two-faced. You can develop a healthy, robust community that lives right with God and enjoy its results only if you do the hard work of getting along with each other, treating each other with dignity and honor.

Along all avenues of our walk, we should carry with us the importance of humility and service to others. It is the foundation of our relationship with God and likewise should be the foundation of our relationship with the people in our lives. Galatians 5:16-18 (MSG) counsels us with these words:

> My counsel is this: Live freely, animated and motivated by God's Spirit. Then you won't feed the compulsions of selfishness. For there is a root of sinful self-interest in us that is at odds with a free spirit, just as the free spirit is incompatible with selfishness. These two ways of life are antithetical, so that you cannot live at times one way and at times another way according to how you feel on any given day. Why don't you choose to be led by the Spirit and so escape the erratic compulsions of a law-dominated existence?

This of course includes the relationships we have with our students, colleagues, and other stakeholders. Even if we are able to reflect Christ's love and passion in our interactions with our students, God does not expect us to limit our influence only to them. God wants to be in every teacher's classroom. Since His name, His Word, and His image are effectively barred at the front door, the best way His message and His character can be present in our workplace is through the example of His followers. Our example, we recall, must begin with humility. In Romans 12:3-8 (NIV), we are counseled, "Do not think of yourself more highly than you ought, but rather think of yourself with sober judgment, in accordance with the faith God has distributed to each of you." A humble person, "[Does] nothing out of selfish ambition or vain conceit. Rather, in humility value others above yourselves, not looking to your own interests but each of you to the interests of others" (Philippians 2:3-4 NIV). A humble person does not seek personal glory. Even Jesus said, "If I glorify myself, my glory means nothing. My Father, whom you claim as your God, is the one who glorifies me" (John 8:54 NIV). In his letter to the Galatians, Paul asks, "Am I now trying to win the approval of human beings, or of God? Or am I trying to please people? If I were still trying to please people, I would not be a servant of Christ (Galatians 1:10)." In John 5:41-44 (MSG), we are told why we should not seek self-glory, recognition, or approval from others:

> I'm not interested in crowd approval. And do you know why? Because I know you and your crowds. I know that love, especially God's love, is not on your working agenda. I came with the authority of my Father, and you either dismiss me or avoid me. If another came, acting self-important, you would welcome him with open arms. How do you expect to get anywhere with God when you spend all your time jockeying for position with each other, ranking your rivals and ignoring God?

This is not saying that all praise or recognition is bad. If we are recognized for the right thing, I cannot imagine how that would not please God. But praise for the wrong thing or self-praise does not please God. Proverbs 27:2 says, "Let someone else praise you, and not your own mouth; an outsider, and not your own lips." Praising one's self, boasting, means one is interested in self-glory rather than glorifying God.

Words are Powerful

Our influence on others is also greatly affected by what comes out of our mouths. It has been said that actions speak louder than words, but all of us are aware of just how much damage words can cause. James 3:5 (MSG) warns, "A word out of your mouth may seem of no account, but it can accomplish nearly anything—or destroy it!" The words that come out of our mouths often define us for people who may not know how we might *behave* more like Christ in other ways. Sixth century Chinese philosopher, Lao-Tse once wrote:

> Watch your thoughts, for they become words.
> Watch your words, for they become actions.
> Watch your actions, for they become habits.
> Watch your habits, for they become character.
> Watch your character, for it becomes your destiny.

The Bible counsels us repeatedly to pay attention to what comes out of our mouths:

- Proverbs 10:19 NIV- The one who talks much will for sure sin, but he who is careful what he says is wise.
- Proverbs 13:3 NLT- Those who control their tongue will have a long life; opening your mouth can ruin everything.
- Proverbs 21:23 NIV- Those who guard their mouths and their tongues keep themselves from calamity.
- Proverbs 30:12 MSG- Don't imagine yourself to be quite presentable when you haven't had a bath for weeks.
- James 3:9-10 NIV- With the tongue we praise our Lord and Father, and with it we curse human beings, who have been made in God's likeness. Out of the same mouth come praise and cursing. My brothers and sisters, this should not be.
- Proverbs 4:23-24 NLV- Keep your heart pure for out of it are the important things of life.
- Matthew 15:18-19 NIV- But the things that come out of a person's mouth come from the heart, and these defile them. For out of the heart come evil thoughts-murder, adultery, immorality, theft, false testimony, slander.
- Ephesians 4: 29 NLT- Don't use foul or abusive language. Let everything you say be good and helpful, so that your words will be an encouragement to those who hear them.
- James 1:26 NLT- If you claim to be religious but don't control your tongue, you are fooling yourself, and your religion is worthless.

My mouth has caused a lot of problems for me throughout my life. I frequently say things without giving them a lot of forethought. In my defense, part of it is a cultural thing. I am a New Englander, a Downeaster from coastal Maine. We tend to be very direct in what we say. We don't beat around the bush or sugarcoat things. We sometimes feel like we are doing a person a great service by enlightening them in this manner. This directness was not well received when I first moved to the South. I was not generally trying to offend anyone with my directness, but I learned over time that I must try to be more tactful in expressing my thoughts. Sir Isaac Newton once said, "Tact is the art of making a point without making an enemy." It is one of the things I have worked hardest on the past several years, and while I believe I have come a long way, sometimes when I am "in a tizz" my bluntness reappears. In some cases, the words that come from us are intentionally critical, judgmental, or slanderous. I have been guilty of all of these, but the most dangerous manifestation of my words are when I am using them to tear a person down. Many of us possess the sinful ability to know exactly what to say to hurt a person the most. Sometimes we assume the rule of judge or enforcer and use caustic words to "put someone in their place." The flip side of that is that these same people usually know the exact thing to say to build a person up. The key is turning this ability into an asset rather than a weapon. Just as words can drive a person into the dirt, they can also lift a person up from the dirt. In the book of Proverbs, we find a number of verses that confirm this for us:

- Proverbs 12:18 NIV- The words of the reckless pierce like swords, but the tongue of the wise brings healing.
- Proverbs 12:25 NIV- Anxiety weighs down the heart, but a kind word cheers it up.
- Proverbs 15:1 NIV- A gentle answer turns away wrath, but a harsh word stirs up anger.
- Proverbs 15:23 MSG- Congenial conversation—what a pleasure! The right word at the right time---beautiful!
- Proverbs 15:30 MSG- A twinkle in the eye means joy in the heat, and good news makes you feel fit as a fiddle.
- Proverbs 16:24 NIV- Gracious words are a honeycomb, sweet to the soul and healing to the bones.

The mouth is also the gate through which gossip and slander leave the body. I have already addressed gossip as a violation of "Love Protects," but it is such a cancer in some places that it is worth further scrutiny. Like anger and complaining, gossip is often fueled by something else: jealousy, a need to seem important or valuable, bitterness, attempts to make ourselves look good compared to others, or resentment. Gossip is harmful on so many levels, both to the gossiper and the target of the gossip. Gossip almost always places the person spreading or eagerly gobbling up the gossip in the role of being the judge of someone. Proverbs 10:18 (NIV) says, "Whoever conceals hatred with lying lips and spreads slander is a fool." Gossip is a sin. In James 4:11-12 (NLT), we are warned that such behavior will not be overlooked by the Lord:

> Don't speak evil against each other, dear brothers and sisters. If you criticize and judge each other, then you are criticizing and judging God's law. But your job is to obey the law, not to judge whether it applies to you.

Even listening to gossip is considered a sin. In Ecclesiastes 7:21-22 (MSG) we are warned, "Don't eavesdrop on the conversations of others. What if the gossip is about you and you'd rather not hear it? You've done that a few times, haven't you—said things behind someone's back that you wouldn't say to his face?" Gossip also frequently involves commentary that is based on incomplete or inaccurate information. Chronic gossipers want to get out ahead of others, to be the first to "share the news." In Proverbs 11:12 (NIV), we read, "Whoever derides his neighbor has no sense, but one who has understanding holds his tongue." While not specifically addressing gossip, to me this passage of scripture warns that a spiritually mature person avoids slander in general but is particularly conscientious about commenting without knowing all the information. It may also suggest that even when we know all the information, the Lord denies us the right to share certain information if we are doing so in a self-serving, judgmental manner. I may be reading far more into the passage than what is there, but I believe other passages throughout the Bible support this view.

The Complain Train

We also model Christ by not being a constant complainer. Thoreau once wrote, "If misery loves company, misery has company enough." I have already made it clear that listening to people complain is one of my major pet peeves. It's not that there isn't room for expressing legitimate concerns which I think is a necessary and healthy part of any home or workplace. The complaining I'm talking about is more like the whining of a spoiled child. It is seldom productive and quite often contagious. It is laced with judgment and at times even ill-intent. I hate how it wears me down, but I also hate how easy it is for me at times to fall into that pattern of behavior when I am exposed to it. We need to face the truth about our vocation: a lot of what we are asked to do makes little to no sense at all, is counterproductive, consumes vast amounts of time with little gain, is frequently inconsistent, is not "fair," and requires large amounts of time that certainly can be put to much better use developing lessons, collaborating, tutoring struggling students, etc. Many veteran teachers complain about how much more difficult things have gotten since they started teaching years ago. This is certainly an accurate and valid observation, but Ecclesiastes 7:10 tells us that wise people do not always go around pining away for the "good old days." There is no shortage of things to complain about and I have no doubt the list will increase as it has year after year in our chosen profession. But folks, it is what it is. Do we imagine that other professions are free from this kind of drag? Where in the Bible does God tell us that any part of our lives is going to be a cake walk? Another very prominent theme of the Bible (which will be addressed in later chapters) is this: God allows adversity in all areas of our lives because *adversity is a tool He used to help build our character*. In a life with no adversity, there would be no need for anyone to know God, to need God. A life free of adversity creates a being free from empathy. Adversity is the obstacle course through which we build our strength, our endurance, our determination, our confidence, and our faith---IF we understand and accept its purpose. God wants and needs us to be assertive at times when change is needed, but whining and complaining must be far, far more offensive to his ears than it is to ours. After all, He hears it all.

When I listen to people in my profession complain day in and day out, the thought that crosses my mind is, "If this is such a terrible place, why don't you find something else to do as a career?" I suspect that chronic complainers will be chronic complainers regardless of where they work because their nature is a reflection of their character more than it is a result of challenging work demands. I have been *blessed* to have worked with some very challenging students in some very challenging schools, and I think I have developed a pretty good sense of what a truly challenging school environment is like. I have worked with youth offenders, many of whom were members of organized gangs. I have worked with students who were diagnosed with behavior disorders. I have worked in schools where cussing at the teacher gets you a day out of school at best. I have known people who work in schools where the students must pass through a metal detector before entering the school, where the teacher parking lot is enclosed by a tall metal fence topped by barbed wire! I have worked in schools where the degree of apathy toward learning was so pronounced that it was a wonder that many of the students came to school at all. I have worked in districts where the high school dropout rate was thirty to forty percent. I have walked a mile in the shoes of the teachers who work under these conditions every day, so I know without a doubt just how good I have it now.

I now work in a system that is the envy of many other schools in southeastern Georgia. We have, for the most part, a fabulous student population, community support, great facilities, a strong cadre, and a wise school board. And yet, I oftentimes hear more complaining in my school than I did in schools with none of these things. Some of the people who complain the most have worked in more challenging schools, so it baffles me how they could complain so overtly and so regularly in our system. When the person doing the complaining is a veteran teacher, many newer teachers may come to understand that complaining is "just what teachers do." So, instead of infusing the system with fresh energy and optimism, the kettle of milk becomes all the more spoiled. I've also observed that the people who seem to do the most complaining often have very little to offer that is constructive or productive. They complain, but they offer no viable alternative or solution. I don't mind participating in a meeting where people have the opportunity to vent and sometimes just venting is enough. However, at some point as professionals we need to discuss how to address the issues that are troubling us. When we leave a meeting with a plan it leaves the door open for hope or optimism. When we leave a meeting having accomplished nothing more than complaining about an issue, there is little room for either. On the contrary, the group will most likely be revisiting the same issue again and again.

Chronic complainers also seldom reflect upon how their own attitude might be part of the problem. I certainly didn't when I was stuck in that cycle. People who constantly complain seem to feel simply miserable about their lives. Part of me wants to be sympathetic and supportive, but another part of me just wants to yell "snap out of it!" It also puzzles me when I hear certain people complaining about how much work they have to do and how little time they have to complete it, yet during their planning period I frequently observe them sitting and chit-chatting with a colleague for extended periods of time. Certainly it is important to be social. I would even agree that venting our frustrations from time to time is an effective way of relieving some tension. Everybody has bad days when they are more irritable than usual. We should all have one person in our lives mature enough to allow us to vent without jumping on the complaint wagon themselves. That's not what I am referring to. Again, my concern is with the chronic complainer.

Chronic complaining is annoying, distracting, exhausting (I suppose to both the complainer and those exposed to him or her), unproductive, and most of all, *sinful.* Unless they have lived their lives in a bubble, even new teachers know from the start that teachers are overworked, asked to do things that don't make sense, have to deal with constant changes and legislative mandates, are expected to do ten hours of work in an eight hour day, are often underappreciated, frequently have to deal with discipline issues with little support from home, are asked to do or change things at the last minute, and so on. In order for us to remain focused on the job and the kids in front of us, we must be able to set aside all of these things. Constant complaining from colleagues makes this impossible. When we are bombarded by constant complaining, it is impossible for most of us to divert our attention away from the negative and onto the task and the child in front of us. I have worked with so many constant complainers that I have lost track. You frequently hear other colleagues "laugh it off" by saying something like, "She's so funny," or "He's such a hoot." Those comments send the message to this person or group that people want to continue hearing this constant complaining because it is entertaining. It validates their sinful and toxic behavior. I believe we all know that to be true. Ask yourselves this: If the situation involved a student who was a chronic behavior problem in class and who was constantly encouraged to behave in such a way by students who laughed at him or gave him positive attention for his behavior, would you think it was "a hoot?" Would you think it was hilarious? It is absolutely *not* entertaining to those of us who are fighting to stay positive and productive. It is not funny. It is not cute. It is destructive to every aspect of our job.

If you are such an "enabler," please understand that you are as much a part of the problem as the person or group complaining. I have confessed that my response to them is not a whole lot better. I'm a coward. I do not confront the person because I don't like confrontation with colleagues. But neither do I encourage them in any way. If I can walk away I do so. Sometimes this is next to impossible to do if the person is on your team or in your department. Sometimes we have to be part of these conversations. We can't always walk away. As Christians, this can be a tough spot to be in if the atmosphere is not conducive to confrontation related to the dialogue, the tone, or the purpose for the meeting. People perceive our actions through their own life filters. Two people who observe us from a distance interacting with a group may have very different interpretations of what is taking place. A different phenomenon can happen with regards to the people *in* the conversation group. I *try* very hard not to complain much. I *try* very hard to focus on student or parent *behavior* without personalizing by making derogatory statements about the student, especially ones that have absolutely nothing to do with the issue at hand. I *try* not to be judgmental about these children or their families. We cannot always avoid conversations related to students or parents where the dialogue of some group members becomes personalized or judgmental. But here's the rub: if we are unwilling to confront people about the tone or the language, then even if we remain behavior-focused and refrain from making personalized statements *people within that group may not notice that we are behaving differently in any way.* Seen through the filters of the others who are part of the conversation, we may seem as though we are contributing to the process of tearing a student, colleague, or parent down even if we are trying to stay focused on the behaviors rather than the individuals. As an inherently quick-tempered and impatient person by nature, I am often not able to hide my frustration about these behaviors, so my own tone may contribute to the negative atmosphere even if I am not making inappropriate personal remarks. This further obscures how my approach may be different.

Years ago I had a bit of a reputation for being able to pin back the ears of even the most difficult parents. Most of the time, my team members in that discussion thought that it was awesome. I thought it was awesome too. An outside, impartial observer, however, may have seen smugness, self-righteousness, attention-seeking, pride, professional immaturity, and arrogance. Move ahead several years where my approach to dealing with difficult parents has changed, in large part to lessons I learned from being a parent. I am much better at putting myself in the parent's position. I am still able to express my concerns, but I think I am able to do so in a much more compassionate way rather than trying to "put the parent in his or her place." I have been told by impartial observers that my tone, language, and affect are often different from some of the others in the group but in a favorable way. I have had parents share with me their appreciation for the way I approached the conversation. The challenge for us as Christians is that we are involved in conversations every day about students, parents, administrators, colleagues, etc., and when they start to go sour there is usually no "third party" observer to distinguish whether our behavior is somehow different and more appropriate than the behavior of some of the other participants. To the people in the conversation, it may appear that I am riding the same Complain Train with them. As stumbling blocks go, it's a huge one. "Modeling" a different approach will seldom be effective if others do not perceive the difference and the benefits that come from this different approach. A certain degree and type of assertiveness may be necessary, but it must be assertiveness that is gentle in nature but clearly expresses that the dialogue or tone of the conversation needs to be readjusted.

Chronic complaining also reflects a lack of gratitude for God's blessings. William Arthur Ward in another of his simple but effective analogies once wrote, "Feeling gratitude and not expressing it is like wrapping a present and not giving it." A lack of gratitude can lead to some serious corrective measures from God to bring us back into a right relationship with Him. Any person who doesn't believe God has a right to expect gratitude clearly does not understand what God is offering us through Christ. A lack of gratitude is a personal slap in God's face, and if we have committed ourselves to Christ, He cannot allow it to continue unabated. It will not be overlooked. In Chapter 17 of Luke, Christ heals ten lepers, but only one, a Samaritan, comes back to offer praise to God. When only this one man returned, Christ asks, "Didn't I heal ten men? Where are the other nine? Has no one returned to give glory to God except this foreigner" (Luke 17:17 NLT)? As challenging as it may seem to us, God expects us to honor Him by doing our work without complaint. Our complaints are a window into our frame of mind. They can expose our attitude toward meeting the trials that God promises we will face. Our complaints can expose the weakness of our faith. With regards to complaining, Ward reminded us that our attitude determines our perspective. He once wrote, "The pessimist complains about the wind; the optimist expects it to change; the realist adjusts the sails." Along these same lines, he also wrote, "We can throw stones, complain about them, stumble on them, climb over them, or build with them." In Ephesians 6:7-8 (NIV), we are told, "Serve wholeheartedly, as if you were serving the Lord, not people, because you know that the Lord will reward each one for whatever good they do, whether they are slave or free." In similar fashion, Paul also writes to the Colossian church, "Work willingly at whatever you do, *as though you were working for the Lord rather than for people.* Remember the Lord will give you an inheritance as your reward, and that the master you are serving is Christ" (Colossians 3:23—24 NLT). Mother Teresa once wrote, "There is always the danger that we may do the work for the sake of the work. This is where the respect and the love and the devotion comes in—that we do it to God, to Christ, and that's why we try to do it as beautifully as possible." In his letter to the church in Philippi, Paul counsels them to, "Do everything without grumbling or arguing, so that you may become blameless and pure, children of God without fault in a warped and crooked generation. Then you will shine among them like stars in the sky as you hold firmly to the word of life. And then I will be able to boast on the day of Christ that I did not run in labor or in vain" (Philippians 2:14-16 NIV). St Francis of Assisi once wrote, "It is not fitting, when one is in God's service, to have a gloomy face or a chilling look

I absolutely understand how easy it might be for teachers to become bitter. I have been there. I still "go there" sometimes. But I also understand the drain bitterness has on a person's health, family, work, and faith. I have done more than my fair share of complaining in life and in my profession. I understand the darkness that fuels the dissatisfaction, how blinding it can be. I did not see myself as a complainer. Instead, I saw myself as somewhat of a champion fighting against injustice. Some of my complaining was a result of frustration at some of the ridiculous practices and expectations that exists within our profession. However, it was at times driven by ego, self-righteousness and a need for attention or praise. I was caught up in bitterness and could not seem to pull myself from it. I was angry, resentful, intensely frustrated and felt like lashing out and venting would alleviate these feelings. It did not. In the 73rd Psalm, Asaph finds himself struggling with bitterness at seeing the prosperity of the wicked and the relative poverty of so many of God's people. His bitterness seemed to be consuming him. In verses 2 and 3, he writes, "But as for me, my feet had almost slipped; I had nearly lost my foothold. For I envied the arrogant when I saw the prosperity of the wicked" (NIV). If we jump ahead to verses 21—22, we can perhaps see ourselves or others who cannot seem to shake bitterness from their lives: "When my heart was grieved and my spirit embittered, I was senseless and ignorant; I was a brute beast before you." Asaph regained his foothold by, in his own words, "entering the sanctuary of God." In verses 16-17, Asaph writes, "When I tried to understand all this, it troubled me deeply, till I entered the sanctuary of God; then I understood their final destiny."

While I have come a long way in dealing with my own bitterness, I haven't had as much success helping others with theirs. I have a lot of *excuses*. Sometimes I don't want to interfere because I feel like I don't have the kind of relationship with the person that would make the person receptive to my input. Confronting a person with whom you do have a positive relationship can backfire. We have all experienced that and in some cases it can be disastrous. Confronting a person with whom you do not have a relationship, then, seems an even more daunting prospect. Some people have the type of personalities that enable them to confront people with whom they do not have a relationship. There is a gentleness about them that can open tightly locked hearts. Jesus was like that, though at times He needed to be a lion when confronting others. I have known a handful of people like this in my life and oh, how I envy that gentleness. Only my mother would say I have a gentleness about me and only because she is my mother. Time may also have softened her memories of me as a teenager. Sometimes the lack of success when confronting someone about sinful behavior is a simple matter of timing. There are times when people are less receptive to counsel. Proverbs 27:14 (NIV) reminds us, "If anyone loudly blesses their neighbor in the morning it will be taken as a curse." A lack of success at helping others to change may also be a reflection of our own level of credibility. In my case, I would guess that many people would raise their eyebrows at me for confronting people from the glass house in which I have been known to reside. While I think I have made some positive changes, they may not be all that noticeable to everyone or even anyone (which means I haven't changed enough). To some people I imagine it would seem the pinnacle of hypocrisy to hear me confront someone about sinful behavior. I understand that this is not a good excuse for not confronting people when confrontation is necessary and that my unwillingness to confront people is also at times a wasted opportunity for people to see that I have changed, but I struggle with this none-the-less.

But let's be honest- most people reading this will know right off the bat the main reason why we don't we say anything to people who are constantly complaining, making inappropriate personal comments about others, gossiping, even sabotaging others: because we have to work with these people. We are afraid that by confronting them we will turn them away from us or that they will turn *on* us-and that is a very real possibility! Confrontation can create tension. The person being confronted can become extremely defensive, even combative. It can create divisions not just between you and that person but you and his or her supporters (and your supporters, which would compound the problem). It can make *you* a target. The person whom you confronted and his posse may begin to talk about you behind your back, even undermine you at times. It can adversely affect team or group effectiveness. I will admit that I can be pessimistic at times, but I am speaking from experience here from the perspective of both the person doing the confronting and the person being confronted. It has only been the past few years that I have been able to accept critique from others. I fought many a battle from atop my high-horse. When my thoughts fester over such concerns, when I whine to God that "He might become really defensive," or "She might talk about me behind my back," or "They might try to ruin my reputation," I hear a little whisper in my mind saying, "Uh huh. *And*?"

The Bible tells us that some people will turn from us, that divisions will be created between those who choose to honor Christ and those who do not. Christ tells us some people will *hate* us because of Him. He tells us that we will be persecuted for living a life that honors Him. The Apostle Paul was beaten and imprisoned for confronting people about their ungodly behavior. Jesus was *killed* for it as were most of His disciples and countless Christians throughout history. It seems a bit trifle that some of us worry too much about offending someone or even worrying about how his or her anger might be turned on us. It begs the question: how can any of us serve as an effective model for Christian behavior if we lack the personal or professional courage to confront sin? It is particularly disparaging when we fail to confront sinful behavior that has the potential to harm others, to taint the well we all drink from enabling the sin virus to infect others. I'm not suggesting that we stand directly in front of person with a crucifix extended out in front and calling the person on the carpet while channeling a Puritan minister. I'm also not suggesting in any way that the healthy and effective confrontational skills are something we have naturally. I would hope that any confrontation would involve a great deal of forethought and prayer. I would love to have the ability to use a parable to open someone's eyes like Nathan did with David in 2 Samuel, but I'm not that clever or creative.

No matter what angle we approach the issue from, fearing to confront someone about their sinful behavior primarily because we are afraid of offending him or her or of the potential repercussions that might result is as sinful as the other person's offense. What about the commitment we said we made to the Lord? Where is our faith? And for those of you who enjoy irony, for me this situation is thick with it: I have been aware of people making derogatory comments behind my back for years-many that are well-warranted. For much of my career, the scuttlebutt was sometimes about how arrogant I acted. Sometimes it was for other behaviors I am too embarrassed or ashamed of to even mention. I know some colleagues have resented me because of my popularity with students (though that popularity seems less of issue these days!) I am told that I have been talked about unfavorably by some people who resent all the attention I have received in the past few years for a unique program I developed. I can be moody and distant from others at times which leads people to a host of conclusions. I know there are colleagues who complain about how undeserving I am of the teacher awards I have received. So a handful of people (and more than a handful at times) over the years have already been making derogatory comments about me behind my back. And here I am concerned that people might talk about me behind my back for confronting others who are engaging in inappropriate dialogue about students, colleagues, parents, administrators, or others! Pause a moment if you will to ponder the pure silliness of it.

I certainly don't want my failure to lead by example in this area to discourage others from trying to honor God by confronting bitterness and division in the workplace. The Bible makes it quite clear that God does not want us to become involved in grumbling or complaining. God expects us to pray about it, contemplate it, find scripture to support and strengthen our resolve to provide *loving assistance* to people who are mired in a wallow of negativity and bitterness. Certainly building relationships with others is a logical starting point. Depending upon the relationship you have with the person complaining, you may be able to express a different way of looking at an issue. You can let the person know that you share in their frustrations, but that you have found a way of dealing with frustration that works better for you. This may or may not lead into a further discussion about how God works in your life to help you deal with your frustrations, but I bet the other person will watch you closer from then on to see whether you really do have a handle on things. If he or she sees that you really do seem able to remain, "calm as a baby when all hell breaks loose (Psalm 27:3 MSG)," he or she may seek to learn more about your way, which of course is really God's way. It also pays to offer them a compliment when you notice them handling a particular situation without grumbling or complaining. This can be effective with others as well when you offer compliments to people who listened to a person complaining on and on about something but did not join in the complaining him or herself. Even if the person has issues with you for some reason, most people will internalize a favorable remark. The familiarity that results from having a relationship with someone, of course, can be a double-edged sword. The person engaged in the sin may operate under the assumption that he can "be himself" around you and so you bear the brunt of their sinful behavior. The exact opposite should happen of course: if the relationship is healthy, we should be the very person who lovingly confronts a person about his or her behavior. If, however, the Holy Spirit is working in that person, however angry and hurt he might become at first toward you, he will feel the conviction of the Spirit. Without the conviction of the Spirit, that person can never change. If the Holy Spirit is not working in that person either because of that person's absence of faith or because the Spirit is buried under the fallout from a complicated life narrative, confrontation could cost you the relationship. And we should be willing to take that risk. Unfortunately, most of us (me especially) practice spiritual cowardice when it comes to loving confrontation, though we may feel quite comfortable and self-righteous when it comes to sinful confrontation.

It may be that certain people whom I have worked with over the years will wonder, "Is he talking about me?" The answer may be "yes." But not just you, me as well. There is almost no sinful behavior related to my role as a teacher mentioned in this book that I have not engaged in and sometimes engaged in to a degree that makes many of the educators around me look like saints. I have been the gossiper, the chronic complainer, the self-righteous buffoon, the saboteur, the attention-seeker, the judge of others, the one who refused to acknowledge his faults, the one who lacked courage, the one who ridiculed Christian behavior, and worse. I have said already in this book there are certain sins I struggle with and will continue to struggle with perhaps the rest of my life. I keep going back to the Apostle Paul's struggle in Romans 7:14-20 (NIV), "for I am not practicing what I would like to do, but am doing the very thing I hate." I am often unable to live out or model the types of Godly behavior I write about. Part of the challange is that I was broken a long time ago and the darkness still seeps through the cracks. God has used and allowed a lot of different trials to build me into His vision for me, but there are still a lot of cracks in my clay. I am still on the pottery wheel. God is repairing those cracks, but until He is done darkness will continue to leak out from time to time. Another part of the problem is that I view the world largely through the lens of clinical depression and anxiety disorder. With God's help and help from a number of other sources, I have managed to live successfully with these "thorns" throughout my adult life, but the lens is always there. Those of us with these disorders have to be particularly conscientious about focusing on the positive because by our very nature we are glass-half-full people. We have to give extra consideration to how we think and what we feel because sometimes how we feel has more to do with the disorder than the reality of our current situation. We are not inherently social by nature, so we must *compel* ourselves to function appropriately and effectively in a calling that is profoundly social. Even when I do act in a way that honors the Lord, it often goes unnoticed because people are not accustomed to looking for that behavior in me.

I may never be a *great* role model for many or even most of these behaviors. The difference now is that I actually give a rip about it. I acknowledge my sins and pray for God's help to overcome them if not permanently than at least one battle at a time. I cannot say that I love God's timetable, but whether His timetable makes sense to me or not I have to trust things are progressing for me in accordance to *His* plan for me rather than my own. It may very well be that some of what I have written will help others far more than or perhaps more quickly than it has helped me. I find myself praying this will be the case because there are weeks when I feel like I have made no progress at all. I have questioned whether I will ever at my three steps forward, twos steps back pace become a mature enough Christian to serve as a role model to others. I have been worried that after sharing this book with others, people will look closer at my words and actions and notice every way possible that I fail in that manner. I am not so much afraid of being held accountable because the Lord knows I need it. Rather, I am concerned that people may dismiss the notion of reading this book because they look at me and think there could not possibly be anything in it worthwhile for them which I do not believe is the case. In fact, I am certain others can benefit far more from this book than I have. At some point several months ago when I was considering whether to self-publish this book or not, I was close to deciding that I would just keep it as a personal resource because I felt that if I was still struggling so much than

I was not the person to share something like this with teachers, *especially* in my district. I was caught up once again in the "me" mode of thinking. Why am *I* not seeing as much change as I had hoped? How can something like this possibly help anyone else if it isn't really helping *me* as much as I hoped or believed it would? Somewhere during this process of self-centered thinking, I felt the Lord respond to my heart with one simple statement: "I appreciate your concern, but you need to stop thinking this is just about *you*. Let *me* worry about whether anyone else will benefit from this book."

Anger

How we express or control our anger can also influence others. We already covered anger a bit in an early chapter, but it is worth revisiting because it is such an issue for so many of us. Anger is an emotion we must learn to manage effectively. In Chapter Four, we distinguished between righteous anger and sinful anger. It is the latter that can cause us the most problems when it comes to reflecting Christ's character. In Ecclesiastes 7:9 (MSG) we are warned, "Don't be quick to fly off the handle. Anger boomerangs. You can spot a fool by the lumps on his head." In Proverbs 15:18 (MSG), Solomon tells us, "Hot tempers start fights; a calm, cool spirit keeps the peace." In James 1:19-20 (NIV), we are told, "Everyone should be slow to speak and slow to become angry, because anger does not produce the righteousness that God desires." It is during periods of anger that we say and perhaps do the most hurtful things. A person in the throes of sinful anger simply cannot show love because all rationale and reason may be temporarily suspended. Hence Paul's warning to the Ephesians, "In your anger, do not sin. Do not let the sun go down while you are still angry, and do not give the devil a foothold" (Ephesians 4:26-27 NIV). He continues in verse 31, "Get rid of all bitterness, rage, and anger, brawling and slander, along with every other form of malice." We need to face our anger honestly when it afflicts us. We should not pretend we are not angry when we are. Though it may take much more to provoke us to anger as we develop mature wisdom, we are a sinful people. We cannot ever fully escape anger. Everybody feels sinful anger at one time or another. To deny that would lead others to doubt our level of honesty or perhaps even our sanity. The goal for us, then, should be to deal with our anger in a Godly manner so that others might learn by our example. I've already acknowledged that I can be quick tempered, but I have learned that a heartfelt admission of my wrongdoing and an apology can often patch up the wound I inflicted. If I dress a student down in front of his peers, I make it a point to apologize to him in front of his peers and admit that my behavior was wrong. I have known many teachers who believe they should never admit they were wrong about anything to their students. To me, that is a total waste of golden opportunity to teach God's nature and build a more trusting relationship with the students. Likewise, if I lose my temper with a colleague, I usually seek to make amends once I have calmed down and the nature of my sin compels me to do so.

I admit that I can be far more judgmental and critical of my colleagues than I can be of my students. I have different expectations of them than I do for my students, and because of this I am much more easily frustrated or annoyed when I feel like they are not acting in a professional manner, not doing an adequate job of teaching, or not treating students properly. I fully acknowledge that nobody made me their judge and that my feelings toward them are sinful and hypocritical, so I have learned to either bite my tongue (not always the right thing to do) or set a different example in hopes that I might influence them to act differently. Most teachers don't like to be corrected or have their behavior or teaching style critiqued by their peers, which in many ways is sad because there is so much benefit from open and honest discourse. Ephesians 4:25 (NIV) says, "Therefore each of you must put off falsehood and speak truthfully to your neighbor, for we are all members of one body." Proverbs 24:26 (NIV) says, "An honest answer is like a kiss on the lips." Unfortunately, some people are not prepared for people to be honest with them. At one point in my career, my pride was so blinding that I dismissed most critique. Proverbs 13:10 tells us that pride leads to conflict, and I can certainly testify to that. I would either argue with them in an attempt to justify my behavior or I would simply write the critique off. I was right. They were wrong. It was as simple as that. Let's face it: while honesty may be the best policy, honesty can also sting. Our ability to offer our comments or the willingness of another teacher to seek our counsel depends upon the relationship you have with the other teacher. The relationships we foster with our students, their parents, our colleagues, and our school leaders will determine whether people value our input or reject it. This is why we must make every effort to build these relationships. At the very least, we must be able to get along with each other despite the differences that exist among us if we are to foster the kind of work atmosphere that leads to success for all the stakeholders.

Getting Along

One of the most prominent themes in the New Testament is the need for followers of Christ to get along with each other. Psalm 133:1 (NIV) says, "How good and pleasant it is when God's people live in unity." While the New Testament was written by followers of Christ, we understand the Bible is timeless and applies to the way we treat people regardless of whether they share our faith or not. How effective would our mission to lead others to Christ be if we only showed Christian behavior toward other Christians? "Getting along" is one manifestation of a person's ability to act in a loving way toward others. It is a reflection of God's belief that we are able to fulfill His mission for us much more effectively when we work together. In Chapter 12 of Romans, Paul explains how all of us are endowed with certain gifts, and that together we make one body. In this body, everyone has a role, a purpose. The body works best when everyone is working together to help each other fulfill their roles. Working for the greater good may require compromise or sacrifice. The same concept applies to the workplace. A workplace where people get along is likely to function much more effectively than a workplace sown with discord. That is true at the school level all the way down to the department and team level. Proverbs 27 tells us, "As iron sharpens iron, so one person sharpens another." "Getting along" doesn't mean that everyone necessarily agrees with one another, that everyone is friends with all the others, or even that a person likes every other person with whom he or she works. "Getting along," like love, humility, patience, and many other virtues is sometimes something that comes naturally, but quite often is something that requires an intentional effort. The author of Hebrews 13:16 (MSG) advises us, "Make sure you don't take things for granted and go slack in working for the common good; share what you have with others. God takes particular pleasure in acts of worship—a different kind of "sacrifice"—that take place in kitchen and workplace and on the streets."

If you are a person in a position of authority or influence, your relationship with the people in your workplace may be different, but your role will still be to bring out the best in people for the common good. Good leaders understand that they don't know everything. I doubt there is a principal on the planet, for example, who has taught every subject at a variety of levels including special education. Many have been out of the classroom environment for a number of years and therefore may not fully understand how the demands of the modern classroom are different than when he or she was still teaching. I believe the most effective principals are those who regularly consult with veteran teachers in order to understand something better. Teachers appreciate this greatly. Thoreau once wrote, "The greatest compliment that was ever paid me was when one asked me what I thought, and attended to my answer." Similarly, it is our job to support the role of our leaders and bring out the best in them as well. There is an abundance of good counsel to be found throughout the Bible on how to get along with others and what this might look like. Consider the following:

- 1 Thessalonians 5:13-15 MSG- Get along among yourselves, each of you doing your part. Our counsel is that you warn the freeloaders to get a move on. Gently encourage the stragglers, and reach out for the exhausted, pulling them to their feet. Be patient with each person, attentive to individual needs. And be careful that when you get on each other's nerves you don't snap at each other. Look for the best in each other, and always do your best to bring it out.

- Romans 12:6-8 MSG- If you preach, just preach God's Message, nothing else; if you help, just help, don't take over; if you teach, stick to your teaching; if you give encouraging guidance, be careful that you don't get bossy; if you're put in charge, don't manipulate; if you're called to give aid to people in distress, keep your eyes open and be quick to respond; if you work with the disadvantaged, don't let yourself get irritated with them or depressed by them. Keep a smile on your face.

- Romans 12:14-19 MSG- Bless your enemies; no cursing under your breath. Laugh with your happy friends when they're happy; share tears when they're down. Get along with each other; don't be stuck up. Make friends with nobodies; don't be the great somebody. Don't hit back; discover the beauty in everyone. If you've got it in you, get along with everybody. Don't insist on getting even; that's not for you to do. "I'll do the judging," says God. "I'll take care of it."

- Romans 12:20-21 MSG- Our Scriptures tell us that if you see your enemy hungry, go buy that person lunch, or if he's thirsty, get him a drink. Your generosity will surprise him with goodness. Don't let evil get the best of you; get the best of evil by doing good.

- Romans 14:19-21 MSG So let's agree to use all our energy in getting along with each other. Help others with encouraging words; don't drag them down by finding fault.

- Romans 15:1—2 NLT We who are strong must be considerate of those who are sensitive about things like this. We must not just please ourselves. We should help others do what is right and build them up in the Lord.

- 1 Peter 3:8-9 NLT- Finally, all of you should be of one mind. Sympathize with each other. Love each other as brothers and sisters. Be tenderhearted, and keep a humble attitude. Don't repay evil for evil. Don't retaliate with insults when people insult you. Instead, pay them back with a blessing. That is what God has called you to do, and he will bless you for it.

- 1 Peter 4:8-9 NIV Above all, love each other deeply, because love covers a multitude of sins. Offer hospitality to one another without grumbling.
- Colossians 3:13 NIV- Bear with each other and forgive one another if any of you has a grievance against someone. Forgive as the Lord forgave you.
- Ephesians 4:2-3 NLT- Always be humble and gentle. Be patient with each other, making allowance for each other's faults because of your love. Make every effort to keep yourselves united in the Spirit, binding yourselves together with peace.
- Ephesians 4:32 NIV- Be kind and compassionate to one another, forgiving each other, just as in Christ God forgave you.
- Hebrews 10:24 NLT- Let us think of ways to motivate one another to acts of love and good works.
- Matthew 5:9 MSG- You're blessed when you can show people how to cooperate instead of compete or fight. That's when you discover who you really are, and your place in god's family.

Matthew 5:9 applies as much to your students as to your colleagues. Students need someone to teach them the benefits of collaboration and cooperation, which sometimes involves sacrifice. This is something they will most likely not learn from t.v. and movies, and it is most assuredly not something they will learn if they pay attention to the words and actions of the legislators and executives at the highest level of our government. Part of that is a media issue. I have no doubt there is a great deal of collaboration and cooperation going on in the halls of Congress, but collaboration and cooperation are not nearly as newsworthy as dissention, mudslinging, and partisan politics.

- Matthew 5:43-47 MSG- You're familiar with the old written law, 'Love your friend,' and its unwritten companion, 'Hate your enemy.' I'm challenging that. I'm telling you to love your enemies. Let them bring out the best in you, not the worst. When someone gives you a hard time, respond with the energies of prayer, for then you are working out of your true selves, your God-created selves. This is what God does. He gives his best—the sun to warm and the rain to nourish—to everyone, regardless: the good and bad, the nice and nasty. If all you do is love the lovable, do you expect a bonus? Anybody can do that. If you simply say hello to those who greet you, do you expect a medal? Any run-of-the-mill sinner does that.
- Luke 6:31 MSG- Here is a simple rule of thumb for behavior: Ask yourself what you want people to do for you; then grab the initiative and do it for *them*! Don't grumble against one another, brothers and sisters, or you will be judged. The Judge is standing at the door.
- Philippians 2:2-4 MSG- If you've gotten anything at all out of following Christ, if his love has made any difference in your life, if being in a community of the Spirit means anything to you, if you have a heart, if you *care*— then do me a favor: Agree with each other, love each other, be deep-spirited friends. Don't push your way to the front; don't sweet-talk your way to the top. Put yourself aside, and help others get ahead. Don't be

obsessed with getting your own advantage. Forget yourselves long enough to lend a helping hand.

- Galatians 5:13-15 NLT For you have been called to live in freedom, my brothers and sisters. But don't use your freedom to satisfy your sinful nature. Instead, use your freedom to serve one another in love. For the whole law can be summed up in this one command: "Love your neighbor as yourself." But if you are always biting and devouring one another, watch out! Beware of destroying one another.

- Galatians 6:1-4 NLV Christian brothers, if a person is found doing some sin, you who are stronger Christians should lead that one back into the right way. Do not be proud as you do it. Watch yourself, because you may be tempted also. Help each other in troubles and problems. This is the kind of law Christ asks us to obey. If anyone thinks he is important when he is nothing, he is fooling himself. Everyone should look at himself and see how he does his own work. Then he can be happy in what he has done. He should not compare himself with his neighbor.

- 2 Timothy 2:14-18 MSG- Repeat these basic essentials over and over to God's people. Warn them before God against pious nitpicking, which chips away at the faith. It just wears everyone out. Concentrate on doing your best for God, work you won't be ashamed of, laying out the truth plain and simple. Stay clear of pious talk that is only talk. Words are not mere words, you know. If they're not backed by a godly life, they accumulate as poison in the soul.

- 2 Timothy 2:23-26 MSG- Refuse to get involved in inane discussions; they always end up in fights. God's servant must not be argumentative, but a gentle listener and a teacher who keeps cool, working firmly but patiently with those who refuse to obey. You never know how or when God might sober them up with a change of heart and a turning to the truth, enabling them to escape the Devil's trap, where they are caught and held captive, forced to run his errands.

- Proverbs 17:9 NLT- Love prospers when a fault is forgiven, but dwelling on it separates close friends.

- Proverbs 17:14 NIV- Starting a quarrel is like breaching a dam; so drop the matter before a dispute breaks out.

- 2 Corinthians 13:11-13 MSG- And that's about it, friends. Be cheerful. Keep things in good repair. Keep your spirits up. Think in harmony. Be agreeable. Do all that, and the God of love and peace will be with you for sure. Greet one another with a holy embrace.

There may be a times when you feel compelled to comment on a colleague's conduct when you see they are behaving in an unprofessional or perhaps even unethical behavior. This is never easy, even when you have a good relationship with the person. Again, much of it depends upon whether you have conducted yourself in a way that has earned the person's respect. It is particularly challenging when you are compelled to speak to someone with whom you have a less developed relationship. This is where I think many of us fail as teachers. I have already confessed it is an area where I have displayed a great deal of moral cowardice. I do not feel comfortable confronting most colleagues about inappropriate behavior. The ability to "bite one's tongue" is not always what God wants. Imagine if Jesus "bit his tongue" instead of confronting people about their sin. A few years back a scandal in Georgia involved groups of teachers changing student answers on the state test so the scores would look better. Dozens of teachers in several school districts were indicted for this. I have no doubt that others were aware of what was going on but did not dare to intervene, just as I did not dare to say anything when I listened to teachers at one school years ago plot to set off certain students so the student would react and be removed from their classes. The teachers never ended up doing it, but I wonder how I would have reacted if they had. Today I would never allow something like that to happen, but at times I still am not comfortable saying something when I see someone has treated a child unfairly. I know that part of my role as a teacher is to be an advocate for children, yet more times than I have been able to keep track of I have listened uneasily to teachers bashing students (or parents, or other teachers, or admin) and not said a word to them about it. I have watched teachers get in a child's face and speak to him or her in a demeaning manner in the middle of the hallway and not say a word to the teachers later. I will listen to a person talk in the most poisonous ways about colleagues or administrators though I suspected they did not have all the information or even the right information and not confront them about it. I have been on the other end of that as well as the person doing the hollering and belittling, the gossiper. God confronted me, but no one at work usually did. We have to work with these people, and we fear that confronting them will adversely affect our working relationship. We worry about offending the offender, or perhaps about people not liking us. This itself is a sin. The Bible warns us that doing the work of Christ will sometimes make us unpopular. The Bible teaches us that confrontation is sometimes necessary. God confronted the Jews through the prophets about their sinful behavior. Jesus also regularly confronted people about their sin. Sometimes His language was direct and to the point, no holds barred, no sugar coating it (in true New Englander fashion). He referred to the Pharisees as a "brood of vipers" and called them on the carpet for their blatant hypocrisy. Most of the time, though, Jesus rebuked people in a more gentile manner. Proverbs 17:10 (MSG) says, "A quiet rebuke to a person of good sense does more than a whack on the head of a fool." Paul knew that his protégé, Timothy would have to confront people in the church who were acting in an ungodly manner. He offered Timothy this counsel:

> Opponents must be gently instructed, in the hope that God will grant them repentance leading them to a knowledge of the truth, and that they will come to their senses and escape from the trap of the devil, who has taken them captive to do his will.
>
> 2 Timothy 1:25-26 NIV

People are less likely to respond to or learn from our counsel if we deliver it in a condescending, judgmental, or belittling manner. In Matthew 7:1-2 (NIV) we are told, "Do not judge, or you too will be judged. For the same way you judge others, you will be judged, and with the measure you use, it will be measured to you." The Message translation of these verses says, "Don't pick on people, jump on their failures, criticize their faults—unless, of course, you want the same treatment. That critical spirit has a way of boomeranging." Luke also warns us about the dangers of judging others Luke 6:37—38 (NIV): "Do not judge, and you will not be judged. Do not condemn, and you will not be condemned."

Paul also warns the Roman Christians about hypocritical criticism and judgment:

> But if you think that leaves you on the high ground where you can point your finger at others, think again. Every time you criticize someone, you condemn yourself. It takes one to know one. Judgmental criticism of others is a well-known way of escaping detection in your own crimes and misdemeanors. But God isn't so easily diverted. He sees right through all such smoke screens and holds you to what you've done. You didn't think, did you, that just by pointing your finger at others you would distract God from seeing all your misdoings and from coming down on you hard? Or did you think that because he's such a nice God, he'd let you off the hook? Better think this one through from the beginning. God is kind, but he's not soft. In kindness he takes us firmly by the hand and leads us into a radical life-change.
>
> Romans 2:1-4 MSG

Later, in Romans 14:10 (MSG), Paul continues:

> So where does that leave you when you criticize a brother? And where does that leave you when you condescend to a sister? I'd say it leaves you looking pretty silly—or worse. Eventually, we're all going to end up kneeling side by side in the place of judgment, facing God. Your critical and condescending ways aren't going to improve your position there one bit.

If we are uncertain about when to "bite our tongue" and opt for the time being to lead by example, Paul provides us with some assistance:

> Welcome with open arms fellow believers who don't see things the way you do. And don't jump all over them every time they do or say something you don't agree with—even when it seems that they are strong on opinions but weak in the faith department. Remember, they have their own history to deal with. Treat them gently.
>
> Romans 14:1 MSG

The verses above remind us that we are not the judge of others in large part because we are all guilty of sin as well. 1 Corinthians 10:12 warns us, "If you think you are standing firm, be careful that you don't fall." We are in no position to counsel others if we live in a manner that lacks integrity.

Service

In Chapter Two, we learned that one of the defining characteristics of humility is service to others. We read how the Lord of Lords demonstrated humble service when He washed the feet of His disciplines during His last meal on earth. In Mark 41-45 (MSG), Christ tells His disciples,

"You've observed how godless rulers throw their weight around," he said, "and when people get a little power how quickly it goes to their heads. It's not going to be that way with you. Whoever wants to be great must become a servant. Whoever wants to be first among you must be your slave. That is what the Son of Man has done: He came to serve, not to be served—and then to give away his life in exchange for many who are held hostage."

In his letter to the Galatians, Paul writes,

It is absolutely clear that God has called you to a free life. Just make sure that you don't use this freedom as an excuse to do whatever you want to do and destroy your freedom. Rather, use your freedom to serve one another in love; that's how freedom grows. For everything we know about God's Word is summed up in a single sentence: Love others as you love yourself. That's an act of true freedom. If you bite and ravage each other, watch out—in no time at all you will be annihilating each other, and where will your precious freedom be then?

Galatians 5:13-15 MSG

In his letter to the church at Corinth, Paul wrote,

Even though I am free of the demands and expectations of everyone, I have voluntarily become a servant to any and all in order to reach a wide range of people: religious, nonreligious, meticulous moralists, loose-living immoralists, the defeated, the demoralized—whoever. I didn't take on their way of life. I kept my bearings in Christ—but I entered their world and tried to experience things from their point of view. I've become just about every sort of servant there is in my attempts to lead those I meet into a God-saved life. I did all this because of the Message. I didn't just want to talk about it; I wanted to be in on it!

1 Corinthians 9:19-23 MSG

I Corinthians 10:24 (NLV) counsels us, "Do not work only for your own good. Think of what you can do for others." The Message interpretation of Romans 15:2 says, "Strength is for service, not status. Each one of us needs to look after the good of the people around us, asking ourselves, 'How can I help?'"

Some teachers may not feel like they have a whole lot to offer to others. They may be new to the profession, new to the school, new to the subject, a person who teaches outside the "regular" classroom, or someone who has been struggling to be a more effective teacher. The Bible tells us that *all* people have been bestowed with gifts that we are to use to serve others:

There are different kinds of gifts. But it is the same Holy Spirit Who gives them. There are different kinds of work to be done for Him. But the work is for the same Lord. There are different ways of doing His work. But it is the same God who uses all these ways in all people. The Holy Spirit works in each person in one way or another for the good of all.

1 Corinthians 12:4-7 NLV

It may take some time for a person to figure out what his or her gift *is*, but no one should question whether or not they actually have a gift. In 1 Corinthians 12:8-10, Paul lists a few of these gifts, but to many people these "gifts" can see a bit archaic or out-of-place in our modern society. While the gifts of wisdom, preaching, and faith seem reasonable and applicable, the gifts of healing, prophesying, discerning demons, working miracles, speaking in tongues, or interpreting the speech of tongues seem quite extraordinary to believers and downright supernatural to people who may be new to the faith. One should not think, however, that these are the only types of gifts God bestows upon people. These are the gifts of *The Holy Spirit*, which means they are things God can do through His Holy Spirit living in us if He chooses. But there are many other gifts or abilities that are mentioned directly and indirectly throughout the Bible. One may have the gift of compassion, the gift of listening, the gift of empathy, the gift of being able to see beyond someone's façade, the ability to spread joy and laughter, the ability to comfort, the ability to teach, the ability to promote teamwork, the ability to bring out the best in people, the ability to inspire, the gift of a complimentary spirit, the gift of physical strength, the gift of a charitable heart, the gift of intelligence, the gift of discernment. Everyone has a gift or gifts. I frequently wish that I had the gift of spreading joy and laughter. I wish I had the gift of spreading feelings of peace and calmness. Sadly, those are not among my gifts. I have suffered with depression and anxiety all my adult life. I have been told at times that I present an outward image of someone who is too serious all the time. I can come off as someone who is distant and at times easily agitated. I usually do not present as someone who is joyful and who feels the peace that comes with a personal relationship with Jesus. I used to be funnier, more outgoing, capable of gut wrenching laughter, but as I have grown older the depression and other health issues have taken a bit of a toll on me. When I appear light-hearted, jovial, am joking around with others, even something as simple as smiling, it is often something very intentional. It is not usually a projection of what is going on inside. I am not necessarily covering up anxiety or depressed thoughts. Sometimes I am feeling relatively calm inside, but that in my case does not automatically manifest itself as outwardly joyful behavior. I am not wired for these things, or perhaps I was at one time but these connections have become corroded as my body ages. My body does not produce enough of the right chemicals to enable me to feel over-the-top "happiness," but it is absolutely critical in my line of work, as a husband, and as a father that I present an outgoing, social face to the world. I don't feel like I am "faking it." I am projecting the behavior that honors God and feeds my family and students because I know that it is an illness that affects my thought patterns rather than a true manifestation of dissatisfaction with my life. The Bible tells us to wear the outward appearance of joy which comes from knowing we are saved. It does not tell us to wear the outward appearance of happiness which comes for the world.

I know without a doubt how incredibly blessed I am and I will fight to demonstrate gratitude for those blessings especially when that fight is against faulty wiring. But it is no easy fight. My form of depression with associated anxiety is mild in comparison to people I have known with depression so crippling they can hardly get out of bed. Never-the-less, anyone who has experienced either condition knows that these conditions at any clinical level, even mild, become one of the filters through which we process our world and as such can at times drive our actions. Those of us with these conditions face the choice of dealing with their effects by a.) dampening them down a bit with some help from meds and therapy so that we can still feel or b.) numbing ourselves on higher doses of meds that strip of us of our ability to feel much of anything. Though he was never diagnosed as having depression, I am convinced that my father suffered from it and did his dampening with alcohol. He was seldom able to just have one drink. When he drank, he almost always became intoxicated. For much of his adult life, he drank almost daily. In the first situation we are able to feel passionately but that passion at times becomes misguided and causes us to focus on what isn't right in our lives even though we may recognize that these negative feelings are completely illogical. With numbing, we are stripped of passion altogether. In the lesser-medicated situation we may do a hundred God-honoring things that may go unnoticed but then become focused on the negative and do or say one really stupid thing that stands out to others. Because the one hundred little things are easily overlooked or easily forgotten, the negative behavior ends up leaving the impression that those unfavorable attributes of our character are the sum of who we are.

I have prayed for years to be healed and God knows that I feel cheated and sometimes angry at Him because He has not chosen to heal me. I argue with Him that I cannot be "a light in the darkness" if I focus on the negative or when I come off to others as having a flat affect or periodically say or do something stupid that sticks out in people's minds. Each time I am directed back to Paul in his second letter to the church at Corinth. God would not remove Paul's thorn from his life. It served a purpose that Paul may not have understood and for some length of time apparently found hard to accept. The same must be true for those of us with emotional disorders. Depression will always be part of our fallen world. I live with it and have a good life. I still love and try to honor the Lord. It seems logical that God needs people like me to show that one can live a productive life with anxiety disorder and anxiety. Perhaps one day God will cure me and I will then become a different kind of example for people, from persevering throughout the illness to gaining victory over it with God's help. These conditions are a gift, not one I would choose on my own but a gift that enables me to serve others by showing them we can live a productive and satisfying life even with these particular thorns. In 2 Corinthians 12:9 (NIV) God tells Paul, "My grace is sufficient for you, for my power is made perfect in weakness." God did not create useless people who have nothing to offer, who simply take up space and breathe the common air. Whether or not we discover our gifts and then choose to use them to serve others and honor God is not the same as not having gifts. In 1 Peter 4:10 (NIV), we are told, "Each of you should use whatever gift you have received to serve others, as faithful stewards of God's grace in its various forms." How can we use our gifts to help our colleagues? Here a few suggestions, many of which fall under the category of being charitable:

- Be a good listener when people are frustrated and need to talk to someone about it.
- Help a new teacher develop his or lessons, grade papers, or develop activities. Provide him or her with suggestions on how to establish good classroom management procedures, build relationships with students or colleagues, or communicate with parents.
- Cover someone's duty for them. You may do this when you see they are feeling a bit frazzled, but you may offer to do it simply as a gesture of kindness.
- Offer your classroom as a place to send students who need a "time out" from one of your team or department member's classes.

- Offer to do the least desirable duties or serve on the committees that require the most work.
- Offer to create the worksheets, do the photocopying, or develop the common assessments your department uses based on feedback about which questions or types of questions the members would like to incorporate.
- Offer frequent, sincere compliments when you notice a colleague acting admirably.
- "Gossip" about the good things you see your colleagues doing in your discussions with other colleagues, with parents, and with school leaders.
- Be a calming presence in the midst of a tense situation.
- Model cooperation, support, collaboration, relationship building.
- Offer to work with a person whom others may find particularly challenging to work with.
- Share your concerns in a productive and effective manner without complaining.
- Carrying out your duties and responsibilities without complaining, even if they are unpleasant or don't seem to make a whole lot of sense.
- Be willing to make sacrifices, even if it means you will go without so that another teacher does not have to (however, be careful not to compromise the needs of your students or the quality of your instruction by doing so).
- Surprise your colleagues by bringing in a batch of brownies or some fresh vegetables from your garden.
- Offer your services freely with no expectation that you will be repaid in kind.
- Model optimism and enthusiasm for your work. Focus on the positive. If someone asks you how your day is going, don't lie or pretend all is well when it isn't but don't go on and on about how bad it has been. Instead consider saying something like, "The kids are acting a bit wild today, but we're going to work through it."
- Show a sincere interest in your colleagues. Ask about their children, their grandchildren, about their trip to the beach, or about their interests. Somewhere in these discussions you may find ways to connect with them.
- During your planning period, offer to cover a class for someone who needs to step out for a while to attend a child's holiday party.
- Establish that you are open to and value critique from others, even if it is offered in a less than tactful manner. If the person's comment accurately reflects something you did or said, thank them and tell them you will try to do a better job at it next time. Don't start arguing back and forth that you have "seen them do the same thing or worse" even if it is true. If the person's observation about you is not accurate, calmly say, "I think you may have misunderstood what I said or what actually happened. If you'd like, I can explain to you." I have already discussed how admitting that you said or did something wrong to students is a powerful way to build a positive relationship with them. The same thing is true with your colleagues, though it will take your colleagues a whole lot longer to change their perceptions about you.
- Organize a mini potluck at the end of the quarter where everyone brings in a dish to share during planning. In big schools like mine, it makes sense to limit this to the grade level.
- Have some fun. Thomas Aquinas once wrote, "It is for the relaxation of the mind that we make use, from time to time, of playful deeds and jokes."

How often do I do the things mentioned above? Not nearly enough, and when I do a very long time may go by between one act and the next. I used to do a whole lot more, but the work load over the past five years has increased so much that I find it difficult just to keep my head above water. If this is true for me, then it is most likely true for others and it is now more than ever that people need a "gift" from us. It requires intentionality. In the whirlwind of all the varied tasks we try to balance, finding time for random acts of kindness can be a challenge. I keep telling myself I need to put a note up on my computer that reads, "do some random act of kindness today." Perhaps that would help. When we do these things for our colleagues, we should not try to make a show of it. We are not doing it to earn praise from others. Remember what is written in Matthew 6:1-4 NLT:

> Watch out! Don't do your good deeds publicly, to be admired by others, for you will lose the reward from your Father in heaven. When you give to someone in need, don't do as the hypocrites do—blowing trumpets in the synagogues and streets to call attention to their acts of charity! I tell you the truth, they have received all the reward they will ever get. But when you give to someone in need, don't let your left hand know what your right hand is doing. Give your gifts in private, and your Father, who sees everything, will reward you.

This doesn't mean that you should do everything anonymously. It's hard to influence people if you do everything as though you were a secret agent. The passage simply means that we should not draw attention to our service. If the person you are serving chooses to share or if others notice, that is fine. If they choose not to share and nobody else knows about it, which may be the case sometimes, then that is fine too. God knows.

I would like to end this line of discussion by challenging each of us to *observe the actions of others* and *take note of the small things they are doing that honor God* whether they are intentionally trying to honor Him or not. If we are intentional about *looking for* acts of Godly behavior we will most likely become aware that they are happening far more than we realized and that can not only be inspiring but can lead us to see others in a different light. We also need to be conscious not to become "closed off" from others. I have worked in schools that were very cliquey and in schools where a large number of teachers kind of "did their own" thing without a whole lot of collaboration or interaction with colleagues. For much of my career, I have preferred to do things primarily on my own. It was not easy for me to transition to working as a member of a professional learning community. I still prefer to design my own lessons, activities, assessments, and enrichment opportunities. Part of the reason for this is that I like to tailor my lessons to my students. Another reason is that I tend to learn the content and teach the content better when I design my own lessons. I do share what I develop with my grade level department. And while I develop most of my own materials, we collaborate closely in most of the things we do. I have little doubt God finds this more desirable than my being an island unto myself. It has been my experience that schools which foster and nurture true collaboration (as opposed to meeting just for the sake of meeting) between educators run smoother, have more content staff members, and are more successful at getting the best out of their particular population of students. I have also found that people in these types of schools "get along" better most of the time as well. The Bible tells us we are all parts of the same body. We should make every effort to get along with each other and promote the greater good. We should act in a loving way toward our students, their parents, our colleagues, and our leaders. When Jesus sent out the twelve for the first time, he didn't send each one alone. He sent them in pairs. We are not hard-wired to "go it alone" in life nor in our Christian walk. We need others who can support us, help us work through things, gently rebuke us when needed and help us with accountability.

> Two people are better off than one, for they can help each other succeed. If one person falls, the other can reach out and help. But someone who falls alone is in real trouble. Likewise, two people lying close together can keep each other warm. But how can one be warm alone? A person standing alone can be attacked and defeated, but two can stand back-to-back and conquer. Three are even better, for a triple-braided cord is not easily broken
>
> Ecclesiastes 4:9-12 NLT

One person is good; more are better. We have a lot of small groups at our church, but I know of none that are arranged by one's profession. I have often thought about starting a small group for teachers, but truth be told I have been afraid to do so. With God's guidance I have managed to write a book, yet I still do not feel like I am a worthy candidate to start a Christian teacher small group. Part of my problem is that I have an unusual "thorn" for someone who is in front of people as much as I am: one of the characteristics related to my depression is a social anxiety in certain types of small group settings and even settings like family reunions. I can talk to an auditorium full of people, but put me in a small group and weird things start happening. You would never notice my restlessness because I hide it very well, but it is always there. My wife, also a teacher, suffers from the same type of anxiety. We are better together, but that doesn't necessarily mean it comes easy for many of us.

William Arthur Ward once wrote very eloquently about the "trails" we leave behind us during our lifetime, and I would like to end this chapter with this passage:

> Every person has the power to make others happy.
> Some do it simply by entering a room –
> others by leaving the room.
> Some individuals leave trails of gloom;
> others, trails of joy.
> Some leave trails of hate and bitterness;
> others, trails of love and harmony.
> Some leave trails of cynicism and pessimism;
> others trails of faith and optimism.
> Some leave trails of criticism and resignation;
> others trails of gratitude and hope.
> What kind of trails do you leave?

CHAPTER SEVEN

Trials

The tests of life are to make, not break us. Trouble may demolish a man's business but build up his character. The blow at the outward man may be the greatest blessing to the inner man. If God, then, puts or permits anything hard in our lives, be sure that the real peril, the real trouble, is that we shall lose if we flinch or rebel.

Maltbie Davenport Babcock

I took a burden to the Lord
To cast and leave it there.
I knelt and told Him of my plight,
And wrestled deep in prayer.

But rising up to go my way
I felt a deep despair,
For as I tried to trudge along,
My burden was still there!

Why didn't You take my burden, Lord?
Oh, won't you take it, please.
Again I asked the Lord for help, His answering words were these:

My child, I want to help you out
I long to take your load.
I want to take your burdens too
As you walk along life's road.

But this you must remember,
This one thing you must know...
I cannot take your burden
Until you let it go.

Betty Curti

'Tis easy enough to be pleasant, When life flows along like a song; But the man worthwhile is the one who will smile when everything goes dead wrong.

Ella Wheeler Wilcox

By pressing into the kingdom of God is denoted a breaking through opposition and difficulties. There is in the expression a plain intimation of difficulty. If there were no opposition, but the way was all clear and open, there would be no need of pressing to get along. They therefore that are pressing into the kingdom of God, go on with such engagedness, that they break through the difficulties that are in the way. They are so set for salvation, that those things by which others are discouraged, and stopped, and turned back, do not stop them, but they press through them.

Jonathan Edwards

In order to find the worth of the anchor, we need to feel the stress of the storm.

Corrie Ten Boom

We are always on the anvil; by trials God is shaping us for higher things.

Harriet Ward Beecher

God, who foresaw your tribulation, has specially armed you to go through it, not without pain but without stain.

C.S. Lewis

Foundational Concepts

- ✝ The Bible promises that we will all experience trials in our life. Even Jesus faced many trials.
- ✝ Trials are used by God to develop faith, strength, and perseverance in order to prepare us for an eternity with our Lord.
- ✝ God is always with us through our trials.

Central Questions

1. Why must we face trials in our life?
2. How do we face these trials so that we may grow from them as God desires?
3. What does the Bible tell us about worrying?

I think one of the greatest misunderstandings people have when they first give their lives to Christ is that somehow the trials of life will no longer plague them. This could not be farther from the truth. I recently learned this lesson the hard way (discussed in the epilogue). A life changing relationship with Christ should change the way we perceive, accept, and handle trials, but in no way will it eliminate the trials from our lives. On the contrary, Satan's army upon seeing you give your life to Christ work to increase your trials in hopes that you will give up on your new faith. Before becoming discouraged, remember that even Jesus experienced trials throughout His life of Earth. He was born in a stable to outcast parents and spent the first few years of his life on the run in a foreign land. He began His ministry by fasting for forty days in the desert. During his ministry he was accepted by many but violently rejected by others-even in His own home town. Many days He may not have been certain where His next meal might be or where He would sleep. He was challenged repeatedly by the powerful and influential religious leaders of His time. In the Garden of Gethsemane, Jesus' intense anguish showed just how human He was. On top of all this His constant companions, His disciples, were at times argumentative, doubtful, whiney, self-centered, unreliable, hot-tempered, and just plain dense when it came to understanding Christ's mission. They eventually "got it" and would go on to face severe trials of their own including martyrdom.

Another well documented life of trials is exposed in the life of the Apostle Paul. Beaten nearly to death on several occasions, shipwrecked, imprisoned repeatedly, maligned, challenged, abandoned; Paul experienced more than his fair share of trials. The aforementioned trials were external. As with all of us, I have no doubt that Paul also experienced inner trials that may have been even more of a challenge for him because they were with him at *all* times. Paul constantly battled his sinful nature and, if we are to glean anything from his own words, often lost. As mentioned previously, Paul wrote of an ongoing trial, his "thorn," though the exact nature of this thorn is unknown. It has been suggested by some that Paul suffered from poor eyesight. Failing eyesight is certainly a trial for anyone. In addition to earning a living as a tentmaker which would have required a coordinated effort between his hands and his eyes, Paul most likely had to rely upon a competent scribe whom he could trust to accurately pen his letters for him. I have also heard it suggested that while Paul was an extremely eloquent writer, he was not a dynamic public speaker. Public speaking was an art form in the Greek-speaking areas of the Mediterranean and in western Asia. People were accustomed to the dynamic, theatrical speaking style of skilled Greek orators whose speeches were as much a performance as a message. As a culture we are still drawn to a great public speaker; unfortunately, we too are often mesmerized by the presentation rather than compelled by the message. I am certainly guilty of this. Before choosing Savannah Christian Church (now Compassion Christian), I visited a number of churches. Some of the pastors presented a great message, but their speaking style was not dynamic enough for me. I admit I did not feel moved by the message. Others were very dynamic, but the message did not move me. Some were simply too dynamic. I was raised Catholic, and could never make the adjustment to the over-the-top, theatrical evangelistic style of some ministers. The first time I heard the head pastor at my now home church speak, though, I knew this was the church God meant for me to be a part of. The head pastor delivers the message of God in an incredibly dynamic, effective, and passionate manner. During his time as head pastor, our church has grown from several hundred to over 8,000 members who now attend services in one of several satellite locations. We love the combination of a dynamic presentation and a compelling message. This human characteristic, I believe, had its roots in ancient Greece. If Paul was indeed great at writing his thoughts but not so eloquent and powerful in person, one can imagine how difficult that might have been for him given the nature of his calling.

In addition to these trials I also believe that one of Paul's greatest trials, perhaps even the one he referred to as his "thorn," was the challenge of living a life of humility. Paul himself says he was given the thorn to "keep [him] from becoming conceited." He was Christ's chosen apostle to bring *The Word* to the whole known world, the man responsible for establishing churches throughout the Mediterranean and Western Asia. What a tremendous challenge it must have been for him to remain humble. What a challenge it must have been not to think or say to people who were maligning or challenging him, "Don't you know who *I* am and what *I* have done?" I do not doubt that he desperately wanted to feel a deep sense of humility, but Paul was human. He may have been able to demonstrate humility most of the time, but I think there is evidence in his writings that he struggled with it as well. What is most important when considering Paul's thorn is Christ's response to Paul when Paul asked three times for his thorn to be removed. The Lord told Paul, "My grace is sufficient for you, for my power is made perfect in weakness" (2 Corinthians 12:9). It helped him to remain humble. Our thorns, our trials, have a purpose. Neither external nor internal trials will ever leave us as followers of Christ. They can't. For one thing, we live in a fallen world where trials are inherent. More importantly, though, trials are *necessary* for us to grow in our faith. That is not to say that everyone's faith grows through facing trials. As I mentioned above, the way we perceive, accept, and handle trials will determine whether the trial builds us up or tears us down. But there is simply no way around it: if Jesus Christ was not exempt from trials then surely we cannot expect His followers to be exempt either.

So the first understanding we must have about trials is that they will happen to all of us in all areas of our lives: family, personal relationships, work, the world at large. Some trials will certainly be the result of a self-inflicted wound: poor money management, bad choices, misguided priorities. Many, though, are trials that hit us from out of the blue. Ironically, I would argue that it is the more prevalent, ever-present, day-to-day trials that most of us fail at the most. When we are torn, battered, and bleeding; when we are watching a child fight a potentially terminal illness; when a spouse is killed by a drunk driver on her way home from work-at times like these even many non-believers will turn to God. But we usually forget to see the day-to-day challenges of work, marriage, parenting, life, for what they are: trials. As with Job, trials are not sent by God but may be sanctioned by Him for a higher purpose.

Teachers face trials every day. All of us have or have had students, colleagues, or parents who test every bit of our skill and patience. We deal with students and even entire families who are apathetic toward education. We are tasked with finding ways to teach students with a myriad of different learning styles, ability levels, family situations, disabilities, and development stages. The "public education system" is often maligned in the media as the cause of all the problems in our nation. I have read a good bit about the educational systems of other developed nations to whom we are often compared, and I am convinced that no other nation has an educational system that goes to such great lengths to teach such a diverse population. We also face the challenges of an increasing workload. Curriculum standards change every few years because the last "great thing" somehow ends up being not such a great thing at all to the new reformers. We have new instructional methods mandated nearly every year. No sooner do we feel that we have started to get a handle on one thing than it changes to another. The amount of documentation required of teachers for a whole host of things takes, I would estimate, up to 25-35% of the teacher's time. I'm not referring to planning lessons or grading papers. I'm talking about parent communication logs, individual intervention plans for struggling students loss of instructional time, redundant backups of the same information in several different places. And all the while class sizes are increasing though planning time in many schools is decreasing. We have "additional duties and responsibilities" also written into our contracts. I have never been the kind of teacher who clocks in and out right on the eight-hour mark, but neither did I ever anticipate that my job (if I do it at a high level) would become impossible to do in less than a ten-hour day plus some time on weekends. I face the challenge of getting all my work done and the challenge of not becoming resentful toward my work at the same time.

For teachers in high-risk schools, concerns about one's own safety and the safety of students is constantly lurking in the background like some ominous shadow. I was watching some videos on YouTube recently where students were captured on film disrupting a classroom. I observed students running around the classroom making fun of or taunting the teacher. In some cases, students got in a teacher's face and threatened to harm him or her. The picked up chairs and held them high like they were going to strike the teacher. Does it matter that they really didn't intend to hit her with the chair? Some even put their hands on the teacher. In one case, an elderly teacher was thrown to the ground because she took a cell phone from a student who was texting in class. There was absolutely no recognition of the teacher's authority nor for the classroom as a learning environment. I have seen this kind of behavior in schools before and the most disturbing part of it is how minimal the consequences are for this type of behavior in these schools. When a teacher in an environment like this snaps and goes off on the students or when a campus police officer uses excessive force (which is wrong) it is all over the news and the web in a matter of hours. We should not condone this adult behavior, but what we almost never see and seldom hear of on the news is the side of the coin, mainly the rampant abuse of teachers that exists in schools where students acting like thugs are allowed to rule the school. In a period of years, we have gone from the extreme of being able to paddle students in our classes (which I am not advocating for) to becoming far too concerned with how we might damage the self-esteem of a child who tears our learning environment apart by disciplining him or her too sternly. We have become enablers of misconduct and this is so contrary to what the Bible calls for us to do with regards to discipline. In some cases, we have lost the ability to protect our learning environment from these students. Even in some of the best schools I have witnessed a student behave in a way that would realistically result in arrest for disturbing the peace or even criminal threatening outside of school. It's hard not to feel powerless and intensely frustrated as teachers. In this overblown effort to protect a child's self-esteem in cases like this we have reinforced in them behavior patterns that will ultimately be as harmful as self-esteem issues. This may fit the category of a "trial," but in this case it also fits the category of being a "crisis," and a crisis situation should be dealt with in a much more immediate and firm manner. This is not the kind of trial we should be expected to "endure" any more than a spouse should be expected to endure being physically abused and to stay with the abusive spouse. I consider this far more than just a personal trial: it is a community, state, or national crisis. I do not think it is an exaggeration to say that teachers in some schools enter a war zone every day and they ought to receive combat pay on top of their regular salaries. They fight this battle on the front and with very, very little backup from "the command." But even so-called "safe" schools are at risk. With the number of random acts of violence and homicides that have happened in these "safe" schools, all of us must now look differently at that particular withdrawn child who seems not to fit in. Some school districts are even contemplating arming teachers, though if the world is any example, sooner or later that could backfire when one of those armed teachers "snaps" or perhaps harms or kills an innocent bystander in the process of trying to protect others from a potential threat.

There has to be a balance, of course. Thug-like behavior is one thing, general misconduct another. If we treat students who act out as though they are thugs, we very well could create a self-fulfilling scenario. We need to treat criminal behavior in our classrooms like criminal behavior, but on the other hand we need to help students who engage in lower level misconduct to learn a better way of dealing with whatever issue exists that is at the root of the behavior. We should care very much about a child's self-esteem and dignity, but that does not mean that we withhold discipline. I have seen far too much harm come to students when we lose the battle during one of our trials and treat children in a condescending manner that strips them of their dignity, hope, and self-esteem. Again, I am not advocating that we always treat kids with "kid gloves." I believe in tough love, but the important word in that phrase is "love." Love does no harm. Love builds up. I haven't worked in many other professions, but enough to know that trials come with all jobs. But I selfishly believe that much more is at stake in our profession than most because there is no other like ours when it comes to exposure to the youth of our nation. Regardless of where you end up in life, you will have passed through dozens of teachers on the way. If we can learn to deal with the trials of our job, we can change lives for the better. If, on the other hand, our trials constantly keep us on the edge or even over the edge, at best we might "do no harm" to our children. Unfortunately, the danger of trials is that they can destroy us and those around us if we allow the trials rather than our faith to dictate our lives.

So how then do we deal with these trials? First, we must anticipate them. In John 16:33 (NIV), Christ tells us, "In the world you *will* have much trouble." I enter every school year knowing that I will experience trials as opposed to putting energy into hoping that I will not. When we anticipate trials, we can begin the process of preparing ourselves spiritually and mentally for them by studying God's Word. We can work to build relationships with believers who can provide us with love and support throughout our trials and whom we can serve as well through their trials. We can work to develop spiritual courage. Trials will at times merely nag us, at other times distract us, slow us down, discourage us, cause us to worry excessively, divert us away from something important. At times, though, trials may rip the limbs from our body, crush us beneath an avalanche of boulders, burn our homes to the ground, steal from us the people we love most. Anticipating trials does not mean we can predict them nor that we should sit around worrying about or waiting for them. Most of us carry a spare tire on our vehicle but don't drive around worrying the whole time that this will be the day we have to use it. Being prepared for trials is not the same as worrying about them. In fact, The Bible explicitly commands us *not* to live lives consumed by worry or "stress." In Matthew, Chapter 6:25-27 (NIV), the Lord tells us,

> Therefore I tell you, do not worry about your life, what you will eat or drink; or about your body, what you will wear. Is not life more than food, and the body more than clothes? Look at the birds of the air; they do not sow or reap or store away in barns, and yet your heavenly Father feeds them. Are you not much more valuable than they? Can any one of you by worrying add a single hour to your life?

In verse 34, He continues, "*Therefore do not worry about tomorrow, for tomorrow will worry about itself. Each day has enough trouble of its own.*"

In his letter to the church at Philippi, Paul counsels,

> Don't fret or worry. Instead of worrying, pray. Let petitions and praises shape your worries into prayers, letting God know your concerns. Before you know it, a sense of God's wholeness, everything coming together for good, will come and settle you down. It's wonderful what happens when Christ displaces worry at the center of your life"
>
> Philippians 4:6-7 MSG

Anxiety can attack all areas of our lives. During the day it distracts or even consumes us. At night it floods our mind. I totally get that "not worrying" or not experiencing anxiety is easier said than done. I am an expert on the topic of anxiety. I have suffered with anxiety issues much of my adult life and that has at times resulted in crippling anxiety attacks. I sometimes wake up in the morning and feel my body already sliding toward an attack maybe as a result of a dream or because I went to bed knowing that when I awoke I had a long list of tasks ahead of me but not enough time to accomplish them-at least in my mind. Some of this is a result of genetics, but much of it is a result of holes in my faith, failing to recognize my limitations, not establishing boundaries when it comes to work, and not taking care of my health as well as I should. This is a constant trial for me, mostly self-inflicted! For example, I have been on vacation all this week and yet I have spent perhaps a total of sixteen hours on school related work. I still have three days left but have hours more work to do just to get my lessons planned for when we return. There have been times when I simply could not turn off the worries that were coursing through my mind. Midnight rolls around. Then 1:00 a.m. I know that in a few short hours the alarm will sound and I will have to get ready for work. That increases the stress even more because I begin to worry that I will not be as alert, energetic, or sharp as I need to be. Try facing one hundred or more tweenagers or thirty rambunctious first-graders when you are not alert, energetic, or sharp. These lovely creatures of God will eat you alive. Never underestimate the value of a good night's sleep. In my case the amount of sleep I get has a tremendous effect on my blood pressure. The less sleep I get, the more difficulty I have keeping it under control the next day.

A couple years ago, anxiety launched a sneak attack on me. I was working a brutal schedule, much of which was self-inflicted, but I did not *feel* consciously stressed. I had developed some gradually escalating health problems that often caused chest complications and pronounced fatigue. One day while sitting at my desk during my planning I was going over my "to do" list when my whole body went numb. I started feeling like I would pass out. My chest tightened and I had difficulty breathing. Given my family history of heart disease on both sides, I felt certain it was a heart attack. The panic that came with that thought increased my sense of panic and fear even more. I left the school that day in an ambulance. My daughter was in my 4th block class, and I felt certain the word would get around because a number of students saw me wheeled out. The diagnosis turned out to be a major anxiety attack. I had had anxiety attacks before in my twenties, but those mostly wreaked havoc on my intestinal system causing nausea and violent muscular spasms in my digestive system. You can guess what comes with that. Imagine a four-hour flight with a spastic colon and only one bathroom for over one hundred passengers. Other underlying issues were discovered during my battery of tests, but the anxiety was ready to wreak havoc with or without that compounding factor. For months I experienced the aftershocks of this event. I would have anxiety attacks that resulted even from stressful dreams. Through a recommitment to prayer, reviewing my own work in this book and the Bible, and with the assistance of medication my family and I continue to work through my health issues. We are adjusting to a "new normal."

While no one enjoys living with a medical condition that can be debilitating at times, I understand that in my life it was necessary to bring me back to God. During the ten-day period when I was waiting to hear the results of a biopsy of some swollen lymph nodes in my lungs, I was forced to take a serious look at my life. My daughter was baptized during that ten-day period and she did not know during this time there was a possibility that I might have cancer. As I stood there in the lake with her and our pastor, I remember thinking to myself, "I may never get to see her graduate, walk her down the aisle, or hold her children, but I am seeing this and this is what matters most." My life had become and still has a tendency to become too much about work and too little about God and my family. God did what He had to do to break through my stubborn resistance.

My illness keeps me connected to God. I still wrestle with Him for control, easily falling back into the path of a workaholic. But the frequent discomfort in my chest, the fatigue, my bouts of anxiety and mild depression-these things are referred to as thorns for a reason. They hurt. They also serve to remind me that God's grace is enough and that I need to maintain a Godly perspective about my priorities. So while I know first-hand it may not be easy to turn our worries over to God, particularly for those of us with more serious anxiety or depression, it is still crucial that we pray as often and as long as is necessary for God to wrestle this anxiety back from us. It may be a long process for some of us who have ignored God's counsel even though we certainly know what He expects from us. Some days are better than others for me. I sometimes need help sleeping, help with the depression, and help with anxiety. I turn to God more now than I ever have because even meds can only help so much. I had become complacent and that is not where God wanted or needed me to be. God wants us to trust Him and believe that He will see us through our trials. When we are willing to turn our worry over to God, sleep comes easier. Psalms 4:8 says, "In peace I will lie down and sleep, for you alone, LORD, make me dwell in safety." When David's son, Solomon became king, he inherited his father's faith. In Proverbs 3:24, he echoes, "You can go to bed without fear: you will lie down and sleep soundly.[1]" We have

---

[1] Later in Solomon's life, he found it increasingly difficult to follow his own advice. In Ecclesiastes, we are provided an intimate look into Solomon's self-reflection and his thoughts about the meaningless of life. Solomon was considered one of the wisest men in history. He was fabulously wealthy and indulged in whatever his heart desired. Some people may find Solomon's despair worrisome; if Solomon who was renowned for wisdom and for providing counsel struggled to follow his own teachings, how then can we follow sound counsel? I have a different take on it. Solomon in all his greatness was still subject to failure, to feelings of worthlessness, futility, and emptiness. If someone of his stature, one who received such enormous blessings from God, can fail then certainly I should not beat myself to death when I fail. We sometimes picture the "heroes" of the Bible as somehow above the kind of failure we experience. Nothing could be farther from the truth. Moses, Jacob, David, Solomon, Paul, the disciples- they each experienced failure many times. The Bible does not hide the failures of these important figures or the failures of others in the Bible. To be human is to be prone to sin, to failure. That is precisely why we need Jesus. His death erases our failures and gives us a fresh start each time we repent. We have hope because we no longer need to fear our own imperfections. We know that we can fail and be forgiven, that we can fail and yet still have a place in heaven. Only Christ was perfect.

to forge in our memory the fact that we made it through trials in the past because we tend to forget that in the stress of the moment.

Those familiar with the life of Corrie Ten Boom know that if anyone had cause to worry it was her. She never knew when Nazis would storm her home and carry her and/or a family member away to a death camp. Her family was never certain where the next meal might come from. When she and her sister finally did end up in a death camp, neither she nor any of the other captives knew what type of tortuous treatment awaited them each day. They ate bread made partially with sawdust and soup that contained only the peelings of the potatoes. Their bunks were infested with parasites like fleas and their bodies were emaciated. Yet Corrie praised God for the fleas because they kept the Nazi guards from entering the sleeping areas. In their absence, Corrie and her sister were able to spread the hope of Christ to captives who needed hope more than anything else. Miss Ten Boom referred to worry as, "...an old man with bended head, carrying a load of feathers which he thinks are lead."(Ten Boom, 168). "Worrying," she wrote, "is carrying tomorrow's load with today's strength- carrying two days at once. It is moving into tomorrow ahead of time. Worrying doesn't empty tomorrow of its sorrow, it empties today of its strength." God wants us to trust Him enough that we live a life without worrying. Pray as King David did in Psalms 16:8 (NLT): "I know the Lord is always with me. I will not be shaken, for He is always with me. In Psalms 27:1 (NLT), David asks, "The Lord is my light and my salvation, so why should I be afraid?" In Psalms 118:5 (NLT), the psalmist testifies, "In my distress I prayed to the Lord, and the Lord answered me and set me free." This doesn't mean nothing bad will happen. In his psalms, David goes back and forth from praising God to being angry at God for "abandoning" him. In the balanced moments of our lives, we need to believe God will always be there for us when we need Him the most. A number of years ago, a new, very promising young teacher was hired at our school. He came in with tremendous enthusiasm. By his second year, he admitted that he dreaded coming to work every day, that he was miserable most of the day and couldn't wait to leave once school was over. He lasted two years. The trials he faced as a teacher defeated him. Two other young, enthusiastic teachers with great potential also left during that time period after only a couple of years. I work at a pretty good school that, as trials go, present far fewer than many other places I have worked. We are one of the systems teachers in our region want to work for. I would have liked to have seen these young teachers work through the trials because I know they would have come through them stronger teachers, but they chose a different path. The one in my department had three strong female teachers mentoring him but the one male in our department, me, didn't enter into the fray until he was too far gone. I failed him both as a mentor and as a Christian. It wasn't that I didn't care. I was simply too wrapped up in my own trials to remember that sometimes serving others is the way through our own trials.

Secondly, we must understand and accept the nature and the importance of trials. As mentioned above, trials are not only inevitable but necessary. My trials were necessary because I had ignored God's whispers to me. If God does not allow my body to rebel against me when I start to overdo it, I will begin to neglect Him and my family and push myself into even more serious health problems. In Romans 5:3—4 (NIV), we read, "...we also glory in our sufferings, because we know that suffering produces perseverance; perseverance, character; and character, hope." James writes, "Consider it pure joy, my brothers and sisters, whenever you face trials of many kinds, because you know that the testing of your faith produces perseverance. Let perseverance finish its work so that you may be mature and complete, not lacking anything" (James 1:2—4). Paul tells us in 1 Thessalonians 5:16—18 NIV, "Rejoice always, pray continually, give thanks in all circumstances; for this is God's will for you in Christ Jesus." This does not, of course, mean that we should *feel* joyful when beset by trials. Jesus certainly was not "feeling" joyful when contemplating what was about to happen in the Garden of Gethsemane. In fact, the Bible tells us He was in anguish. Whether or not Jesus actually began to sweat blood (an actual condition called hematohydrosis that can be caused by great stress) or whether this was a symbolic representation to illustrate the intensity of Christ's anguish, our Lord and Savior was facing the trial of His life. He told Peter, John, and James "My soul is overwhelmed with sorrow to the point of death" (John 26:38 NIV). But as Christ prayed, He put His faith in God the Father and submitted to His trials because He knew they were necessary. Obviously, none of what followed over the next few days was in any way joyful for Christ or His closest followers. The joy that is spoken of is not feeling joyous about the suffering nor expressing joy during the suffering, but refers rather to that seed of joy we hold on to during these tough times because of our belief that God will help us through our trials and that our trials will prepare us for an eternity with Him. In his second epistle to the Corinthians, Paul wrote, "Therefore we do not lose heart. Though outwardly we are wasting away, yet inwardly we are being renewed day by day. For our light and momentary troubles are achieving for us an eternal glory that far outweighs them all. So we fix our eyes not on what is seen, but on what is unseen, since what is seen is temporary, but what is unseen is eternal" (2 Corinthians 4:17-18 NIV).

Our trials also create in us the gift of empathy. We are able to provide comfort to others who are facing or will face similar trials. In 2 Corinthians 1:3-4 (NIV) Paul writes, "Praise be to God and Father of our Lord Jesus Christ, the Father of compassion and the God of all comfort, who comforts us in our troubles, so that we can comfort those in any trouble with the comfort we ourselves have received from God." Some of the trials I faced as the child put me at enormous risk of being at least an academic failure. Now, however, I understand those trials were necessary for me to become the kind of teacher who can empathize with students who are struggling with some of the same challenges I faced. God is always with us and will provide us with the comfort, the strength, and the support we need to face the trial. Recall what David wrote in Psalms 16:8 (NLT): "I know the Lord is *always* with me. I will not be shaken, for He is right beside me." Later in chapter 46 he continues, "God is our refuge and strength, always ready to help in times of trouble ." David repeats this theme again in Psalms 52:22 (MSG) when he writes, "Pile your troubles on God's shoulders—He'll carry your load, He'll help you out." In a similar expression Solomon would write, "I looked for the Lord, and He answered me. And He took away all my fears" (Psalms 34:4 NLV).

Corrie Ten Boom once wrote, "If God sends us stony paths, He provides us with strong shoes." Christ understands how difficult trials are. He knows how ill-equipped most of us are to deal with stress as well as the devastating effects stress can have on our lives and on the lives of those around us. He loves us deeply and passionately and neither desires nor intended for us to deal with trials on our own. Instead, He encourages us to turn our worry over to Him. If you are not convinced by David or Solomon, consider the words of the Lord Himself. In Matthew 11:28-30 (NLT), Christ extends this invitation to all of us:

Come to me, all of you who are weary and carry heavy burdens, and I will give you rest. Take my yoke upon you. Let me teach you, because I am humble and gentle at heart, and you will find rest for your souls. For my yoke is easy to bear, and the burden I give you is light.

God is not a distant God that must come from afar to help us. Before ascending to Heaven, Jesus promised His apostles that He would ask God the Father to send them an Advocate: The Holy Spirit. In some translations, advocate is translated as "comforter," encourager," or "counselor." God is with us, in us, at all times in the form of the Holy Spirit. Paul encourages the people of Corinth to remember this with these words:

We have this light from God in our human bodies. This shows that the power is from God. It is not from ourselves. We are pressed on every side, but we still have room to move. We are often in much trouble, but we never give up. People make it hard for us, but we are not left alone. We are knocked down, but we are not destroyed. We carry marks on our bodies that show the death of Jesus. This is how Jesus makes His life seen in our bodies. Every day of our life we face death because of Jesus. In this way, His life is seen in our bodies. Death is working in us because we work for the Lord, but His life is working in you.

2 Corinthians 4:7-12 NLV

Even during those times when we are so overwhelmed that we don't even know where to begin our prayers, the Bible provides us with guidance:

In the same way, the Spirit helps us in our weakness. We do not know what we ought to pray for, but the Spirit himself intercedes for us through wordless groans. And he who searches our hearts knows the mind of the Spirit, because the Spirit intercedes for God's people in accordance with the will of God

Romans 8:26-27 NIV

Christ wants us to put our faith in Him and promises this faith will bring us His peace:

I am leaving you with a gift—peace of mind and heart. And the peace I give is a gift the world cannot give. So don't be troubled or afraid.

John 14:27 NLT

His message is clear: nothing in *this* world can give us freedom from stress or peace of mind and heart like the Lord can especially since it is this world that is causing us this anxiety. Only a life-changing relationship with Him can give us this peace. Several years ago, I asked Jesus to carry my burden, to help me escape the debilitating stress I felt as a teacher. I was reborn as a teacher, and next four years were some of the best of my career. But then my priorities once again became confused and once again I found myself robbing God and my family of their time and love. God did and continues to do what is needed to keep me connected to Him and to stop robbing my family of an "all-in" father and husband. When I have this balance, I feel greater enthusiasm for my work as well. I feel less resentment toward the stack of responsibilities associated with being a teacher and coordinator of a time-consuming ecological studies program. I never find my job easy to do, and there are aspects of it that I may never find enjoyable. However, now when I face the trials that are inherent in my profession, I remind myself of Colossians 3:23: "Whatever work you do, do it with all your heart. *Do it for the Lord and not for men* (my emphasis) NIV." I am where He wants me to be doing what He has called me to do.

CHAPTER EIGHT

Fighting the Good Fight

So we're not giving up. How could we! Even though on the outside it often looks like things are falling apart on us, on the inside, where God is making new life, not a day goes by without his unfolding grace. These hard times are small potatoes compared to the coming good times, the lavish celebration prepared for us. There's far more here than meets the eye. The things we see now are here today, gone tomorrow. But the things we can't see now will last forever.

2 Corinthians 4:16-18 MSG

Let me tell you something you already know. The world ain't all sunshine and rainbows. It's a very mean and nasty place and I don't care how tough you are it will beat you to your knees and keep you there permanently if you let it. You, me, or nobody is gonna hit as hard as life. But it ain't about how hard you hit. It's about how hard you can get hit and keep moving forward. How much you can take and keep moving forward. That's how winning is done! Now if you know what you're worth then go out and get what you're worth. But ya gotta be willing to take the hits, and not pointing fingers saying you ain't where you wanna be because of him, or her, or anybody! Cowards do that and that ain't you! You're better than that!

Rocky Balboa

Don't burn out; keep yourselves fueled and aflame. Be alert servants of the Master, cheerfully expectant. Don't quit in hard times; pray all the harder. Help needy Christians; be inventive in hospitality.

Romans 12:11-13 MSG

Therefore, my dear brothers and sisters, stand firm. Let nothing move you. Always give yourselves fully to the work of the Lord, because you know that your labor in the Lord is not in vain.

1 Corinthians 15:58 NIV

Let us not become weary in doing good, for at the proper time we will reap a harvest if we do not give up.

Galatians 6:9 NIV

And now, dear brothers and sisters, one final thing. Fix your thoughts on what is true, and honorable, and right, and pure, and lovely, and admirable. Think about things that are excellent and worthy of praise. Keep putting into practice all you learned and received from me—everything you heard from me and saw me doing. Then the God of peace will be with you.

Philippians 4:8-9 NLT

Foundational Concepts

- ✝ God desires for us to fight the good fight of the faith.
- ✝ God will provide us with the weapons we need to fight this fight.
- ✝ The choice to fight must be our own.
- ✝ We cannot allow the battles we lose to turn us away from or quit the "good fight."

Central Questions

1. What components comprise "The Armor of God?"
2. What is our role in this fight?
3. How do we "fight the good fight?"
4. How do we deal with our failures?

A while back, I was reading an article in which the lead pastor of Compassion Christian Church (formally Savannah Christian) in Georgia, Cam Huxford, was asked "What does a Christian do to Live Dangerously?" I'm not sure what I expected as his answer, perhaps something like, "Carry the message to people everywhere at all costs and regardless of the risks." After all, Compassion Christian Church supports missionaries and churches all over the globe, many in places where Christian persecution is rampant. Instead, Cam replied with an answer which comes from a life of being tested and of maintaining a dogged commitment to honoring the Lord. Though he will be the first to tell you he has been abundantly blessed by the Lord, he has shared in a number of his sermons some of the trials his family has experienced, any one of which would knock a person to their knees. He lost his father when he was only eleven years old. Both he and his son were involved in very serious car accidents in their youth. He and his wife, Sara, experienced the pain of miscarriage twice and the frightening battle against breast cancer. Pastor Huxford's response was simple yet incredibly powerful:

Obey. <pause> They obey God's Word. They obey the leading of the Spirit of God. They live a life of joyful submission to the kingdom agenda. And when it gets hard they don't run, they don't quit, they don't start compromising things. They hang tough. They persevere.

Mature Christians like the Huxfords understand that the hardest thing we will be asked to do is continue to fight the good fight when times get tough. It is a battle just to obey. While most of us may not realize it, our fight is mild in comparison to what others had to endure in the battle for our faith. The apostle Paul, Dietrich Bonhoeffer, Corrie Ten Boom-could we have fought the good fight as effectively and faithfully as they did were our lives subject to the tremendous trials each of these people faced? In our world it is so easy to give in, compromise, or give up when it comes to our walk with the Lord. Individuals do it. Groups of people do it. Entire churches do it. *Saying* that we will give our lives to Christ is usually the easy part. Actually doing so is quite another thing. At best, many of us give bits and pieces of our lives to God, but few of us really have the courage to give our lives to Him completely. We may support the war effort in ways. We may even fight in a skirmish here and there when we feel moved to do so. But when it really comes down to it, very few people are willing or perhaps able to enlist for life and be willing to fight on the front lines day after day. These battles aren't just in some distant land where we are trying to bring the word of Christ to those who do not know Him. They are in the minute by minute decisions we make in every aspect of our lives. The battles we face are not just against Satan and his league of distracters but against our own fallen nature. In his letter to the Galatians, the Apostle Paul wrote:

> So I say, let the Holy Spirit guide your lives. Then you won't be doing what your sinful nature craves. The sinful nature wants to do evil, which is just the opposite of what the Spirit wants. And the Spirit gives us desires that are the opposite of what the sinful nature desires. These two forces are constantly fighting each other, so you are not free to carry out your good intentions.
>
> Galatians 5:16-17 NLT

Our flesh is not hard-wired to hold fast to commitments, but the Holy Spirit that lives within us is. Our flesh lives in this world, but the perfect Spirit is of another. There is almost never a time when I don't find myself engaged in this struggle to one extent or another. Some of the engagements are small. Others are epic battles. One of the most challenging aspects of this fight is dealing with the defeats I suffer on such a regular basis. Once we begin the process of truly turning our lives over to God, the conviction of the Holy Spirit brings our sins to light in a way many of us never experienced before knowing Christ. Before I asked Christ into my life, I don't recall spending a whole lot of time feeling ashamed of these failures. In many cases, I was not even aware of them. Now that I have accepted Christ one of the struggles I have had to deal with, ironically, is feeling such grave disappointment and shame at times when I fail miserably. But I never feel that God has or will give up on me. The truth is many of us are more apt to give up on ourselves, failing to understand in this process that giving up on ourselves is giving up on God. Giving up means not trusting God's process for hardening us for battle or for preparing us for eternity with Him. When my wits are about me, I understand that once we give ourselves to Him, God will not give up on us. He may remain at the distance from us that we put Him, but that is not the same as giving up. God is with us for the long haul, through thick and thin, for better or worse, through sickness and health, 'til death brings us together for eternity. The Bible tells us very clearly in Romans 8:38-39 (NIV):

> For I am convinced that neither death nor life, neither angels nor demons, neither the present nor the future, nor any powers, neither height nor depth, nor anything else in all creation, will be able to separate us from the love of God that is in Christ Jesus our Lord.

Instead of giving up, God wants us to *get up*. Get up from being knocked down. Dust ourselves off. Look inward to the Spirit, upward to the Father, and forward toward Christ's promise. Go all "Rocky Balboa" on the problem. We have already talked about how trials are both necessary and inevitable. Failure may not be "necessary," but it is inevitable. If it were possible for any person to live a life without failure when it comes to sinning, there would be no need for a Savior. The Bible tells us *nobody* is righteous. *Nobody is without sin*. James, the brother of Jesus reminds us, "We all stumble in many ways" (James 3:2). Failure is not something to be proud of, for sure, but neither should it be something we simply blow off because hey, everybody sins. Our failures should also not bury us in shame once we have acknowledged them to God and repented. I have failed a whole lot in my walk with Christ. On some days I am lucky if I break even especially if my thoughts convict me along with my actions. As teachers we interact with so many different people, have to adjust to so many different changes, and have to balance so many different responsibilities that it is easy to become overwhelmed and blow it. In truth, though, it is in large part my history of failures that allows me in many situations to empathize with others who are facing the same struggles I have faced and that I continue to face even as I slowly grow in wisdom and Christian maturity. My failures allow me to feel genuine empathy, and empathy is a far more powerful characteristic than mere sympathy. Obviously God did not wish for me to fail in my walk so that I could develop empathy, but He certainly didn't let that failure go to waste.

So how do we fight the good fight? How do we obey, stand our ground, persevere is this world with so many different forces working against us? In Ephesians 6:10-12 (NIV), Paul counsels the members of the Church at Ephesus to:

> Finally, be strong in the Lord and in his mighty power. Put on the full armor of God, so that you can take your stand against the devil's schemes. For our struggle is not against flesh and blood, but against the rulers, against the authorities, against the powers of this dark world and against the spiritual forces of evil in the heavenly realms.

Not our armor then, not our weapons, but the weapons of the Lord. His Word, His example, His people, His Holy Spirit. What is our role in this if it is all God providing the armaments? Simple: God will not dress us in His armor. He will not force us to read and study His Word nor to assemble with an army of believers who can strengthen us. He will not wield the sword for us. He will not force us to make Godly decisions, live a Godly life, nor share His word with others. He will not force us to lead others to a life-changing relationship with Him through the example of our lives. He will not force us to love others. He will not force us to love Him. These things we must do willingly. We must *obey*. Doing these things willingly does not always mean eagerly. We may not be eager to show love to a certain person, to sacrifice our time or money, to put others' needs above our own, to accept becoming alienated from friends or family who cannot support our decision to honor God. Were we perfect like God, eagerness to do such things would come easy to us. But we are not perfect. We are fallen. We are sinners. Willingness, then, often means denying our self-serving desires in order to honor God regardless of whether or not we "want to." The good news for us is that God will give us everything we need to fight in this battle.

I started this book using an analogy of an old coach; I will end it the same way. Our commission is immeasurably more important than even the most important game of an athlete's life and so I am not comparing it to a "game." I am simply returning to the coach analogy because I feel it might help some people to understand what I am trying to say a little better. Great coaches are known for their inspirational and motivational locker room speeches, and while I am neither great nor a coach, I have assembled passages from scripture into a scriptural version of a "locker room" speech. In order to allow the reader to read the passage without interruption, I have footnoted the passages.

Fight the Good Fight of the Faith

Fight the good fight of the faith. Take hold of the eternal life to which you were called when you made your good confession in the presence of many witnesses.[2] As long as it is day, we must do the works of him who sent me. Night is coming, when no one can work.[3] A life frittered away disgusts GOD; he loves those who run straight for the finish line. So roll up your sleeves, put your mind in gear, be totally ready to receive the gift that's coming when Jesus arrives. Don't lazily slip back into those old grooves of evil, doing just what you feel like doing. You didn't know any better then; you do now. As obedient children, let yourselves be pulled into a way of life shaped by God's life, a life energetic and blazing with holiness. God said, "I am holy; you be holy."[4] Be strong in the Lord and in his mighty power. Put on the full armor of God, so that you can take your stand against the devil's schemes. For our struggle is not against flesh and blood, but against the rulers, against the authorities, against the powers of this dark world and against the spiritual forces of evil in the heavenly realms.[5] It is true, we live in a body of flesh. But we do not fight like people of the world. We do not use those things to fight with that the world uses. We use the things God gives to fight with and they have power. Those things God gives to fight with destroy the strong-places of the devil[6].

The first thing I want you to do is pray. Pray every way you know how, for everyone you know. Pray especially for rulers and their governments to rule well so we can be quietly about our business of living simply, in humble

---

[2] 1 Timothy 6:12 NIV

[3] John 9:4 NIV

[4] 1 Peter 1:13-16 MSG

[5] Ephesians 6:10-12 NIV

[6] 2 Corinthians 10:3-4 NLV

contemplation. This is the way our Savior God wants us to live.[7] Don't worry about anything; instead, pray about everything. Tell God what you need and thank him for all he has done. [7] Then you will experience God's peace, which exceeds anything we can understand. His peace will guard your hearts and minds as you live in Christ Jesus.[8] Ask and it will be given to you; seek and you will find; knock and the door will be opened to you. For everyone who asks receives; the one who seeks finds; and to the one who knocks, the door will be opened.[9] In the same way, the Spirit helps us in our weakness. We do not know what we ought to pray for, but the Spirit himself intercedes for us through wordless groans.[10] When life is heavy and hard to take, go off by yourself. Enter the silence. Bow in prayer. Don't ask questions: Wait for hope to appear. Don't run from trouble. Take it full-face. The "worst" is never the worst.[11]

Test yourselves to make sure you are solid in the faith. Don't drift along taking everything for granted. Give yourselves regular checkups. You need firsthand evidence, not mere hearsay, that Jesus Christ is in you. Test it out. If you fail the test, do something about it. I hope the test won't show that we have failed. But if it comes to that, we'd rather the test showed our failure than yours. We're rooting for the truth to win out in you. We couldn't possibly do otherwise.[12] No temptation has overtaken you except what is common to mankind. And God is faithful; he will not let you be tempted beyond what you can bear. But when you are tempted, he will also provide a way out so that you can endure it.[13] On a good day, enjoy yourself; on a bad day, examine your conscience. God arranges for both kinds of days so that we won't take anything for granted.[14] We want each of you to show this same diligence to the very end, so that what you hope for may be fully realized. We do not want you to become lazy, but to imitate those who through faith and patience inherit what has been promised.[15]

So let's not allow ourselves to get fatigued doing good. At the right time we will harvest a good crop if we don't give up, or quit. Right now, therefore, every time we get the chance, let us work for the benefit of all, starting with the people closest to us in the community of faith.[16] So we're not giving up. How could we! Even though on the outside it often looks like things are falling apart on us, on the inside, where God is making new life, not a day goes by without his unfolding grace. These hard times are small potatoes compared to the coming good times, the lavish celebration prepared for us. There's far more here than meets the eye.

---

[7] 1 Timothy 2:1-3 MSG
[8] Philippians 4:6-7 NLT
[9] Matthew 7:7-8 MSG
[10] Romans 8:26-28 NIV
[11] Lamentations 3:28-30 MSG
[12] 2 Corinthians 13:5-9 MSG
[13] 1 Corinthians 10:13 NIV
[14] Ecclesiastes 7:14 MSG
[15] Hebrews 6:11-12 NIV
[16] Galatians 6:9-10 MSG

The things we see now are here today, gone tomorrow. But the things we can't see now will last forever.[17] Whatever happens, conduct yourselves in a manner worthy of the gospel of Christ.[18] As a prisoner for the Lord, then, I urge you to live a life worthy of the calling you have received. Be completely humble and gentle; be patient, bearing with one another in love. Make every effort to keep the unity of the Spirit through the bond of peace.[19] I don't want anyone strolling off, down some path that goes nowhere. And mark that you do this with humility and discipline—not in fits and starts, but steadily, pouring yourselves out for each other in acts of love, alert at noticing differences and quick at mending fences. You were all called to travel on the same road and in the same direction, so stay together, both outwardly and inwardly. You have one Master, one faith, one baptism, one God and Father of all, who rules over all, works through all, and is present in all. Everything you are and think and do is permeated with Oneness.[20]

And now, dear brothers and sisters, one final thing. Fix your thoughts on what is true, and honorable, and right, and pure, and lovely, and admirable. Think about things that are excellent and worthy of praise. Keep putting into practice all you learned and received from me—everything you heard from me and saw me doing. Then the God of peace will be with you.[21] May the God who gives endurance and encouragement give you the same attitude of mind toward each other that Christ Jesus had, so that with one mind and one voice you may glorify the God and Father of our Lord Jesus Christ.[22]

Therefore, my dear brothers and sisters, stand firm. Let nothing move you. Always give yourselves fully to the work of the Lord, because you know that your labor in the Lord is not in vain.[23] Be on your guard; stand firm in the faith; be courageous; be strong. Do everything in love.[24] Don't burn out; keep yourselves fueled and aflame. Be alert servants of the Master, cheerfully expectant. Don't quit in hard times; pray all the harder. Help needy Christians; be inventive in hospitality.[25] I consider my life worth nothing to me; my only aim is to finish the race and complete the task the Lord Jesus has given me—the task of testifying to the good news of God's grace.[26] Not that I have already obtained all this, or have already been made perfect, but I press on to take hold of that for which Christ Jesus took hold of me.[27] [Our Lord tells us], "Remain in me, as I also remain in you. No branch can bear fruit by itself; it must remain in the vine. Neither can

[17] 2 Corinthians 4:17-18 MSG

[18] Philippians 1:27 NIV

[19] Ephesians 4:1-2 NIV

[20] Ephesians 4:3-6 MSG

[21] Philippians 4:8-9 NLT

[22] Romans 15:5-6 NIV

[23] 1 Corinthians 15:58 NIV

[24] 1 Corinthians 16:13-14 NIV

[25] Romans 12:11-13 MSG

[26] Acts 20:24 NIV

[27] Philippians 3:12

you bear fruit unless you remain in me. I am the vine; you are the branches. If you remain in me and I in you, you will bear much fruit; apart from me you can do nothing."[28] Do your best. Prepare for the worst. Whatever happens, conduct yourselves in a manner worthy of the gospel of Christ.[29] Trust God to bring victory.[30] Fight the good fight of the faith.[31]

And all the Lord's people said...

[28] John 15:4-5 NIV
[29] Philippians 2:27
[30] Proverbs 21:31 MSG
[31] 1 Timothy 6:12 NIV

EPILOGUE

In Chapter Four, I wrote about a time when envy ruled in my life. I decided to include some of the more recent things that have happened in my life because many of these events have been life changing-though not always in the way one might expect. The past few years have been full of trials for me, but from an outsider's perspective, a casual observer would have never seen it as such. I reached what some people would argue is the pinnacle of success for a teacher, and with it came trials I had never anticipated.

In 2014-2015, I *was* honored as the teacher of the year for our school. It didn't stop with that. I received a state-level teaching award. Shortly after that award I was honored with the first of four national science teaching awards. I was profiled on a local broadcast news stations as a "Hometown Hero." A little over a year earlier I had thrown a mini tantrum about simply not being nominated for a school-level award. So, you can imagine how elated I must have been when I learned about each of these awards. You can imagine how I beamed with pride. You can imagine it, but that is not at all what happened. Instead I fell apart. I was overcome with a tremendous sense of guilt and shame. My anxiety level skyrocketed in part to this and in part to the demands I had placed on myself at work. The person who had fallen apart momentarily because of envy received what he had desired and now was being torn apart by guilt, anxiety, shame, and a pronounced feeling that I was not worthy. If this was not a "be careful what you wish for" situation, I'm not sure what would qualify as such. My anxiety continued to increase because of the attention that was regularly being focused on me at school, at Board meetings, in the papers, in the news. When I completed the narrative packets for each of these awards, I didn't feel like I was *consciously* competing for these awards out of some sense of pride despite how I had responded to not being nominated in the past. I saw them as my "marathon." I thought it would be a fun challenge, the same way marathon runners feel---to put myself out there against others to test my mettle. My principal had shared at a Board meeting his thoughts that I was "one of the best science teachers in the state." The superintendent of schools whose daughter I had taught shared similar thoughts. "OK," I thought. "Let's put that to the test *just for the fun of it*." Some marathoners run to win, some to push themselves to improve on their personal best, and others for the mere satisfaction of simply finishing such a grueling competition. National teaching awards do not generally recognize anything beyond "1st place." One either wins or does not. As humans, we like the challenge of winning something. Our school culture is full of competitions. There is nothing inherently wrong with wanting to compete in an arena where you feel you can compete. The issue is the motivation behind wanting to compete. There is no escaping that while I enjoyed the "challenge" of it, at some level I still wanted attention no matter how hard I tried to convince myself that was not the case. God responded by working on me to cure me of that need for attention in a very pronounced manner. He humbled me. *Hard. Repeatedly.*

The competition was "fun," for the lack of a better word. Winning was rewarding, "fun" as well-at least initially. The awards directly or indirectly funneled thousands of dollars into my class and ecological studies program which has provided students with some pretty fantastic opportunities. Had I the forethought and the ability to keep news of these awards a complete secret from everyone at work and in my community, I think I would have been fine. But that's not how these things work. After the first national award, I tried to keep the next award out of the news. We kept it quiet at school as well, but a release was sent directly by the award sponsor to the local papers. What I had not anticipated in 2015 was that the "fun" for me, and I emphasize this was a personal issue, ended instantly when the public recognition started. The Hometown Hero recognition came in March shortly after the state and the first national award. A few days prior to this, my anxiety level had become so high that I ended up in the hospital with chest pains, a tingling sensation in my left arm, and a blood pressure of 188/102 even though I was already on blood pressure medicine. This combined with other job stress and other health issues and I was tormented. I had a hard time focusing on anything else.

Throughout this entire time, once of the questions that kept flowing through my mind was "Is this recognition from God or from Satan to serve as a distraction away from my calling, away from humility?" Were my medical conditions now a punishment for my vanity? Mid-way through the year, I called John Mark Romans, one of the pastors at our church, to help me sort through what was happening. After all, if you can't trust the counsel of a pastor who has three books of the Bible in his name, who can you trust? I explained to him that while I should be enjoying all this, I was not. Go ahead: laugh at the irony. To add to my anxiety, I knew there were a few people at my workplace who were, to put it politely, irritated at all the recognition and attention I was receiving because so many other teachers were doing great things and not feeling the love—kind of like I had felt at times during my career! I imagined the condescending whispers to be far greater than they actually were so paranoia added to my list of issues. The notoriety also took me away from my class. I was out a total of sixteen days that year at special meetings and award ceremonies. I suffered. My students suffered. My family suffered. The whole ship took on water and I was taking others down with me to some extent.

The awards I received were mostly based on a unique ecological field studies program I had developed. This program quickly became a part-time job. In addition to the fifty hours a week I spend on my regular teaching duties, the program adds another ten hours onto that. It has also required me to volunteer a number of Saturdays and, on average, about two days out of every vacation because most of the activities we are involved in take place outside of school hours. It is a wonderful program and I believe it is inspiring the students who are involved to become more interested in ecology, but when one wins local, state, and national attention for something there is a chance that it will become an idol. I did not "idolize" the program in the sense that I worshipped it, but rather I felt the pressure to commit more and more time to it each year. Something becomes an idol when it starts to consume your thoughts and rob your attention away from other, more important things. It can become an addiction of sorts, and anyone who has ever suffered from any type of addiction knows that you cannot easily "talk yourself out of it." I prayed for months that God would whisk away the challenges associated with balancing my priorities, but God does things at His own pace and reason because God knows what is best. The problem for me was not really the rewards and not really work demands, it was how I handled both. As Captain Jack Sparrow says in *Pirates of the Caribbean*, "The problem is not the problem. The problem is your attitude about the problem. Do you understand?"

The 2014-2015 school year was tough. In addition to the guilt I felt at times from being away from my own family doing Field Studies, I often felt completely overwhelmed and exhausted both mentally and physically. At times I had trouble keeping up with the curriculum map. I had more difficulty establishing and maintaining relationships with the students and their families that were as deep as relationships I formed over the past several years. I sometimes fell behind in grading, getting my lesson plans in on time, doing labs with my students. When I became unbalanced, my classes became rote and tedious to teach. The students became bored and it became more difficult for me to get them engaged. My daughter was in one of my classes and what she was experiencing was nothing like what she had anticipated based on all the times she had heard about her father's awesome class from former students and parents. That is a lost opportunity I will never get back—having her experience me and my style of teaching at its best. I imagine it was quite a let-down for her because her closest friends also suffered through my struggles that year along with her. Because of the manner in which I dealt with stress related to work, the program, and the awards, the quality of my life deteriorated in most areas rather than improved.

As they say in the South, I had become a "hot mess." I have seen people become completely unglued as a result of work stress and I felt I was headed down that same path. I was feeling a level of anxiety that I had not experienced in several years, and it was being reflected outwardly for others to see and was affecting my whole life. The person who only months earlier had testified in front of his colleagues that he almost never experienced work-related anxiety since turning that anxiety over to God was sinking in a quicksand of anxiety. It was, in retrospect, an invitation to the Devil. I can almost picture him in my mind saying, "Oh yeah? We'll see about this no anxiety thing." Like the apostle Peter, I had made a bold statement that demonstrated my ignorance and just has he had done with Peter I belief Satan asked to sift me like wheat. And just like with Peter, God let him. I felt the added pressure of this. I wasn't supposed to be stressed out. I tried to keep it bottled up, which of course only made things worse. I suffered and everyone and everything around me suffered as well.

As I processed this with John Mark, he listened intently and offered his views. I shared that my greatest reason for believing these events were not from God was that I felt I did not deserve this kind of reward from Him. I was still not consistently adhering to enough of what I have written about in this book. I had made some progress, but I was, no am, still *so* far from the mark. This was not just limited to my work. In my personal life, I was so preoccupied with work that I had stopped serving at the church. Some weekends I was so tired or preoccupied with work I simply could not even generate the energy or will to go to church. Our giving had dropped significantly, in part to the birth of a wonderful but unplanned son, partly to several financial hits we took over the course of the recession, but also because of poor stewardship. I continue to be plagued with doubts as to how much of Christ people see in me which troubles me a great deal since I had spent many summers writing this book on that very subject! I was so completely stressed out that I honestly cannot recall much of what John Mark and I discussed, but one thing he said stood out. He suggested, "Maybe you really don't deserve these rewards from God's perspective. Maybe, though, he has allowed these things to happen to see what you will do with them." That put me on the road to reconciling some of the anxiety I was feeling, but I was still embattled with negative thoughts. When one already suffers from issues with anxiety (though I had somehow tricked myself into thinking that was no longer the case), feeding anxiety causes it to grow exponentially.

Over the next couple of months I read several books that focused on hearing God in our lives, and it became abundantly clear to me that a large part of my struggle was a result of not spending very little time in communication with God. I was praying to God about my condition, but I was not *communicating* with Him. Communication is a two-way process. I did not doubt that God could communicate to us through means other than the Bible, but I was simply never setting aside time to *communicate* with Him. I was praying, asking for something, pleading, but then checking out before He even had a chance to answer. I believe God was trying to communicate to me, but I simply wasn't listening. So, when God really needs to get your attention, a trip to the ER is sometimes in order. After my first trip to the ER (which in addition to being terrifying ended up costing us thousands) I finally set aside time to listen. I heard what I believe to be God's response. I asked Him to tell me whether this recognition was a blessing from Him or a sinful distraction from the Adversary. Before I even had a chance to finish asking the question, a thought came instantly to my mind: "It doesn't matter. That is not important." I tried asking again and heard the same response. At that moment, I believe God opened my eyes and I knew what His message meant. I truly believe had God not put this thought in my mind, it would never have occurred to me to think the source of the recognition did not matter. My mind would have come up with something black or white: "yes," it was from God or I felt more likely in my case "no," it was not from God. What I was hearing was an extension of what John Mark had told me before. It didn't matter whether this recognition was from God or from an agent of the devil. What's done is done. What mattered is *what I did with it*.

By July, 2015, I finally felt that I was finally getting a handle on the anxiety. A long overdue trip to see my family in Maine went a long way to recharging my batteries. I certainly turned to God more and felt that I had been largely "healed" by God. I took that into the new school year with me, but soon found myself once again living among the thorns. In the Parable of the Sower, some of the seed (God's word) fell among thorns which grew up and choked the plants so that they were unable to grow and mature enough to produce grain. I, like so many people today, have struggled with having my walk choked by the stress of this world rather than living my life in accordance to God's desire. Though I had managed to revert back to a more dynamic instructional experience for my students, I fell back into my unhealthy patterns and God, my family, and my church once again began to take a back seat to my work. My program continued to prosper. I had created a program that had, in addition to my awards, received two state-level awards and I felt the pressure to put a great deal of my time and energy into it. But the program is a thief. It steals as much pleasure as it provides. Once again I found myself living in the briar patch.

In April, 2016, my anxiety level finally boiled over again resulting in a serious anxiety attack that once again resulted in a trip to the ER. While I did not know it at the time, there was another underlying medical condition that had contributed to the pressure and discomfort in my chest. The anxiety was simply the tipping point. With my family history of heart disease, I once again felt certain I was having a heart attack. The 2016 trip to the ER came on as a sneak attack. The difference between this event and the event that landed me in the ER the year before was that I had not been *feeling* outwardly stressed at work most of the time- but apparently my body was. The anxiety attack I suffered was my body's way of saying (through God, I believe), "Buddy, if you don't dial it down I am going to dial it down for you." I hadn't learned my lesson from my trip to the ER the previous year and God knew it. God needed to make a bold statement to me and since I had stopped listening again, I honestly believe such a measure was necessary.

I have failed in more ways than I can list, not the least of which in my belief that turning my anxiety over to God would end my work anxiety completely. I had allowed myself to be lulled into the sense that I was impenetrable to work stress. Four relatively stress-free years only bolstered this arrogance. What I should have understood is that while Christ may carry much of our anxiety, He cannot remove all trials from our life because trials are necessary to build us up and bring us closer to Him. As I have mentioned several times, anxiety is an old and very familiar enemy of mine. I was diagnosed with clinical anxiety and mild depression years ago which resulted in therapy and medication I continue taking to this day. Heredity need not be destiny, but certainly I feed my genetic predispositions whenever I allow my connection to God to weaken. On my list of priorities serving God and others had dropped significantly. I have come to learn an important lesson about my life through these trials: without them my relationship with God suffers. His power is made great in *my* weakness. I needed a serious reminder of my priorities and God used my illnesses for that purpose. I needed some serious lessons on humility, so God humbled me, and humbled me, and humbled me some more. Hammering away, chiseling me into His image of me. Even today when I fall back into patterns like doing web-searches on myself or checking blogs several times a day to see how people responded to my posts, God brings something into my life to humble me again. The humbling never ends because in one manifestation or another the sinful pride never ends. When I allow my world to become more about me than about Him or the others in my sphere, I trust God will continue to allow things to take place in my life that will turn my focus back to where it needs to be. But oh how I dislike it when I am having to go through the character-building process.

Our lives are full of events. Some of these events are a result of direct action by God. Many, however, are a result of responding to our own sinful inner voice or to the whispering from an agent of evil. Regardless of their origin, any event can provide us with an opportunity to honor God. With regards to the awards, I have eventually come to accept in my heart that it really is not important for me to drown in anxiety over whether the awards were a blessing from God or a distraction from Satan's army. They were moments of recognition that were fleeting and thank God for that and now they are not a factor in my work at all except that I present at science conferences every now and am perhaps better known throughout certain science teacher circles in the state. I can count on my fingers the number of people at my school and in my community who even know about the awards. I have accepted what I have experienced in the past several years as part of God's ultimate plan for me. I am not certain what that plan is, but I trust God is using these experiences to keep me humble and to strengthen me. The Bible tells us that once started, "He who began a good work in you will carry it on to completion until the day of

Christ Jesus" (Philippians 1:6). Because of God's hand, I have become what I should not have become. I have already shared that I grew up in conditions that predisposed me to academic failure. Poor. Single parent household. Substance abuse by a parent. Limited parental education. Marginal supervision as a youth. The only block that was not checked on my "at-risk" profile was that I came from a home where English was our first (only actually) language. The odds were considerably against me in terms of what I "made of my life." Yet now in my fifties I have received four national, one individual and two ecological studies program state-level awards, and one local teacher award. I am God's testimony to students at risk. I am God's testimony to parents in impoverished or otherwise troubled households who fear for their child's future. God can point to me and say, "Why are you worrying? Have faith. *Look what I did with him*!" Look what He did with such a hot mess.

I expect the "good works" He has in mind for me will continue to involve a lot of "trials by fire." I am also reminded through this time of trial that during these times when Christ is not carrying the anxiety for us, He is still right beside us to comfort us as we deal with the trial. When He doesn't carry the trial itself, His love is there to carry us through the trial when we feel like it is more than we can handle. I was asking the wrong thing. Instead of *expecting* Him to carry my anxiety on his own shoulders, I should have been asking Him for help to get through each trial. Carrying the load for us is not always what is best for us. I should have been asking Him the right questions, and I should have set the rest of the world aside at times to listen for His answers. I should have thanked him for forging my character through these trials.

I think I understand a bit better the nature of my trials. One thing is very, very clear to me: God has used events on two very different ends of the spectrum, winning awards and battling serious health issues, to humble me and bring me back to Him. Perhaps the awards never factored into His plan. Even without the awards, I am a living testimony for at-risk children. Perhaps He was thinking, "Well, I'm not ready for this to happen for you right now, and you're not ready either. But you opened that door without praying to me about it, so I'll let you go through it. Ready or not..." If I did not have a proper measure of humility before, I certainly have a fuller measure of it now. I was also reminded that while our faith should make a difference in how we deal with the challenges life throws at us, it is not a silver bullet to protect us from these trials. I remain hopeful. While writing the majority of this book from 2010-2014, I felt I was doing a decent job at living out at least some of what I have written. I was energized by the process. But here's the rub: once the core of the book was done, *I set it in my desk drawer and almost never pulled it out* to strengthen my walk by reflecting Christ-like behavior in my workplace nor other areas of my life. I had developed a unit plan then failed to use it. The irony is inescapable because I thought I had written this book largely for *me* so *I* could lead a life that honored Christ. It was never clear at any point during the main period when most of this was written that I would ever share it with anyone else let alone submit it for publication. To be perfectly honest, I felt I had a credibility issue and that has not changed in the eyes of many because of how often I shoot myself in the foot. Never-the-less, I feel compelled to share this book because, as I have said, I believe I was inspired by God who worked through me to enable me to write it.

I no longer feel like I have written something that will only have value if the results focus exclusively on me becoming a radically changed person, a stalwart reflection of Christ. I have been broken for a very long time and I have issues that may result in my never passing muster for that level of credibility in the eyes of many people who know me. I fully understand the implications. When the demonstration of my faith lacks credibility, God also lacks credibility in the eyes of people who see me and hear me profess my Christian faith. Though I believe with all my heart what I have written in this book, I continue to struggle to live it out day to day. I have professed on several occasions in this book that I am a work in progress. But this isn't just about me. It is about *you*. I have been working in education since 1991. I am in the twilight of my career as a teacher. I don't have many more years to set an example as a teacher. Whether I leave this profession because it is time to go or because I am no longer able to continue due to health issues, I feel the time for me to model Christ in that capacity is coming to an end and I haven't done a very good job of it in the short time I have endeavored to do so. This is why I now believe I have been mistaken in my understanding of God's intent or purpose for this book. The original title of this book was "Christ in *My* Classroom." I thought it was about me and it largely was at first, but it has now become something more. This book is about how to bring God into *your* classroom and workplace and will hopefully inspire others to succeed far more than I have been able to.

I would like to end by saying that it has certainly not been my intention to make any award-winning teacher feel guilty or convicted because he or she won a teaching award. As I stated, few people know about the last three awards because of my request for privacy and we now have over thirty teachers working at our school who weren't there in 2015 when I won the first two awards. I asked our principal, district office staff, and the local papers not to share the information for my own personal reasons. I am very grateful to be have been honored in such a way, but I learned that public recognition is simply not something that "works" for me. My choice should in no way should discourage anyone from allowing the news of a personal award to be made public. A colleague of mine recently won a national science teacher award and I would be terribly disappointed if she hid the honor from our community because she is so worthy both from a teaching perspective and from a faith perspective. Another colleague won Teacher of the Year for our district and I was thrilled for him. Other colleagues have since been recognized and I am happy for them to have received the recognition. I have played a role in the nomination of some of these colleagues for teaching awards and will continue to support other colleagues in the future. I would simply encourage one to embrace such an honor with humility, accept it as a blessing, and pay it forward however you can. But here's the thing: if my awards become *the* measure of my "effectiveness" in the eyes of my students, their parents, and my colleagues, they will reflect my absolute failure as an ambassador for Christ. When the Twelve were arguing about which of them was the greatest, Jesus explained clearly that each person's "greatness" would be reflected by how well he served others, not how high he rose in society. Years from now if someone asks a former colleague or administrator about me, will he or she say, "Yeah, I remember him. Didn't he win a bunch of awards or something?" Or will they say things like, "He would always help us if we needed it," "He shared all his materials with us without us ever having to ask," "He was selfless when it came to a lot of things," "He worked hard to help people remain positive and hopeful," "He was a very good teacher but didn't consider himself above anyone else," "He really cared about his students and their families," "He used to bring in home-baked stuff and stuff from his garden to share with the rest of us," "He was my mentor and really helped me a lot during my first few years," "He covered my duty for me when he saw I was really worn out and needed a break," "He was quick to offer a pat on the back or a compliment to us or to our supervisors about us," or even, "Yeah, he won a bunch of awards but he didn't let it go to his head. He never acted like he was better than the rest of us. He always recognized others when he was being recognized." The awards are immaterial. It is more important to me that my students and their parents remember that I tried to give them my best effort, that I acted toward them with decency and compassion, that I owned my mistakes, and that I was interested in the child as a person not just as a student. If I did these kinds of things "every now and then," it would certainly not constitute a "life of service," nor would most people recall these occasional acts. This type of service would have to be such a regular part of my life that others would recognize them as an overall pattern of behavior. I'm not there yet. I don't know how many more years left in this profession so the next few years will be very important for me. Winning awards or achieving high levels of job success that somehow "elevate" your status in the secular world has nothing to do with the Kingdom of God *unless* it is part of God's plan for you. When I stand before the Lord in Heaven, I imagine among the questions He might ask are, "How did you show love toward others?" "How did you serve others?" "What did you do with the gifts I gave you?" "How did others see me through you?" "How many people did you directly or indirectly lead to me?" At no point in the conversation do I ever envision Him asking, "So, what kinds of awards did you win?"

BIBLIOGRAPHY

1. Scriptures marked (NIV) taken from the Holy Bible, New International Version®, NIV®. Copyright © 1973, 1978, 1984, 2011 by Biblica, Inc.™ Used by permission of Zondervan. All rights reserved worldwide. www.zondervan.com The "NIV" and "New International Version" are trademarks registered in the United States Patent and Trademark Office by Biblica, Inc.™

2. Scripture marked (AMP) taken from the Amplified Bible, Copyright © 1954, 1958, 1962, 1964, 1965, 1987 by The Lockman Foundation. Used by permission.

3. Scripture marked (ESV) taken from The Holy Bible, English Standard Version. ESV is adapted from the Revised Standard Version of the Bible, copyright Division of Christian Education of the National Council of the Churches of Christ in the U.S.A. All rights reserved.

4. Scripture marked (NASB) taken from the NEW AMERICAN STANDARD BIBLE®, Copyright © 1960, 1962, 1963, 1968, 1971, 1972, 1973, 1975, 1977, 1995 by The Lockman Foundation. Used by permission.

5. New Life Version (NLV) © Christian Literature International.

6. Scripture quotations marked (NLT) are taken from the Holy Bible, New Living Translation, copyright © 1996, 2004, 2007 by Tyndale House Foundation. Used by permission of Tyndale House Publishers, Inc., Carol Stream, IL 60188. All rights reserved.

7. Scripture marked (MSG) taken from *The Message*. Copyright © 1993, 1994, 1995, 1996, 2000, 2001, 2002. Used by permission of NavPress Publishing Group.

8. Scripture marked (NKJV) taken from the New King James Version®. Copyright © 1982 by Thomas Nelson, Inc. Used by permission. All rights reserved.

9. Lewis, C. S. (1952, 1980) C.S Lewis Pte. Ltd. *Mere Christianity*. Paperback, New York: Harper Collins (p. 202)

10. Boom, C., & Sherrill, J. L. (1971). *The hiding place*. Washington Depot, Conn.: Chosen Books.

11. Boom, C. (1985). *Jesus is victor*. Old Tappan, N.J.: Revell.

12. Interview with Cam Huxford. (2008, February 18). *Christian Standard*. http://christianstandard.com/2008/02/interview-with-cam-huxford/

13. Blake, D. (2012). Gabby Douglas Praises God; Christian Gymnast Thankful After Winning All-Around Gold at Olympics 2012. *The Christian Post*. *http://www.christianpost.com/news/gabby-douglas-praises-god-christian-gymnast-thankful-after-winning-all-around-gold-at-olympics-2012-79386/*

14. Herd, A. (2012). Missy Franklin, Olympic Swimmer, Trusts the Lord to help her "shine a little light" on Hurting in Aurora, Colorado. *Breaking Christian News*. *http://www.breakingchristiannews.com/articles/display_art.html?ID=10388*

ABOUT THE AUTHOR

Robert Hodgdon is a middle school Life Science teacher and ecological studies program coordinator at Richmond Hill Middle School in Richmond Hill, Georgia where he lives with his wife Stacey and his two children Abigail and Connor. Robert grew up on the doorsteps of Acadia National Park on Mount Desert Island, Maine. He is a graduate of the University of Maine, Orono and St. Michael's College in Vermont where he received degrees in education. Following high school, he served his country in the United States Army then remained in the Army Reserve while attending university. Since 1991, Robert has worked with youth of all ages as a high school teacher, behavioral intervention specialist, special education teacher, and as a middle grades science and social studies teacher. When time allows, Robert presents at science and STEM conferences in Georgia and writes articles for state science publications. Robert and his family are members of Compassion Christian Church in Savannah, Georgia. Robert is the recipient of several state and national science teaching awards.